W9-AQK-902

AN INTRODUCTION TO
Plato's Laws

For Ellen

AN INTRODUCTION TO
Plato's Laws

R.F. STALLEY

Hackett Publishing Company

Contents

Preface

To most students of philosophy Plato's *Laws* must appear something of a mystery. It is obviously an important work but, by comparison with dialogues like the *Republic* or the *Phaedo*, it has received little attention. The reasons for this neglect are not far to seek. The style is difficult and sometimes obscure but even greater problems stem from the structure of the dialogue. The philosophical content is interwoven with a mass of legal material that is now largely of historical interest. So, although an adequate appreciation of Plato's thought must take full account of the *Laws*, the average reader cannot, I think, be expected to make very much of it without some kind of guide. This introduction is intended to fulfil that role. In writing it I have emphasized those aspects of the *Laws* that have most significance for the problems of philosophy as we now understand them. I have treated Plato as a thinker with whom one can argue, not as a figure to be regarded with awestruck admiration nor merely as a source for the understanding of Greek culture and society. I have tried to initiate debates and to stimulate the reader's own philosophizing rather than to give conclusive answers.

Given these aims, it has not been possible to follow closely the order of discussion as it develops through the twelve books of the *Laws*. Plato's manner is to return repeatedly to the same subjects. I have therefore discussed the *Laws* topic by topic rather than taking it book by book, though there is a rough correspondence between the order I have adopted and the order in which different themes are brought to prominence in the text. At the head of each chapter there is a list of relevant passages from the *Laws* and from other dialogues. These lists are not exhaustive, but they indicate the passages which have most influenced my interpretations and which I would recommend as starting points for the reader's own reflections.

There is very little modern literature about the *Laws* and most of what there is deals with historical and philological matters rather than with the philosophy of the dialogue. I have listed those modern discussions which I feel able to recommend in the suggestions for Further Reading. I have also included some modern discussions of related topics and some of the many passages from Aristotle that bear on the *Laws*. The latter may prove more helpful than most of the modern works.

Like most academic authors I owe much to the colleagues and students with whom, over the years, I have discussed problems of ancient philosophy. In particular I wish to record the debt that I and every other English-speaking student of the *Laws* must owe to Professor T.J. Saunders. His translation has made the *Laws* accessible to the ordinary reader in a quite remarkable way and he has contributed enormously to our understanding of the dialogue by his scholarly articles and bibliography. I am grateful too for the friendly interest he has shown towards my own work.

1

Reading the *Laws*

1 *The importance of the* Laws

The *Laws* is Plato's longest as well as his last work. Of its twelve books the first three suggest the basic principles which should underlie any satisfactory system of law. Attention then shifts to a scheme for the foundation of a new city somewhere in Crete. Books IV and V deal with various preliminaries to legislation, and the remaining seven books describe in considerable detail a constitution and system of law for this new city.

It is obvious that a work of this kind must deal, at least by implication, with most of the fundamental questions of political and legal philosophy. But since Plato takes the province of law to include every aspect of public and private life, the scope of the dialogue is wider than one might at first suppose. For example, it contains a full account of the aims and methods of education, a systematic treatment of the theory of punishment and responsibility and an elaborate proof of the existence of a god or gods. The discussions of the moral basis of the state include Plato's final thoughts on topics, such as the nature of virtue and the role of pleasure, that had concerned him throughout his life.

Since Plato is, by any reckoning, one of the greatest of political philosophers, we might expect the *Laws* to occupy a prominent place in all histories of political thought. But in practice it has often been ignored. In the eyes of most students and teachers of political philosophy the only real source for Plato's doctrine is the *Republic*. This tendency to forget about the *Laws* can infect even the finest scholars. Sir Ernest Barker, for example, gives us one of the fullest and most sympathetic treatments of the dialogue, yet he is apt to leave it out of account when he generalizes about Plato or about the history of Greek political thought (1960, pp. 14, 207–8, 226–7; cf. 42–6).

There are two mains reasons for the neglect of the *Laws*. In the first place it is much less attractive than the Republic as a work of literature.

In the second place there is a long tradition of scholarship that identifies the authentic Plato with the doctrines of the *Republic* and of a few closely related dialogues (the dialogues which are now ascribed to Plato's middle period and which give prominence to the theory of transcendent Forms). The *Laws* adopts a quite different approach to the problems of politics from that of the *Republic*, it says virtually nothing about the Forms, and its doctrine appears inconsistent with the *Republic* on many points of detail. It is not surprising therefore that those who saw the author of the *Republic* as the only true Plato tended to play down the *Laws*.

So far as logic, metaphysics and epistemology are concerned, the traditional *Republic*-centred view of Plato is now extinct, at least among English-speaking scholars. Those trained in the analytic tradition of philosophy have found that they can learn as much, if not more, from late dialogues such as the *Sophist* as they can from those of the middle period. As yet there has been no corresponding change with regard to political philosophy. Attention is still focussed on the *Republic*, with the *Laws* treated as a kind of appendix. In so far as the present volume has any single aim it is to argue that this approach is mistaken and that a re-evaluation of the *Laws* is overdue. It is as one-sided to focus exclusively on the *Republic* when discussing Plato's political philosophy as it is when we consider his metaphysics or epistemology.

2   *Date and style*

The accepted view of the *Laws* as Plato's last work is based on external as well as internal evidence. Diogenes Laertius, the most important of the external sources, gives the following account of the *Laws* and of its short companion-work the *Epinomis*:

> Some say that Philip of Opus transcribed the *Laws* which were in the wax. They also say that the *Epinomis* is his. (III.37)

The natural reading of this is that when Plato died in 347 BC he left the *Laws* as a rough draft, presumably written on wax tablets. His pupil, Philip, prepared this draft for publication. The *Epinomis*, on the other hand, is said to be Philip's own work.

It is not clear from this account whether Philip's contribution to the *Laws* consisted simply in copying out what Plato had written or whether he edited it at all extensively. The former is likely to be nearer the truth. The text contains errors and discrepancies that could easily have been removed by an editor had he wished to do so. Their presence suggests that Philip generally reproduced Plato's words as he found them.

So far as the *Epinomis* is concerned, scholars are divided quite evenly between those who follow Diogenes Laertius in ascribing it to Philip and those who regard it as a genuine work of Plato. Fortunately we can, for present purposes, ignore this controversy. The *Epinomis* is not an integral part of the *Laws* and does not cast much fresh light on any of the philosophical questions I shall consider. I shall mention it only in passing.

Within the text of the *Laws*, 638b may possibly refer to the defeat of the Locrians by the Syracusans in 356 BC. If this is right, Book I, at least, must have been written during the last eight years or so of Plato's life. More subjectively, most readers agree that the main bulk of the work must have been composed after the period of Plato's involvement in Syracusan politics (i.e. after about 360 BC). The frequent harping on the virtues of old age also suggests that this is an old man's work.

The most striking confirmation of the lateness of the *Laws* comes from the style of writing and manner of composition. On a superficial reading, at least, the work often appears rambling and ill-structured. This is particularly apparent in the first two books with their long digression on the subject of drinking parties. The style is characterized by long rambling sentences in which the author himself sometimes seems to lose track of the grammatical structure. There are inconsistencies of detail (e.g. about the age of the third chorus (664d, 812b–c) and the age at which a man should marry (721b, 772d–e, 785b)). The characterization is generally weak, at least when compared with dialogues of the early and middle periods, and in Book V the dialogue form is dropped altogether. Book XI and the early part of Book XII read like a collection of disconnected fragments. Some of these anomalies are most naturally explained on the assumption that Plato died before he could give the *Laws* its final polish. Others may result from a decline in his literary powers. Whichever way one takes it, they support the view that the *Laws* is the product of Plato's old age.

Scholars hostile to the *Laws* have sometimes emphasized that it is an old man's work, with the implication that it is likely to show a decline in philosophical power. There is, I think, a straightforward answer to this. It would indeed be remarkable, if not inconceivable, that a man of, say, seventy-nine should suddenly develop new and original ideas of lasting significance. But no one would suggest that this is what happened in the case of the *Laws*. Plato must have been working on the *Laws* for several years before his death. Moreover he had been deeply concerned with political and ethical problems throughout his life. In setting down his final thoughts on these questions, he obviously drew on themes and arguments developed through many years of reflection. So, even if there are some elements in the *Laws* that are feeble or even embarrassing, we may still expect to find within it material worthy of a really great philosopher. The only way to approach the dialogue is to read it with an open mind, being prepared to admire its strengths as well as to criticize its weaknesses.

3   *The structure of the dialogue*

Most readers of the *Laws* at times find it difficult to follow the thread of the argument. This is partly because the work is long and lacks aids, such as chapter headings, that the modern reader takes for granted, but also because the underlying structure is often obscured by surface features. There are lengthy digressions, and in some cases the same ground seems to be worked over again and again. Nevertheless, on a careful reading, the structure does become apparent. In many ways the *Laws* is a more single-minded work than, say, the *Republic*. Certainly it never strays very far from its main topics. If it seems more diffuse than earlier dialogues that is largely because the transitions are less clearly marked and less skilfully handled.

The opening pages of the *Laws* leave the reader in no doubt about the subject or the basis on which it is to be treated. The participants in the dialogue are three old men, an unnamed Athenian who takes the lead, Megillus the Spartan and Cleinias the Cretan. They are walking through the Cretan countryside to the cave where Zeus is supposed to have given instructions to Minos, the legendary lawgiver of Crete.

Sparta and Crete, both of them Dorian cities, were much admired for the stability of their laws and their strict military discipline, but they were distinctly backward in philosophy and art. Athens, the home of democracy, was much less stable but was known for the intelligence and culture of its citizens. In keeping with this picture, the two Dorians both attribute the legal systems of their own states to divine authorship. The Athenian does not deny this — he certainly regards legislation as a more than human matter — but within a few pages he has attacked the basic assumptions underlying the Cretan and Spartan systems. Crete and Sparta were famous for their emphasis on military training and for the practice whereby male citizens took meals in communal dining rooms rather than in their own households. Both practices are directed towards success in war, but war is waged for the sake of peace, and the Athenian shows that the Dorian states have no institutions to secure the inner concord on which true peace depends.

Although it is difficult for us to make much of the contrast between the Athenian and Dorian ways of thought it must have seemed highly significant to Plato's contemporaries. Plato leaves us in no doubt as to his respect for the Dorian way of life, which was much admired by conservative elements throughout Greece, but at the same time he makes it clear that the Dorian tradition is fundamentally defective and needs to be reviewed in the light of Athenian wisdom. He thus distances himself from the orthodox conservatism of his day.

Once the defects of the Dorian institutions are established, the Athenian moves on to describe institutions which might remedy the situation. The rest of Book I and the whole of Book II are therefore occupied by a discussion of drinking parties, which are supposed to achieve beneficial effects by submitting the young to temptations under controlled conditions, and of the educational value of music and dance. Many readers have found this section tedious; Plato, himself apologizes for it (642a, 645c, 890e). From the philosophical point of view, it is important to attend to the underlying motives rather than to the proposals themselves. The aim of the law is virtue. A prerequisite of all virtue is *sophrosune*, self-control, self-discipline, or temperance. The achievement of *sophrosune* depends on being brought up to experience pleasures and pains in the right kind of way. The proposals about drinking, music and dance are designed to ensure this. Thus Books I and II set out what is, in fact, the main direction of the whole work. We are concerned with a system of laws designed to produce the virtue of self-control; lawgiving is largely a matter of education.

The beginning of Book III looks like a completely new start. We are given a survey of the history of human society from its first beginnings after the flood. This culminates in a description of the Dorian League which looked like a marvellous institution but in fact collapsed (682e–689e). The relevance of this whole section becomes clear only when we learn the reason for this collapse: it was due to a lack of the kind of self-control whose importance has been established in the first two books. Sparta alone survived the collapse because it alone had the good fortune to evolve a constitution which combined different elements, each of which acted as a restraint on the others (691b–693c). Here we are introduced to the idea of a mixed constitution. The two fundamental forms of constitution, monarchy and democracy, are exemplified by Persia and Athens. Each of these states has declined because of an unrestrained excess in the ruling principle. The decline of Persia is due to a lack of self-control on the part of its monarchs, that of Athens is due to the unrestrained excesses of the masses. A satisfactory constitution must embody both monarchic and democratic elements so that there is liberty combined with restraint (693d–702b).

The historical and political discussions of Book III pick up the fundamental themes of Books I and II. The aim of legislation is virtue, which can be achieved only by self-control. Legislation must therefore produce a society which ensures this self-control on the part of its citizens and which exhibits self-control in its forms of government. Most existing states have failed to do this and the only way in which it can be achieved is by setting up a mixed constitution. Thus, in spite of their apparent irrelevance and many digressions, Books I–III provide a prolegomenon to legislation, setting out the basic principles to be followed. We should aim to produce a society characterized by self-control and may expect to do this by adopting a form of constitution in which different elements are combined and act as restraints on one another.

At the end of Book III the Cretan reveals that he is a member of a commission established by the cities of Crete to draw up the constitution for a new colony. The rest of the *Laws* in effect consists of the Athenian's suggestions as to what form this constitution should take and what laws should be enacted for the new city. Books IV and V are concerned with the preliminaries to legislation. A description of the site proposed for the new colony gives the Athenian a chance to pronounce on the geographical conditions which are most suitable for a well-governed city (704a–707d). Then there is more general discussion of the problems of constitution making (708c–724b). Laws should be given 'preludes', i.e. preambles designed to persuade citizens to obey the law of their own free will rather than through fear of the penalty. The first part of Book V consists of a long prelude to the legal code as a whole (726a–734d). This is, in effect, a general exhortation to virtue. Then the conversation turns to the size of the population, the distribution of land and the administrative divisions of the state (734e–747e). The arrangements are designed to ensure that each household has an equal amount of land which will be inalienable. There will also be restrictions on the amount of movable property which can be held.

The legislative code proper occupies Books VI to XII. First there is what we might call constitutional law — the arrangements for holding assemblies and electing the council and magistrates and descriptions of their responsibilities. There follows a detailed exposition of the laws by which the city will be governed. It begins with marriage and the family and moves through education and military training to agriculture and economic matters. The central topics of criminal law — theft, murder, wounding and the like — are dealt with in Book IX, where there are substantial discussions of the purpose of punishment and of responsibility. Book X is theoretically concerned with the law against impiety but is in fact a closely argued exposition of the central doctrines of Plato's theology. Although this looks like a digression, it is clearly intended to provide a religious and metaphysical underpinning for the political and moral ideas that occupy the other books of the *Laws*. Book XI and the first part of Book XII are concerned with legislation on a variety of unconnected topics and appear to consist of fragments. The dialogue ends with an account of the nocturnal council. The function of this curious body is to act as the reason of the state by discerning the aims of legislation and the means of achieving them. To this end it will engage in philosophical research, concerning itself particularly with the unity of virtue and the nature and existence of God.

4 The character of the constitution

It would appear that most features of the constitution proposed for the new Cretan city derive from the practice of one or other of the Greek cities (Morrow, 1960). Plato is most strongly influenced by the law and legal practice of Athens, though his model is not so much the 'extreme' democratic constitution of his own day as the 'moderate' constitution supposed to have existed at an earlier period, when the Areopagus, a council of ex-magistrates, was the dominant influence. Some elements of the constitution are based on Sparta and others possibly on less well-known cities. The Athenian often suggests that he is providing only an outline of what should be included in the legal code but on many matters he goes into considerable detail. The *Laws* is, in fact, a systematic attempt to codify and reform Greek practice in the light of a clear understanding of the ultimate aims of law. In this respect it has, quite reasonably, been compared with the work of Bentham in Britain.

The new city is intended to be quite small — the ideal number of citizen households would be 5040. The arrangements for the distribution of land and the restrictions on the amount of movable property that may be held are designed to ensure that the citizen body will consist entirely of small farmers, though Plato presumably envisages that most, and perhaps all, of the actual physical labour will be done by slaves. Trade and manufacture are forbidden to citizens and will be carried out by resident aliens. It is arguable that Plato has not seen, or has ignored, the full implications of these measures, since many of his proposals seem to envisage a large community with a more developed economic life. In particular it is difficult to see how the citizens could find all the time that Plato expects them to spend on civic duties.

The constitutional proposals are elaborate and in many cases it is difficult to assess their full significance. The aim is clearly to produce a balance of different elements along the lines suggested in Book III. There is an assembly attended by all citizens but it is not clear whether it has any real function apart from the election of magistrates. The electoral arrangements are often complex, sometimes combining straightforward elections with selection by lot. It is clearly intended that the 'guardians of the laws' a body of thirty-seven very senior magistrates should exercise the greatest power. So, although ultimate responsibility may rest with the citizen body as a whole, in practice the main influence on policy will be exerted by a small group of elderly men, distinguished by their long experience and their moral and intellectual excellence.

A dominant theme is the sovereignty of law. All inhabitants of the city will be subject to law in all their activities and the legal code will be almost unalterable. Even the activities of the more important magistracies will be strictly regulated — all will be subject to some kind of measures to ensure that they conduct themselves in accordance with law. Thus law in some ways takes the place of the philosopher kings who exercise sovereignty in the *Republic*. Since the ultimate purpose of law is, in Plato's view, to make the citizens virtuous, law and education are so closely linked that at times they become almost indistinguishable. The entire life of the community is to be regulated so that the citizens develop the right kind of character. This is the purpose of the regulations that strictly control the educational arrangements, literary and artistic activities and the religious life of the city. Contacts with the outside world will so far as possible be restricted to avoid subversive influences.

5   *From the* Republic *to the* Laws

There are many differences, certainly of tone and emphasis, and probably also of doctrine, between the *Republic* and the *Laws*. The most striking of these — between the two accounts of the ideal city — will be considered in the next chapter. Equally important is the way in which the *Laws* differs from the dialogues of the early and middle periods in its account of virtue. In dialogues like the *Charmides*, *Laches*, *Protagoras* and *Gorgias*, Plato seems to adhere to the Socratic doctrine that virtue is knowledge, while the *Republic* suggests that only the philosopher can be truly virtuous because only he has knowledge of the good. In the *Laws*, on the other hand, the suggestion seems to be that the citizens can become virtuous if only their desires and passions are disciplined in such a way that they obey the law as a matter of habit. Discrepancies like this are particularly disturbing to those who believe that the author of the *Republic* is the only true Plato. For this reason some German scholars have seen the *Laws* as a chaotic product of senile decline (see Müller, 1951). Those prepared to take a more positive attitude to the *Laws* can explain discrepancies between it and earlier dialogues in either of two ways. One is to suppose that Plato's philosophy had evolved over the years. A long line of scholars has argued that Plato started from a Socratic intellectualism which stressed man's powers of reason to the virtual exclusion of the passions and desires and that he gradually moved from this to a position in which more importance is attached to these 'lower' elements in the soul. As Dodds (1951, p. 212) puts it: 'Plato's growing recognition of the importance of the affective elements led him beyond the limits of fifth century rationalism' (cf. O'Brien, 1967, ch. 6). It is easy to see the *Laws* as the culmination of this process.

The second approach emphasizes the fact that the *Laws* seems to have been written for a different purpose and to be directed to a different readership from that envisaged for the *Republic*. This view is forcefully maintained by Görgemanns (1960) who argues that the apparent discrepancies between the *Laws* and earlier writings can generally be understood if one appreciates that it is supposed to be written at a more 'popular' level.

It is obvious, even on a superficial reading, that the *Laws* has a more practical and less distinctively philosophical orientation than most other dialogues. Apart from anything else, we can point to the amount of space devoted to detailed legislative proposals, something the Socrates of the *Republic* thought it unnecessary to consider (425c–e). There are other indications that the *Laws* may be intended for a different kind of audience. The Athenian's two companions have no enthusiasm for, and no expertise in, the niceties of philosophy. They are represented as serious-minded old men, very interested in the problems of legislation and devoted to their own cities but quite without philosophical sophistication. Perhaps Plato envisages that his readers will share the same cast of mind. At one point (810e–812b) he suggests that the *Laws* or something like it might serve as a textbook for schoolchildren, which presumably implies that parts of the dialogue, at least, are intended to have a morally improving effect on a relatively unsophisticated audience. Then there is the insistence that laws should have preambles designed to persuade the citizens voluntarily to give their obedience. Samples of these preambles occupy much space in the dialogue. Although they sometimes have a substantial philosophical content they are primarily intended to provide moral exhortation. Similarly, if we are concerned with the practical problems of the legislator, there is not much point in dwelling on the 'true' virtue of the *Republic* which can be achieved only by philosophers. We must concentrate, rather, on the 'popular' virtues that are within the capacities of the man in the street. Thus, given what we can glean about the different purpose of the *Laws*, as compared with dialogues that have a more narrowly philosophical aim, it is not surprising that many topics should be treated with a rather different slant.

It must be emphasized that the 'developmental' and the 'change of level' view are not totally incompatible alternatives between which we have to make a once-and-for-all choice. Both are likely to contain an element of truth. We would naturally expect Plato's thought to have undergone some evolution in the period since he wrote the *Republic* and we would also expect him to adapt the content of the *Laws* to suit the particular purposes for which it was written. It is common ground that the *Laws* is a more practically oriented work than the *Republic* and that this practical orientation affects the treatment of almost all its topics. The difficulty is that of determining in what respects Plato believes that his earlier position was mistaken and in what respects he is merely suppressing earlier doctrines as irrelevant to his immediate purposes. Since Plato himself provides no explicit indications, one cannot expect to answer such questions by considering the *Laws* in isolation. Ultimately one has to decide what is plausible in the light of one's overall assessment of Plato's philosophical character.

6 *English versions*

The *Laws* is a particularly difficult work to translate. Its sentences are often long and unwieldy with an unclear grammatical structure, its idiom is sometimes unusual and in many passages there are obscurities which might be due either to corruption of the surviving manuscripts or to the unrevised state in which Plato left the dialogue.

My own interest in the *Laws* was prompted by the appearance of T. J. Saunders' Penguin translation (1970a). Saunders makes it abundantly clear that his main aim is to render the *Laws* easily accessible and intelligible to the modern reader. He divides the text into short sections for which he provides titles, he introduces brief passages of commentary and he distinguishes typographically the actual laws from discussions in which they are embedded. His table of contents and list of crimes and punishments can be very helpful. The translation itself is designed, above all, to be readable, and Saunders freely acknowledges that he often has to write an interpretation into the text, and sometimes even 'over-interprets' it. For these reasons Saunders' version is not the best to use when one needs to examine the detail of particular passages, but I have no doubt that Greekless readers, and perhaps even some who can read Greek, are more likely to find the *Laws* accessible and to achieve an understanding of its overall themes by reading Saunders, than by reading any other English translation.

Among Saunders' predecessors, Jowett (1953) is readable but free. Bury's Loeb translation (1926) is on the whole reliable, though occasionally marred by the adoption of unlikely readings of the Greek text. Taylor (1960a) is also in general accurate, but his use of archaic English can be irritating. The editions of the Greek used by these earlier translators are inferior to the Budé edition (des Places and Diès, 1951–6) used by Saunders, but this seldom affects matters of philosophical interpretation. The best policy for Greekless readers embarking on a serious study of the *Laws* is almost certainly to start with Saunders but to check the details of important passages against Bury, Taylor or the French version of des Places and Diès.

A translation of the *Laws* by Thomas Pangle (1980) has appeared in the United States but is not generally available in the United Kingdom. Pangle, who is not himself a classical scholar, is strongly critical of the 'loose' translations produced by traditional classical scholarship and he is particularly critical of Saunders. He aims to be as literal as possible and believes that he can thereby come closer to providing 'direct undistorted access to Plato's thought, exactly as Plato understood it'. This aim, in my view, displays a mistaken philosophy of language and a related misunderstanding of the purposes of classical scholarship. If texts were composed of words in the same kind of way that walls are made of bricks one could hope to produce a good translation simply by consulting a dictionary and substituting English equivalents for each Greek word. But in reality the context in which a word occurs largely determines its meaning; a translation right for one appearance of a word can easily be wrong for another. Thus, as Karl Popper puts it, 'every good translation is an *interpretation* of the original text' (1976, p. 23). A very literal translation may be misleading, or more usually, devoid of meaning. This is why classical scholars have always left word-for-word translation to schoolboys and have concentrated instead on conveying the thought of the original as they understood it. It is an illusion to suppose that a very literal translation can give us anything like direct access to Plato's thought. I would not therefore recommend the use of Pangle's translation on its own, though it may have value as a check on Saunders or as a 'crib' for those reading the *Laws* in Greek.

2

Plato's Political Philosophy

Charmides, 162e–175d; *Protagoras*, 311b–320c; *Gorgias*, 447b–461b; *Euthydemus*, 288d–292e; *Republic*, 368c–369c, 471c–474c, 479a–502c, 540d–541b, 592a–b; *Statesman*, 291d–303c; *Epistles*, VII, 323–337e, VIII

Even from the brief summary in the first chapter it will be obvious to most readers that the city described in the *Laws* differs quite markedly from the city of the *Republic*. For example, in the *Republic* all power is entrusted to 'guardians' who have undergone a long training in philosophy, but in the *Laws* ultimate sovereignty is supposed to rest with the law rather than with any particular group of citizens, there is much less emphasis on the need for philosophical training than in the *Republic*, and all citizens, not just a select few, are expected to take some part in government. In the *Republic* the rulers and the soldier class are forbidden to have property or even families of their own, but in the *Laws* all citizens are to have their own farms and families. The *Republic* is bitterly hostile to democracy but the constitution of the *Laws* has some decidedly democratic features.

Broadly speaking, there are two ways of accounting for these discrepancies. The first supposes that the change from the *Republic* to the *Laws* represents a change of heart on Plato's part. Most scholars who take this view would associate the change with Plato's own experience of politics. In 367 to 366 he had been invited by his friend Dion to go to Sicily to assist with the education of Dionysius who had just succeeded his father as tyrant of Syracuse. This scheme was totally unsuccessful: Dion was forced into exile and Plato returned to Athens. He was persuaded to go to Syracuse again in 361 but this time things, if anything, went even worse and Plato himself had difficulty in escaping. In 357 Dion led an expedition which seized control of Syracuse, but his attempts at reform broke down amid factional disputes, and Dion was himself assassinated.

It is tempting to suppose that when Plato went to Syracuse he was hoping to turn Dionysius into a philosopher king and to set up a state something like that described in the *Republic*. When the Syracusan fiasco convinced him that these schemes were impractical, he devoted himself to designing a mere realistic blueprint for politics — the city of the *Laws*. So the *Laws*, on this reading, is a product of despair.

An alternative view of the relationship between the *Republic* and the *Laws* suggests that these dialogues differ in their approach, not because Plato has had a change of heart, but because they are written with different intentions. One possibility is that the *Republic* is intended to exhibit in a graphic way the fundamental principles of morality and politics, while the *Laws* seeks to show how these principles might be applied in practice. Saunders, for example, writes, 'Plato could perfectly well have written the *Laws* when he wrote the *Republic* and the *Republic* when he wrote the *Laws*, for they are the opposite sides of the same coin'. In Saunders' view the *Republic* presents a 'theoretical ideal' while the *Laws* 'describes, in effect, the *Republic* modified and realised in the conditions of this word' (1970, p. 28). It has to be said at once that Saunders has overstated his case in suggesting that the *Republic* and the *Laws* could have been written at the same time. On any reading there are divergencies of doctrine between the two dialogues, particularly in matters of ethical theory. But it is still plausible to suppose that there is a broad continuity between the political doctrines implied in the *Republic* and those expounded in the *Laws*.

1   *The philosopher king*

Many of the dialogues argue explicitly or implicitly that excellence in politics is a matter of knowledge, so that the ideal constitution would bestow unimpeded authority on the person(s) who genuinely know what to do. On this view, democracy, with its assumption that all are equally qualified to rule, is an absurdity. The *Charmides* (162e–175d), *Protagoras* (esp. 311b–320c), *Gorgias* (esp. 447b–461b) and *Euthydemus* (288d–292e) compare political knowledge to the skill of a craftsman and point to the conclusion that this knowledge consists in a second-order skill enabling us to make proper use of all other skills. The *Republic* begins, like the earlier dialogues, by comparing justice with everyday skills but goes on to give a much fuller account of the second-order knowledge required by the ruler: it involves an intellectual grasp of the 'Forms', something achievable only by a trained philosopher. The conception of politics as a skill reappears in the *Statesman* (293c–302b), though this dialogue recognizes that the unfettered rule of the philosopher king is not a practical proposition. It is important to see that the doctrine of the philosopher king in itself gives no direct guidance as to what constitutional forms should be adopted. The philosopher king would rule without restriction, but so too would the tyrant, and Plato regards tyranny as the worst degradation (*Republic*, 562a–580c; cf. *Gorgias*, 470d–472d; *Statesman*, 302c–303b). Constitutional forms cannot by themselves guarantee that the ruler is enlightened. If we could find a suitable philosopher we might initiate a revolution to put him on the throne but it would be impossible to ensure that he continued to rule in an enlightened way or that a suitable successor was available when he died.

Since it is impossible to provide any institutional guarantee that the ruler will be wise, two different, but compatible, strategies appear to be available to those who hold politics to be a matter of knowledge. The first is political education: if those likely to gain power are given an appropriate training there is a chance that the state will be wisely governed. The second strategy is to adopt constitutional forms that encourage wise decisions or, at least, help to prevent foolish ones. This can be done in a variety of ways. If the area of discretion granted to rulers is tightly circumscribed by law, they may be prevented from doing some of the most dreadful things; it may also be possible to ensure that political decisions are taken only after prolonged discussion in which all points of view can be heard; and the requirement that candidates for election have appropriate experience or education may help to bar the most unsuitable characters from holding office.

It is natural to suppose that one of Plato's reasons for establishing the Academy was to create a training ground for those likely to have political influence — this was certainly one of the functions it served in practice. To the extent that this was part of Plato's intention, he was, in effect, following the first strategy, that of education. The *Laws* implicitly advocates a combination of the two strategies. The constitution proposed for the new Cretan city consists of a set of interlocking measures designed to encourage wise government, and this is accompanied with a constant emphasis on the need for education. So, although the *Laws* does not advocate the direct rule of a philosopher king, it can be seen as an interpretation at the practical level of the same underlying ideals.

2   *The impracticality of the* Republic

In the *Republic* Plato shows no interest in law or in constitutional procedures. The rule of the philosopher kings is maintained firstly by means of the class system, which ensures that those who come to political power have the right kind of natural endowment and have been protected from the temptations of property and family ties, and secondly by a system of education that is supposed to give the rulers the right kind of philosophical understanding. Most readers of the *Republic* have appreciated that this system could not be actualized among real men. For example, even if human beings could be divided into three different intellectual categories, it is unbelievable that the majority of them would meekly accept the imposition of the *Republic's* class system. The suggestion that the ideal state could be established and maintained only by force does not help, since force could be effective only if a substantial body of the population could be persuaded to support the ideal. It is equally incredible that the rulers, having gained power, should give up all claims to property and family relationships. If Plato did not see these and similar difficulties he would have been remarkably naive. Of course, history has seen a good many would-be reformers conspicuous for their naivety, but Plato gives clear indications that he is not among them: several passages in the *Republic* suggest that its ideal state is not to be seen as a practical possibility. In the *Republic*, V, Socrates is made to emphasize the difficulty of setting up the state he is describing and to maintain that its validity as an ideal does not depend on its practicability. Nevertheless he claims that there could be such a state if philosophers became kings or kings philosophers (471c–474b). Later he says that to establish the state it will be necessary to expel from the city everyone over ten years old (540e–541a). He does not explain who would look after the city in the absence of the adults or who would train the children. When, near the end of the discussion, Glaucon doubts whether the state can ever be realized, Socrates replies that it does not matter whether the state does or will exist. It is a pattern set up in heaven on which whoever wishes may model himself (592b).

Officially, at least, the *Republic* is concerned, not with the state or the constitution, but with the virtue of justice. The state makes its appearance only by way of analogy: Socrates suggests that it will be easiest to look for justice first in the state and then to apply what has been learnt to the justice of the individual soul (368c–369c). To this end he sets off to describe a perfect state which will perfectly instantiate the virtues he is seeking. Sometimes he seems to lose sight of the original purpose, but it is significant that when in the passage quoted above (592b) he finally draws his conclusions from the analogy, the ideal state is offered as a heavenly model for *ourselves* (not for our cities). This method of argument does not permit Socrates to make any concessions to practical difficulties, since, if he did so, his state would be imperfect and could not offer a picture of perfect justice. But he is only too well aware that this is not a perfect world. So, although his doctrine that the city of the *Republic* is the ideal presumably commits him to saying that we should all aspire towards it, nothing commits him to the belief that real men will ever succeed in getting at all close to that ideal. There is, therefore, no reason to suppose that when he went to Syracuse Plato took with him the *Republic* as a plan or blueprint for political action.

3   *The* Statesman

Those who hold that Plato changed his mind between the *Republic* and the *Laws* are apt to believe that the *Statesman* shows him in the act of making this change. The relevant section of the dialogue begins at 291c where the Eleatic Stranger, who leads the conversation, launches into criticism of the ways in which different kinds of constitution are conventionally classified. People classify them firstly according to the number of rulers, whether they are ruled by one man, a few or the many, and secondly according to whether they rely on enforced subjection or voluntary obedience, whether they are rich or poor and whether they follow law or are lawless. For example, the rule of one man according to law is called monarchy, but without law it is tyranny. The Stranger's complaint is that this classification ignores the fundamental question — whether the ruler has the requisite political knowledge. For example, someone is said to possess the knowledge of medicine provided simply that he knows how to make people well; it is irrelevant whether he exercises this skill over few or many, over willing or unwilling subjects. Similarly, since true statesmen know what is best for their cities it does not matter whether they act with or without law, whether they are rich or poor or whether their subjects do or do not consent (292b–293e).

After this apparent reassertion of the philosopher king doctrine, attention shifts to the role of law. Two parallel passages (294a–295b, 295b–302b) argue that laws are theoretically absurd but necessary in practice. The first argument concentrates on the great differences between individual human beings. Because of those differences there is no reason to suppose that a general law laid down for all men will achieve what is best for each individual. But, equally, the statesman cannot sit beside each person all the time telling him what to do. So there is no alternative to the use of law. In this the statesman is rather like a gymnastic instructor who, being unable to specify advice to each member of his class, contents himself with telling them what is good for the majority (295a–b).

The second argument begins by re-emphasizing the theoretical absurdity of law. A doctor who had to leave his patients for a while might leave them written instructions about what to do in his absence, but we would not expect him to bind himself by those instructions if he returned early to find that his patients' condition had changed. Similarly it would be absurd for a democratic or oligarchic government to attempt to regulate by law exactly how sailors were to sail their ships or doctors to heal their patients. In each case the point is that we expect experts to use their own judgement in particular cases rather than to follow general rules laid down in advance. But, the Stranger goes on, it would be even more absurd if, after establishing general laws, we allowed officials chosen by election or lot to set them aside simply to curry favour.

The conclusion of all this is that, since laws are the product of experience and are brought into being only after advice has been taken and the people persuaded to accept them, it is best to make sure that they are obeyed. A ruler with true knowledge would have no need of laws but, as things are now, there are no such rulers. So we must imitate the true constitution by means of law. On this basis the Stranger constructs a new ranking of constitutions. Where law is supreme, the best constitution is the rule of one man, the next best is that of the few and the worst is that of the many. Where law is not followed the order is reversed. The point here is that a single ruler has most power both to do good and to do harm. Democracies are weakest in both respects.

Although the Eleatic Stranger moves from the praise of a philosopher king to the advocacy of a state ruled by law he does not appear to change his mind on any point of principle. He combines the two ideas by showing that they operate on different levels. The aim of statecraft is the good of the city, and it is knowledge which normally enables us to achieve such goals. But a ruler who could direct every detail of the common life in accordance with knowledge would have to be more than human. In the world as it actually is the best we can do is imitate knowledge by means of law. Thus the philosopher king remains valid as a theoretical ideal while the rule of law is recommended in practice.

4   *The letters*

Of the letters that have come down to us under Plato's name, three, all of them widely accepted as genuine, cast some light on the *Laws*. Letter III addressed to Dionysius, purports to be written soon after Plato returned to Athens in 366 or 365. Letters VII and VIII, both addressed to the friends of Dion, purport to be written soon after Dion's death in about 353 BC. Of these, letter VII is primarily a defence of Plato's own involvement in Sicily, though it does offer some practical advice. Letter VIII, supposedly written about the same time, is largely concerned to suggest the policies that the friends of Dion should follow. If genuine, these letters should cast a good deal of light on the development of Plato's political ideas.

In letter VII Plato tells how the experiences of his early manhood, in particular the death of Socrates, discouraged him from active politics. He believed that the laws and customs of Athens and of other cities had become hopelessly corrupt and that philosophy alone could reveal the true nature of justice. So he concluded that the troubles of the human race would not cease until either those who were true lovers of wisdom achieved political office, or those who held political power became lovers of wisdom themselves. It was in this frame of mind that Plato came to the court of Dionysius (325c–326b; cf. *Republic*, 473d, 487c–489b, 501e). He makes it clear that by using his influence on Dionysius he hoped to unite philosophers and rulers (328a). This letter is now seen as an important source for those who believe that Plato hoped to turn Dionysius into a philosopher king. But Plato does not say that he expected to actualize the city of the *Republic* or anything like it. His main emphasis is on law. It was the corruption of the *laws* and *customs* of cities like Athens that disturbed him (325c–d, 326a), and in going to Syracuse he hoped to put into practice his ideas about 'laws and the constitution' (328c). He taught that cities should be enslaved, not to human despots, but to laws (334c–d) and he eschewed violent revolution (331c–d). In letter III, 316a, he mentions that he worked with Dionysius on preambles to laws, which suggests that he had already formulated the idea that laws should have persuasive preambles, one of the more distinctive ideas of the dialogue, the *Laws*, as we have it.

The advice Plato gives to the friends of Dion carries a similar emphasis on the importance of law. Dion, he believes, would have sought power, not for its own sake, but in order to create the best constitution and laws (351c). His followers should likewise seek to equalize the laws, i.e. impose laws for the common good rather than for the benefit of their own faction, and they should induce their opponents to obey these laws by example (i.e. by obeying law themselves) as much as by fear (336c–337b). To this end they should invite fifty wise men from all over Greece to draw up laws fair to all (337b–d). The advice in letter VIII is even more explicit. Plato urges the followers of Dion to establish the supremacy of law and to avoid the excess both of freedom and servitude by establishing a form of constitutional monarchy (354a–356b). He recommends a constitution with three kings (Dionysius, Hipparinus, a half brother of Dionysius who had joined Dion's faction, and Dion's own young son) whose functions seem largely ceremonial and religious. Real power would rest with thirty-five guardians of the laws ruling together with an assembly and council. There should be a special court of select judges to try capital cases. The triple kingship is apparently proposed simply to reconcile the conflicting factions in Syracuse. All the other proposals are to be found in the Laws (though the number of guardians is there increased to thirty-seven).

Assuming that the letters in question are genuine, it is clear that, at least by the end of his involvement in the affairs of Syracuse, Plato was beginning to develop ideas characteristic of the Laws and to put his political faith in the supremacy of law. He attributes similar ideas both to his own younger self and to Dion, and he does not appear to distinguish these ideas at all sharply from that of the philosopher king. On his own account when he first went to Syracuse he worked to establish good laws and thought that, as a prerequisite for this, the tyrant Dionysius would have to be trained in philosophy. When, on the other hand, he gives advice to the followers of Dion he does not suggest that they should engage in philosophical studies. But there is no evidence to show that he ever believed that philosophers could in practice rule unencumbered by law and nothing to suggest that he was conscious of any marked change in his political principles. At most, there seems to be a gradual shift in emphasis from the distinctive wisdom of the philosopher to a more humble kind of wisdom based on experience and enshrined in law.

5   *Plato's politics*

The picture that emerges from this survey of Plato's writings shows him starting with the doctrine that politics is a matter of knowledge. This doctrine culminates in the description of the philosopher kings in the *Republic*. In view of the fact that there is no practical way of guaranteeing that our rulers will possess the wisdom of the philosopher, this ideal of a philosopher king can work only at a theoretical level. But it does nevertheless have some practical implications in that it will lead us to prefer institutions which encourage rationality in the taking of decisions. Similarly, although the social institutions of the *Republic* could never be actualized one who sees them as an ideal will in practice favour institutions which encourage unity and harmony rather than dissent and diversity.

Wherever Plato addresses himself to matters of practical politics he advocates the supremacy of law, a doctrine worked out in great detail in the *Laws*. This is entirely compatible with his doctrines at the theoretical level. If, as the *Statesman* suggests, law embodies decisions of the community taken after careful consideration, the rule of law may be the closest ordinary men can come to the rule of knowledge. So the *Republic* and the *Laws* can be seen as complementary to one another.

Although there seems to be no change of principle between the *Republic* and the *Laws* it is probably no accident that the works which treat politics at a practical level belong to the later period of Plato's life. No doubt events in Syracuse helped to focus Plato's attention on matters of practical politics, but other factors may be equally important. We know that Plato's attitude to the fundamental questions of philosophy changed between the *Republic* and later dialogues such as the *Sophist* and *Statesman*. In the *Republic* and other dialogues of the same period, Plato espouses the theory of Forms. As it appears in these dialogues the theory is concerned with the relationship between particulars and universals. Plato argues that the particular instances of, say, justice in this world may be called 'just' only in so far as they resemble or participate in the Form of the just. The Forms are thus treated as paradigms which the things of this world imperfectly resemble. The role of the philosopher is to turn his back on the everyday world and devote his attention to the Forms. In dialogues such as the *Theaetetus* the *Sophist* and the *Statesman*, the Forms, if they appear at all, are no longer treated as paradigms. Plato is more concerned with the relationships between concepts than with that between universals and particulars. He discusses how and to what extent very general concepts such as 'being', 'sameness', 'difference', 'motion' and 'rest' may combine with one another and devote a lot of attention to the analysis of more specific concepts such as those of the 'sophist' and the 'statesman' or even of the 'angler' and the 'weaver'. These discussions are characterized by a much greater concern for the world of empirical realities. This change in Plato's philosophical method has been the source of much controversy (see Further Reading, section 8). It may be connected with a new emphasis in his political thought. In particular, it may help to explain why he no longer talks of a paradigm city set up in heaven but attends instead to cities in the real world and why he shows so much more respect for experience.

Human beings are imperfect creatures living in an imperfect world. We are not fully rational or virtuous and our needs and desires have an unfortunate tendency to outstrip the means available for their fulfilment. If we are to have any decent kind of life we need to co-operate, yet we constantly come into conflict with one another. The task of politics is, so far as possible, to reconcile conflicting desires and interests and to create unity in place of discord. It would have no place in a golden age when everyone was virtuous and want was unknown. The *Laws* is largely concerned with these practical problems of making a good life possible in the world as it actually is. The *Republic*, on the other hand, has nothing to say on these matters and restricts itself to describing a community in which human imperfections have been abolished. So if we are interested in Plato's political theory — that is, in his answers to what we now understand as political problems — it makes sense to regard the *Laws* as the primary source while treating the *Republic* as a kind of prolegomenon designed to set out the underlying principles.

3

The Nature of Law

Laws, 624a–632d, 644d–645c, 712b–716b, 769a–771a, 772a–d, 874e–876e, 889a–890d, 960c–964a, *Hippias Major*, 284a–285b; *Statesman*, 291c–303c; *Minos* (although this dialogue is probably spurious it makes an interesting commentary on the *Laws*)

1 Law in the Greek city

For most English speakers, the paradigm case of law is a statute enacted by Parliament or Congress. But there is, of course, much law that does not fit this pattern — the common law, early customary law, international law and so on. The Greek word *nomos* (plural: *nomoi*) has, if anything, an even wider extension. It may refer to any form of order which is actually accepted or which ought to be accepted by a social group (Ostwald, 1969, pp. 20–54). Thus it can apply to what we would regard as rules of morality or etiquette, to religious beliefs and practices, to the general way of life of a particular community and even to the habits of mankind as a whole when compared, for example, to those of the beasts. Often the best translation is not 'law' but 'convention' or 'custom'. Ostwald (1969) has argued that the application of *nomos* to what we would call 'statute law' was a comparatively late development, associated in Athens with the rise of democracy. The democrats preferred *nomos* to the older term *thesmos* because it suggested a norm accepted by the people, rather than a measure imposed on them from above.

The wide scope of *nomos* is reflected in the content of the *Laws*. Plato is concerned with all kinds of social norm, including the fundamental principles of the constitution, laws prohibiting crimes such as murder and theft, the regulations that will govern agricultural and commercial activities, standards of religious observance, the ways in which children will be brought up and patterns of sexual behaviour. He is aware that some aspects of human behaviour cannot be governed by written statutes enforced by the courts, but he does not consider that they therefore fall outside the scope of *nomos*. Instead he distinguishes between written and unwritten laws. He uses this distinction in at least three different contexts.

(1)   Sometimes the point is that it is, as a matter of practice, inappropriate to lay down formal rules with penalties to regulate the details of, say, family life or behaviour in the hunting field (788b, 790a–b, 822d–823a).

(2)   At 793a–d he seems to be making the important point that a legal system requires a background of accepted moral beliefs, customs and conventions. These may not be part of the formal legal code, but without them it would collapse.

(3)   At 838a–b and 841b the unwritten laws are apparently sexual taboos, which may influence behaviour more powerfully than any formal legislation.

In none of these cases does Plato suggest that there is a fundamental difference of kind between the written and the unwritten laws. All areas of life fall within the legislator's concern and it is his task to establish appropriate norms of behaviour. Where formal penalties and written laws are inappropriate, he has to rely on exhortation and persuasion, but there is no difference of principle between the two. One consequence of this is that Plato does not recognize a distinction between law and morality. Nor is there an area of private life with which law may not, in principle, interfere.

2   *Law and purpose*

The *Laws* opens with a question about the source of law: 'Do Cleinias and Megillus attribute the Cretan and Spartan systems to a god or to some man?' Both piously attribute their own systems to gods. This suggests that they accept some kind of divine command theory — law demands our obedience because it embodies the edicts of the gods. One implication of that theory would be that established law is beyond criticism because it rests on divine authority. Later the Athenian makes it clear that he too gives law some kind of religious basis, but for the moment he does not dwell on this point. Instead, he alters direction and asks his companions about the purposes of their own cities' most distinctive institutions (625c). In this he sets the tone for the whole dialogue. Attention is focussed on the end or purpose that law is supposed to serve much more than on its source. Unlike the divine command theory, this perspective inevitably lays existing systems of law open to criticism, either as failing to accomplish their purposes or as being directed at ends that are altogether misguided.

In assuming that the institutions of the Dorian states have a purpose, the Athenian does not commit himself to any particular theory of law. On any view, the individual provisions of a legal code may be expected to serve some purpose — after all, the legislators presumably thought that they were achieving something by their enactments. But a stronger conception of law as purposive may be implicit in the Cretan's reply (626a–c). He claims that the lawgiver of Crete directed his regulations concerning both public and private life towards the goal of victory in war. The language implies that victory is the unique end of all the Cretan legislation, not solely of those institutions about which the Athenian had inquired (a point blurred in Saunders' translation). A few pages later the Athenian attacks piecemeal legislation and insists quite explicitly that all the legislator's activities be directed to the one ultimate goal (630d–632d). This single goal is described in a variety of ways, but the Athenian clearly believes that it will involve making citizens completely virtuous, that this will bring about the well-being and happiness of the citizens and that it can thus be identified with the common good of all the citizens (631b, 697d, 715b, 875a–c, 923b, 925e). At the very end of the *Laws* the demand for single-minded legislation provides the main basis for the activities of the nocturnal council (962b–c).

This assertion that there is an unique goal at which all legislation should aim is capable of two varieties of interpretation:

(1)   It may simply mean that laws *ought* to aim at this goal. One can maintain this while agreeing that, in the world as it is, many (perhaps most) laws do not have this aim. Such measures will be bad laws but they will nonetheless be laws.

(2)   On the alternative interpretation it is seen as part of the intrinsic nature of law that it should seek a particular end. A measure not directed to this end is not in the full sense law.

Many of the legal theorists known as positivists would be happy to accept that law should be directed to a particular goal provided that this is understood in sense (1). Bentham and Austin, for example, both believed that law depends on the will of the sovereign but coupled this with the belief that all laws *ought* to be directed to the greatest happiness of the greatest number. If the enactments of a wicked or misguided sovereign were not directed to this end, the resulting provisions would, on their view, be bad laws but nevertheless valid as laws.

The second view, that law by its very nature has to serve a particular end, must be denied by any legal positivist but is characteristic of authors in the natural-law tradition. Thus Aquinas argues that every law is directed to the common good and that this involves making the citizens virtuous. A tyrannical law, therefore, is not properly a law, but rather a perversion of law (*Summa Theologiae*, 1a 2ae, 90, 2; 92, 1; 96, 4). Pushed to its logical conclusion, this might seem to imply that a bad law (i.e. one not conducive to the right end) cannot really be called law, in other words that there is no such thing as an unjust law (Cicero, *De Legibus*, II. v. 11–12; Augustine, *De Libero Arbitrio*, 1.5; Aquinas, *Summa Theologiae*, 1ae 2ae, 95, 2 & 4).

Where does Plato stand on this question? In the *Minos*, 314e, Socrates is made to maintain that there cannot be a bad law and thus to commit himself to the natural-law position. That dialogue is probably spurious, but the same doctrine is affirmed in the *Hippias Major*, 284a–285b, which most scholars now accept as genuine. Nowhere in the *Laws* is Plato so explicit, but there are a number of passages where the Athenian talks as though law must necessarily be good and in accordance with reason and as though the legislator must necessarily be right (e.g. 644c–d, 645a, 659d, 714a, 715d, 728a). Elsewhere he speaks of laws and legislation as correct or incorrect (e.g. 627d, 705e, 707b, 715b) or implies that law has natural standards of rightness (e.g. 631c–d, 690c, 853a).

The fullest treatment of this problem is between 712b and 715d. There the Athenian, while officially discussing what form of constitution should be imposed on the new Cretan city, seizes the opportunity to distinguish between genuine and pseudo-constitutions. Crete and Sparta have genuine constitutions because their laws aim at the common good of the whole state. Other so-called constitutions are simply mechanisms by which one faction in the city imposes its will on the rest. The section is interrupted by a digression on the age of Cronos which leads to the conclusion that in obeying law we are obeying reason, the immortal element within us (713c–714b). Some people, it is true, say that there are as many kinds of law as there are forms of constitution. They believe that laws ought to promote the interests of the rulers and that justice is whatever suits the stronger party (714b–c). The Athenian, however, denies that these are genuine constitutions. In his view laws are not correct unless they serve the good of the whole city (715a–b). He goes on to contrast the fortunate states whose rulers are obedient to law with the wretched ones where law is trodden under foot.

It is natural to interpret this passage as asserting that a genuine law must seek the good of the state and that measures which do not seek the common good are not, strictly speaking, to be called laws. In fact the

Athenian is not quite as explicit as this. He does tell us that corrupt states lack genuine constitutions but he does not say in so many words that they have no laws —merely that their laws are not correct (*orthos*). Other passages suggest the same kind of ambivalence. The Athenian never seems to doubt the validity of existing legislation even though he recognizes that laws vary from city to city and sees it as his task to discover which of these laws is good and which bad (634c, 635a, 637d, 683b, 708c, 770e, 962b-c). The same attitude is evident in his treatment of the Cretan and Spartan systems. These fall short of the ideal in some very important respects (631a, 634c, 705d) but the Athenian does not doubt their legality. The inference is that a misguided measure may still be genuine law.

This may seem to suggest that the Athenian is hopelessly confused — that he is simultaneously trying to sit on both the positivist and natural-law sides of the fence. But there is in fact an interpretation which makes very good sense of his position. In dialogues such as the *Phaedo* (97c ff.) and the *Republic* (508b–509b) Plato argues that we cannot really understand anything until we know how it is related to the good. In other words we need to know what purpose it serves. This is obviously the case with artefacts such as knives. We cannot know what a knife is without knowing the purpose or function for which it is designed — in this case cutting. A knife may therefore be said to be defined by its function. It is characteristic of such items that the line between being a bad specimen of its kind and not being a specimen at all is blurred. For example, we can say that a good knife cuts well and that a bad knife cuts badly. But what do we say if we come across a knife-like object that is quite hopeless at cutting? Do we call it a very bad knife or say that it is not really a knife? The answer may not be clear.

We can apply these ideas to our problem about the object of law. Plato obviously believes that it is part of the nature of law that it should seek the good of the whole community. In other words law is defined by its function of promoting the common good. It follows that we may be uncertain whether to regard a very misguided provision as a bad law or as not a genuine law at all. There will be a continuous gradation from good laws, at one end, to measures at the other end that are so bad as not to merit the title of 'law'. Measures that come between the two may deserve some respect while falling well short of the ideal (see Aquinas, *Summa Theologiae*, 1a 2ae, 96, 4).

On this view the Athenian has no need to make it clear whether misguided measures are or are not law. Law, on his conception of it, has its own intrinsic standards of rightness and wrongness. He can therefore talk about particular laws as correct or incorrect. The nearer a measure comes to fulfilling these standards, the more truly can it be called 'law'. But there is not a black and white division between genuine and spurious systems. Even the misguided codes of existing states have some claim to validity.

3　The role of reason

The Athenian and his companions always appear confident that the good which is the aim of law can be objectively discerned and that it can therefore be *known* whether a particular measure is or is not good law. They see themselves as discussing the natural correctness and error of law (627d) and believe that in doing so they are seeking what is 'true' and 'best' (634c). The author of the *Minos*, whoever he was, accurately reflects this doctrine when he makes Socrates claim that law is a good (i.e. true) opinion of the city and so must aim to be the discovery of what is the case (314d–315a).

Law, in the Athenian's view, is an embodiment or expression of reason and an object of knowledge. The judgements of reason, when embodied in a decree of the city, become law (644c–d; cf. 645a). Reason strives to become law (835e) and in obeying law we are obeying the edicts of reason (713e–714a). The assimilation of law to reason is helped by an etymological connection which Plato (wrongly) discerns between *nomos* (law) and *nous* (reason or intelligence) 713e–714a, 957c; cf. 836e.

This view of law as an object of rational knowledge underlies the account of the nocturnal council. The senior members are the reason of the state and their young assistants its senses; both are needed to ensure its survival (961d). Their main task is to discern the ends and means of legislation (962d). In this they are compared to experts such as navigators, generals and doctors who have knowledge of the end to be pursued and are able to apply this in practice (961e–962b, 963a–b).

The Athenian's theology supports his view of the objectivity of law: 'God holds the beginning middle and end of all things and justice follows him to punish those who break his divine law' (715e–716a); 'God, not man, is the measure of all things' (716c). The connection of these theological pronouncements with the rationality of law becomes clear in Book X. There the Athenian argues at length that the order of the universe shows it to be under the control of reason; we may therefore be sure that there are supremely rational deities who love the just and hate the unjust and that the natural order is so arranged that the wicked will automatically suffer for their misdeeds. The idea that there are irregular movements in the heavens is treated as blasphemous because it contradicts this picture (820e–822c). Thus law is the reflection within the human sphere of the rational order that governs the universe as a whole. In keeping with this there is a vehement attack on those who see law, together with moral and religious beliefs, as products of human invention rather than of nature (888e–890b). The great heresy is the distinction, prevalent among Plato's intellectual predecessors, between *nomos* (law or convention) and *phusis* (nature), with its implication that *nomos* is relative to particular human societies and lacks any fundamental importance. The Athenian, by contrast, seeks to show that genuine law is a part of nature. Indeed one way of interpreting, not only Book X, but the whole of the *Laws* would be to see it as a systematic attack on the *nomos–phusis* distinction. Plato would replace this with a view that unites law and nature by showing that they are both products of the same divine reason and therefore involve the same kind of order. It is the work of human reason to discern the truth about law and it may be aided in this by observation of the orderly movements of the heavens.

Despite its aesthetic appeal the parallel between the order created by law in human societies and the order apparent in the visible heavens does not solve any fundamental problems in the theory of law. The trouble is that the order of the heavens tells us nothing whatever about what we, as human beings, ought or ought not to do. There is no sense in which we can literally emulate the movements of the heavenly bodies. So, even if we were to grant that the universe is under the control of divine reason, we still would not know what forms of law ought to be adopted by human communities. Like other ethical rationalists, Plato can make good his position only if he can show that his moral recommendations are in some way derivable from self-evident principles of reason. In practice he cannot do this. The measures he recommends rest largely on two assumptions, (a) that whatever makes for the stability and security of the state is good, and (b) that conventional standards of morality are to be upheld. The general tendency of his work is to give the dictates of conventional morality the status of divine truths.

Associated with this tendency to identify reason and convention is an unclarity about how political wisdom is to be attained. The general position seems to be that it is a kind of scientific knowledge requiring the awareness of first principles and the ability to put them into practice. The parallel is usually with some kind of trained expert (e.g. 709a–e, 961e–962b, 963a–b). But in practice the Athenian seems to rely on the accumulated experience of mankind rather than on any form of specialist knowledge. This is evident in his ready acceptance of conventional moral beliefs, in his apparent use of existing codes of law, in the praise he gives to Crete and Sparta, and, above all, in the respect he shows for old age. Education, for example, is defined as 'the process of drawing and guiding children towards that principle which is pronounced right by the law and confirmed as truly right by the experience of the oldest and most just' (659d, trans. Bury), and there are many other tributes to the supposed wisdom of the old (e.g. 634d–e, 665d–e, 715d–e). In the constitution of the Cretan city the important magistrates must all be aged at least fifty (755a, 765d, 946a; cf. 951e, 961a).

If we take such passages at their face value there are obvious problems. There is no reason why the judgments of the old should coincide with those of rational insight. Moreover the old, though they have the benefit of experience, are commonly supposed to be prejudiced and inflexible. Thus the assumption that they are the repository of truth might be a recipe for simple conservatism. We may however be able to make a better case for Plato on the hypothesis that he is writing at a 'popular level'. The members of the nocturnal council who will be the experts on legislation are to follow a programme of philosophical study. Presumably out of deference to Cleinias and Megillus the Athenian does not explain this in any detail. It might be the kind of study laid down for the philosopher kings of the *Republic*, though it is perhaps more probable that it would resemble the kind of dialectic described in the *Sophist* (see below, chapter 12, section 5). The members of the nocturnal council will be the experts on legislation. They will also be quite old. It must be these that the Athenian has in mind when he refers, in passages like 659d, to the wisdom of the old. Cleinias and Megillus and the popular audience they supposedly represent could not be expected to understand the philosophical work of the nocturnal council, but they do respect the wisdom of the old and they do admire the order of the universe. It would make sense therefore that the Athenian should choose to emphasise these factors and play down more distinctively philosophical elements.

This interpretation would absolve the Athenian from the charge of confusing reason with convention, but it raises formidable problems at another level. We have to accept (a) that the practice of some form of Platonic dialectic can lead to an insight into the fundamental principles of law and morality, and (b) that it is possible for at least some human legislators to link these insights with the practical business of law making. Plato himself denies that philosophical insight can be conveyed in a book (*Letter* VII 341d-e). Thus we are all to some extent in the position of Cleinias and Megillus. We are forced either to take on trust the possibility of a genuinely philosophical legislation or to fall back on experience as the best available substitute.

4   The role of the legislator

In the real world, systems of law have to govern the daily lives of peoples whose circumstances vary enormously from place to place and time to time. So it is not enough for a legislator to be aware of eternal moral truths, if there are any. He needs to translate any such truths into detailed regulations appropriate to the particular circumstances of his own community. Plato is well aware of this — he emphasizes what we might call the 'contingent factors' in legislation and what he calls the 'opportunities given by God and chance' (709a-c). But he is by no means consistent in his handling of such problems.

In the *Statesman* it is argued that laws, being general, cannot take account of individual circumstances. The ideal would therefore be the unimpeded rule of a wise man who could deal appropriately with each case. A state governed by law is a second-best alternative, needed only because wise enough rulers are not generally available (see above, chapter 2, section 3). The *Laws* also concedes that theoretically speaking, the absolute rule of a wise man might be ideal: 'knowledge is unsurpassed by any law or regulation; reason, if it is genuine and really enjoys its natural freedom, should have universal power' (875c). The difficulty is that, in practice, no human being is capable of exercising untrammelled power: not only do most men lack wisdom but there is also the danger that their desires will get the better of their judgement (713c-d, 714a, 875c-d; cf. Aristotle, *Politics*, III. xv, 1386a 7-35). Thus reason must be embodied in law. But, even then, the legislator should, if possible, leave the courts wide discretion to deal with individual cases. So, where good courts can be established, the legislator will content himself with setting out guidelines or examples of what is to be done (876c-d).

Despite its superficial attractions, this view seems to rest on a misunderstanding. The function of law is not simply to remedy the defects of human rulers but to bring benefits that could be secured in no other way. One of its chief functions is to enable us to co-ordinate our activities by means of rules: if I know that most people will obey the law, I can, within certain limits, predict the behaviour of my fellow men and plan my own life accordingly. To plan my life in a rational way, I also need to know which kinds of act will be penalized by the authorities. This is possible only where there is a settled system of law. But it is not only by regulating pre-existent forms of activity that law enriches our lives; it also makes new forms of activity possible. Only where there is a law of property can we buy and sell things; only where there is a law of inheritance can we bequeath our property to others, and so on. None of this would be possible if an absolute ruler settled all questions on a purely *ad hoc* basis.

In practice Plato not only recognizes the need for a settled system of law but carries it to extremes. He expects the legislator to establish a detailed code that will remain valid for all time with little possibility of change (see below, chapter 8). In part this presumably reflects the general Greek admiration for stability in law and Plato's own dislike of political change, but it must also be connected with his view of law as a product of reason. If we emphasize the role of reason in providing knowledge of eternal truths and regard human laws as the counterpart among men of the divine order that governs the universe, then we will not expect an adequate legal system to be produced haphazardly by piecemeal legislation. It must be the result of a single unified vision, and it therefore requires a wise legislator. Once he has done his work there will be no need for improvements or modifications, because the principles of reason embodied in the law are as permanent and unchanging as the laws of mathematics or of celestial motions. Thus Plato's belief in the power of reason leads him in directions quite opposite to one another. When he emphasizes the variability of human affairs he is led to the ideal of a wise ruler unimpeded by law; when he emphasizes reason's function in the discovery of eternal truths he expects the legal system to be equally permanent and inflexible.

A solution to this problem requires a more complicated account of the relation between law as established by human legislators and the eternal truths supposedly discovered by reason. The point is well handled by Aquinas who distinguishes the roles of natural and human law. Natural law, which remains the same at all times and places, lays down the ultimate ends that are to be pursued, while it is the task of human law to determine the means by which these ends are to be sought in particular circumstances. So human law may vary from place to place and change as conditions change (*Summa Theologiae*, 1a 2ae, 95.2; cf. Aristotle, *Nicomachean Ethics*, V. vii). It follows from this that there are two ways in which human law may be derived from the natural law. Sometimes it is deduced from the principles of natural law in much the same way that a conclusion in geometry is deduced from premises; for example, the precept 'Do no murder' is deduced from the more general natural-law principle 'Do harm to no man'. In other cases the human legislator is more like a creative artist: he has to produce something which will meet the ends of law but has considerable freedom in deciding how to do this.

In practice Plato also sees the lawgiver as a creator of institutions. His legislator is a craftsman rather than a scientist. He knows that a good life can be secured for the citizens only by the cunning design of laws. But he seems curiously unconscious of this when he theorizes about legislation. In spite of a few passages where he compares the work of the lawgiver with that of a craftsman (803a, 858a–b), he is more apt to present it as being like science or philosophy — a search after pre-existing truth. This is especially apparent in Book X with its insistence that law is a product of nature rather than art (888e–890a, 890d).

5 Plato and natural law

It is not accidental that in this chapter a number of points of contact have emerged between Plato's theory of law and that of Aquinas. Scholars have rightly argued that Plato is one of the founders of the natural law tradition of which Aquinas is the most important exponent (Maguire, 1947; Hall, 1956). Plato shares with the natural-law philosophers the belief that there are objective moral principles valid for all time and for all men and capable of being discerned by reason; that there is a fundamental unity between these moral principles and the natural laws that govern the behaviour of the lower animals and of inanimate objects; and that the object of any genuine law is the common good which involves making men virtuous. But there are two qualifications to be added here. Firstly, Plato influenced the natural-law tradition indirectly through Aristotle rather than at first hand. Secondly, the natural lawyers also owed much to Stoicism and, of course, Christianity. Among the ideas derived from these sources is the argument that the natural law is accessible to all men by the use of reason and that, since all thus share a common law, they are all fellow citizens (Marcus Aurelius, 4.4; cf. Romans, 2.14). Plato apparently believes that all men have reason (644d, 713e) but couples this with the view that only certain specially qualified people can discern the law that is 'truest' and 'best'. His theory thus lacks the humanitarian bias of later natural law: he has little sympathy for slaves and aliens.

Natural-law theories have been used to influence practical politics in the direction of both reform and reaction. One who holds that there are objective standards of law may criticize and reject as invalid systems of positive law that do not meet these standards. Thus, in this century, the Nazi regimes indirectly caused a revival of natural-law theories because this way of thought enabled jurists to say that the unjust 'laws' of these regimes were not genuine laws and so had no claim to be obeyed. At other times it has simply been assumed that existing systems of law embody the true natural law and are therefore beyond moral criticism. This is the fault Bentham detected in Blackstone. Plato shows traces of both kinds of argument. His belief in an objective law enables him to criticize the Cretan and Spartan systems and, more virulently, the pseudo-constitutions of faction-ridden states (714b–715d, 832c). But when he comes to propose legislation for the new Cretan city, he generally assumes that existing systems of law and morality reflect the divine law of reason and thus raises them to status of eternal truths.

Whatever the practical influence of natural-law theories, they all share a weakness in their theoretical foundations. We can all no doubt agree on certain very general premises; for example, that good is to be pursued or that some kind of order is essential if human beings are to live a decent kind of life. The difficulty is in seeing how we can argue from these truistic premises to substantive conclusions about what particular kinds of acts ought to be required or forbidden by law. Plato does not succeed in bridging this gap: nowhere does he make any really serious attempt to show that the particular provisions he recommends follow from his general conception of law.

4

The Aims of Legislation

Laws, 625c–632c, 688a–b, 693b–c, 697b–c, 705d–706a, 707d, 718c–724b, 811c–812a, 829a, 857c–859b, 961c–964a; *Republic*, 426c–435a, 441c–445b; *Gorgias* 503d–505c

We saw in the last chapter that law, as Plato views it, must aim at the overall good of the city. As it stands, this doctrine lacks any real content, since it gives no account of the specific forms of good to be sought by legislation. Plato does have plenty to say about this, though it is not clear whether his different accounts of the specific aims of legislation are consistent with one another.

1 *Critique of the Dorian legislation*

The Athenian's enquiry about the purposes of the most distinctive Cretan and Spartan institutions (625c) prompts Cleinias to a general account of the aims of the Cretan laws. The legislator, he claims, has arranged everything with a view to warfare, and in doing so has implicitly criticized the generality of mankind who do not realize that, in reality, they are always at war. What ordinarily passes for peace is in fact a state of undeclared conflict in which all cities are ranged against each other. It is right therefore to concentrate on military preparedness because a state defeated in war loses everything worth having (625c–626b).

The Athenian replies to this by extending the idea that we should continually be prepared to defend ourselves: he applies it, not only to relations between cities, but also to those between villages, households and individuals. He then suggests that perhaps we can even be enemies of ourselves. The Cretan seizes eagerly on this idea: everyone is at war with everyone else and each man is at war with himself. So the most important victory is the victory over self; in other words we all need self-control (626c–e). The Athenian then gets Cleinias to agree that a city too can be vanquished by itself. This would happen if the worse elements in the population seized control over the better. So the political equivalent of the virtue of self-control is a situation in which the best elements dominate the state (an obviously questionable analogy) (627a–c). At this point the Athenian changes direction by arguing that the best situation is not one in which the better elements vanquish and destroy the worse, but one where the weaker elements willingly submit to the better. The ideal therefore is to secure peace and reconciliation and to create friendship by means of law. So victory in war, like medical treatment, is good only as a means. The highest good and true aim of legislation should be peace (627d–628d).

At one level both the Athenian and the Cretan seem to be making good points here. It is true that defeat in war can render most other things valueless and it is equally right to direct attention to the dangers of civil war and to the value of internal peace and friendship. Who could deny these points? But it does not therefore follow that either of these objects should be treated as the sole end of legislation. There are many different goods which can be realised in society and if the legislator pursues any of these to the exclusion of all others he is bound to sacrifice much that is valuable. One might therefore argue that it is wrong to suppose that there could be a single goal of legislation. The legislator must seek so far as possible to realise many different goals. An alternative would be to characterize the ultimate goal in such a way that it can be seen to embrace all the particular goals that are held valuable. It looks as though this is the direction in which the Athenian wishes to move. His objection to the supposed goal of the Cretan and Spartan systems is not that it is wrong but that it is too narrowly defined.

In 629a–630d the Athenian uses contrasting quotations from the poets Tyrtaeus and Theognis to point out the inadequacy of the Dorian ideal. Tyrtaeus, the favourite poet of the Spartans, praises the man who shows courage in war, but Theognis values most the man who can be trusted in civil strife. This trustworthiness, in the Athenian's view, requires not only courage (*andria*) but also justice (*dikaiosune*), self-control or temperance (*sophrosune*) and wisdom (*phronesis*). So a good legislator will design all his laws to inculcate this total virtue. From this, the Athenian infers that it was a mistake to suppose that great legislators aimed chiefly at imparting courage, for courage is only one part of virtue. One should rather say that these legislators aim to impart virtue or goodness as a whole. It is important therefore not to legislate piecemeal, as is generally the custom, but systematically, taking virtue as the starting point (630d–631a).

An important speech at 631b–632d expands this view of the legislator's activity. Correct legislation secures the happiness of those who live under it by securing for them both the human and the divine goods. The human goods are health, physical strength, beauty and wealth (if wisely used), but these depend on the divine goods which are first wisdom, secondly 'a temperate condition of the soul involving reason', thirdly justice, which is a product of the other divine goods, and fourthly courage. So the human goods look to the divine and the latter to reason as their leader. The Athenian then explains at some length how the legislator should supervise the whole of the citizen's lives, from conception to death with a view to imparting these virtues. He lays particular emphasis on the need for the legislator to understand the passions and emotions. Finally, he suggests that guardians should be set over the laws. Some of these will be guided by wisdom and some by true opinion. In this way reason will bind the system together, demonstrating that each element is subordinate to temperance and justice rather than to wealth and ambition.

The idea that virtue is the goal of legislation remains the Athenian's official position throughout the dialogue, and, in theory at least, shapes most of his practical proposals. It is reasserted when he first turns to consider the constitution of the new state (705c–706d, 707d) and receives its strongest reaffirmation in the final account of the nocturnal council. Just as a doctor must understand the aim of his craft (health) and the general of his (victory) so the state must contain some element that understands its object. This is the function of the nocturnal council which must fix its gaze on the single object to which all institutions of the state should be directed, namely virtue. It will therefore need to understand how virtue is both one and many, and be able to instruct the citizens in it (961e–964d).

2 _Virtue and peace as objects of legislation_

The Athenian does not retract his suggestion (628c–d) that legislation should aim at peace and reconciliation. In his handling of the quotation from Theognis (630a–d) he implies that complete virtue is to be sought because it makes people reliable in times of civil strife. The obvious inference is that virtue is to be valued primarily because it promotes peace and security. Yet, within a page or two, the Athenian announces that the virtues are divine goods whose possession is the only guarantee of happiness (631b–d). The implication here is that virtue is the highest form of good — to be sought for itself alone. Thus there appears to be a serious ambiguity. Is virtue itself the ultimate goal or is it to be sought merely as a means to peace?

A similar problem arises elsewhere in the *Laws*, especially towards the end of the historical excursus in book III. Twice in this section the Athenian reiterates the doctrine of 631c–632d that the end of legislation is complete virtue (688a–b, 697b–c). The dominant theme in this part of the dialogue is the need for the virtue of temperance or self-control. Since the Athenian regards this as an essential precondition of the other virtues, his doctrine here is consistent with the idea that legislation should seek to make the citizens virtuous. But he also maintains that the aim of legislation is freedom, friendship and wisdom (693b–c; cf. 694b, 695d, 701d). Later the ideal of friendship is pushed to an extreme. In the truly best state, all citizens would share common feelings about everything — a situation which could come about only if property and family relationships were abolished (739c; cf. 807b). At 693c the Athenian apologizes for characterizing the ends of legislation in so many different ways, but claims that it does not matter whether the goal is described as self-control, friendship or wisdom, since these are all in reality the same.

In these passages the Athenian appears to be working with two basic conceptions of the end to be sought. According to the first conception the end is virtue, which is in itself the greatest good of the soul. According to the second conception the end of legislation is to make the city as peaceful and unified as possible. To be consistent, the Athenian must argue that these two conceptions of the end coincide — that in pursuing virtue we will promote unity and peace in the city and that in pursuing this peace and unity we inevitably promote virtue. He attempts to show this at 828e–829a.

> [The city,] like the individual man must live well. Necessary conditions for living well are not doing wrong to others and not being wronged by them. Of these the first is not very difficult. But it is extremely difficult to acquire the power of not being wronged. One cannot have this power to the full extent without becoming good to the full extent. The same goes for the city. If it is good it will have a peaceful life, but if it is bad it will be subject to strife from within and without.

The argument here seems to be that the virtuous individual and the virtuous city can somehow escape suffering wrong at the hands of others. Virtue and peace thus go together and can be seen as different aspects of the same ultimate goal. But this, on the face of it, seems absurd. It is obvious to everyone that good men are sometimes the victims of injustice. How, then, can the Athenian suggest that virtue protects us from being wronged?

So far as the relationships between individuals are concerned, the Athenian could defend himself by arguing that, where the city as a whole is virtuous, each of the inhabitants will be good. None of them will therefore be willing to wrong his fellow men. Thus those who live in the virtuous city will be certain not to suffer injustice. Each of them would, then, be protected, not so much by his own virtue, as by the virtue of his fellow citizens.

Even if this argument is acceptable, the Athenian would still have to explain how the virtuous city is protected from wrongs done to it by non-virtuous foreigners. His position on this point seems to be that virtue will make the city strong politically and militarily. It will therefore be proof against external attack as well as from internal subversion. This idea has some plausibility so long as one thinks of virtue as a matter of diligently performing one's allotted social role. The virtuous city would then be strong because each citizen would loyally and courageously do whatever the wise rulers told him. Much of the Athenian's legislation does indeed seem designed to encourage this kind of conformist attitude. (See especially 700a–701d, 729d, 793b–c, 942a–d.)

The trouble is that we now seem committed to a quite different view of virtue from that espoused by the Athenian when he speaks of the virtues as 'divine goods' (631b–c). His position there is that the virtues, as divine goods, are the greatest possible blessing on those who possess them. If virtue was simply a matter of conformity to social norms, it would, no doubt, be a blessing to the community but not necessarily to the virtuous man himself. After all, it may not always be in his interests to do what society requires. The Athenian is not very explicit about why he thinks virtue is always a blessing to its possessor, but, so far as one can see, he would adhere to the doctrine of the *Republic* that virtue is good for us because it is an orderly state of the soul in which the passions are properly subordinated to the reason. (See chapter 5 below.) But there is no obvious reason why a person who is virtuous in this sense should necessarily be an obedient citizen, prepared to act as a reliable cog in the machinery of state. There is a significant tension here between two different conceptions of virtue. If virtue is a good state of the individual, there is no obvious reason why the city with virutous citizens should be strong; if virtue means conformity to social norms there is no obvious reason why the virtuous man should be happy.

The difference between these two conceptions could be important. So long as one concentrates on the idea that the object of legislation is virtue one may conclude that the Athenian's fundamental concern is with the happiness and moral fulfilment of the citizens as individuals, and that the value of the individual soul has priority over that of the state (Hall, 1981, p. 97). But this individualist interpretation would be out of the question if the virtue that is to be inculcated consists simply in a disposition to do whatever is required of one in the interests of the state. This problem can be resolved only if Plato can develop his accounts of virtue and of the state in such a way as to show that the two conceptions of virtue could in practice coincide.

3   *Plato's legal moralism*

Insofar as they treat virtue as the object of legislation the Athenian and his companions are logically committed to a form of legal moralism, i.e. to the belief that the law should seek to improve the moral character of the citizens. This view may be disturbing to a modern reader because most of us have been brought up, under the influence of liberal thinkers like J.S. Mill, to regard any kind of legal moralism with suspicion. The main objection raised by these thinkers is that if the state seeks to make people good it pre-empts choices that should properly be left to the individual and thus stifles individuality. These points would not have worried the Dorians but, by implication at least, they ought to have worried some of Plato's contemporaries. For example Pericles, as reported in Thucydides II, 35 ff., praises Athens for the freedom it bestows on the individual citizens. They are free to conduct their private lives and to educate their children as they wish.

Plato's moralism is, no doubt, largely due to the absence from Greek thought and language of the kind of distinction that we would draw between law on the one hand and matters of morality or of convention on the other. But it is also closely connected with some of the most fundamental features of Plato's philosophy. One of these features is the Socratic doctrine, familiar to readers of dialogues like the *Gorgias* and the *Republic*, that the individual can be happy if and only if he has a virtuous soul. From this, together with the innocuous-looking premise that the legislator should seek the welfare of the citizen body as a whole, there follows the conclusion that the legislator should, so far as possible, seek to make the citizens virtuous. So, although Socrates is sometimes represented as a protagonist of the liberal conscience, the doctrines that Plato derived from him lead directly to the doctrine of legal moralism that is anathema to the liberal tradition.

The idea that it is the task of the legislator to make people virtuous implies that the legislator can know what forms of life are required by virtue. So the Athenian's legal moralism rests also on his objectivist view of morality — his view of it as a matter of knowledge. What is more, it involves a particularly strong form of objectivism. The Athenian believes that there is a reasonable prospect of finding a legislator with reliable knowledge of right and wrong and that this legislator will be able to lay down detailed rules of right living. He will regulate every aspect of the citizen's lives with a view to the 'divine goods' (631b–632c).

Someone who wishes seriously to defend a doctrine of individual liberty will almost certainly reject this strong form of objectivism. He may argue that moral values are not objects of knowledge but simply express the preferences of the individual or the group. (It is likely that some of Plato's contemporaries would have developed the distinction between nature and convention in the same way, though the evidence is not very clear.) An alternative would be to replace Plato's strong objectivism with a more limited form. One could then argue (a) that even if moral values are knowable in principle, no one can in fact be trusted to have an infallible knowledge of these matters, and (b) that, while ultimate values (such as peace, freedom and justice) are objectively discernible, they may be instantiated in many different ways so that there is room for each person to determine his own form of the good life.

Even if we cannot accept Plato's account of moral knowledge, it does not, I think, follow that we must reject the whole of his moral and political philosophy out of hand. Liberal thinkers have argued their case not just by attacking the idea that rulers can know what is right for their subjects but also by depicting the attractions of societies that allow a high degree of individual freedom (much as Pericles praises Athens in the funeral speech). Similarly it is open to Plato to paint the attractions of a society committed to the kind of moral order that he admires. He can try to show that only in such a society can human beings satisfy their most fundamental needs. One can read the *Laws* as an attempt to do this, to make the reader feel the attractions of a life committed to Plato's ideal of law. Even if we do not share Plato's epistemological premises a reading of the *Laws* can therefore provoke us into re-examining some of the assumptions that underlie our own political attitudes.

4 *Law as education*

The Athenian's demand that the lawgiver should supervise all the activities of the citizens, and should instruct them as to what is right and wrong by using praise and blame, honour and dishonour as well as by penalizing misbehaviour (631b–632d), implies that the legislator has an educational role. This conception is worked out in two ways. Firstly, there are laws to govern the upbringing of children and to establish appropriate educational institutions. The second, and more distinctive, idea is that legislation itself must involve a kind of instruction, that it should seek to shape the character by persuasion as well as by coercion.

This distinctive view is developed through a medical analogy. There are two kinds of doctor. The first kind are slaves themselves and mostly have slaves as patients. They rush from patient to patient and, on the basis of experience alone, issue orders without explanations. The second kind are free doctors who treat free men. They make careful enquiries about the nature of the illness and explain to their patients what is happening. They give instructions only when they have secured the patient's consent. Thus they heal primarily by persuasion (719e–720e). Similarly there are two methods of legislation, the 'single' method which simply lays down penalties for certain kinds of act, and the 'double' method in which the prescription of the penalty is preceded by an attempt to show why the acts in question are wrong and to persuade people not to do them. The 'double' method is taken to be twice as valuable as the single (720e–722c). The implication of this is that the lawgiver must instruct and educate the citizens (857c–e). He will do this by means of preambles which use persuasion rather than threats to produce the required behaviour (722c–723d). The Athenian follows the 'double' method both by setting out a general preamble or prelude to the whole legal system (726a–734e) and by providing preambles for individual laws. (In practice it is often difficult to distinguish the preamble from (a) the general discussion which introduces a particular section of legislation and (b) the law proper which lays down the penalty.) The Athenian is so proud of his preambles that he attributes them to divine inspiration. He also suggests that the *Laws* itself should be the major textbook used in the education of the young. Schoolmasters must be compelled to learn it, and any similar works, by heart and to teach them to their pupils (811c–812a, 957c; cf. 858c–859c).

The idea that the lawgiver should use exhortation and instruction so that the citizens behave rightly out of a sense of moral duty, rather than through fear of penalties, sounds attractive. Surely, persuading people voluntarily to do what is required is preferable to coercing them by sanctions? But the Athenian's proposals deserve to be treated with scepticism. The difficulty is not that they would be impractical — it is all too clear that government propaganda can be very effective. Rather, the proposals are questionable on moral grounds.

One point raised here concerns Plato's concept of persuasion. In the *Gorgias* (454b–455d) he distinguishes the kind of persuasion effected by rhetoric, which results merely in belief, from the kind which produces genuine knowledge. One would like to think that the preambles to the laws exercise persuasion of the latter kind (Hall, 1981, pp. 93–6), but this is clearly not the case; they are exhortations rather than arguments (see, e.g., 726a–734d, 741a–e, 772e–773e, 823d–824a) and it is their literary qualities in which the Athenian feels so proud (811c–e). This is inevitable, given (a) the view of virtue in the *Laws* which emphasizes the need for correct training of the emotions and (b) the belief that only a limited number of the citizens can come to a fully rational understanding. In any case Plato never pretends that understanding can be conveyed in a few words. On the other hand, there is nothing in the *Laws*, apart from the suggestion that poets should say that justice and happiness coincide even if this were not the case (663d–664a), to support Popper's allegation (1966, p. 270) that by 'persuasion' Plato means largely 'lying propaganda'. The preambles mostly have the character of rather conventional sermons.

Although the preambles are in themselves pretty innocuous, the reliance which the Athenian would lay on them and on other means of persuasion could be very dangerous. There are two points here:

(1) As Plato recognizes, propaganda can extend to areas of life where penalties would be ineffective and the social pressures it creates can be as powerful as the fear of sanctions. So the kind of persuasion advocated by the Athenian could restrict the area within which the individual is free to choose his own way of life.

(2) Persuasion is unlikely to be effective if people are free to propagate views opposed to the official line.

So if a government wishes to use persuasion as a major means of achieving social conformity it cannot tolerate freedom of speech. Thus the idea of law as education is inextricably linked to one of the features of the *Laws* that a modern reader is likely to find most disturbing: its failure to allow room for self-expression on the part of the citizens.

5

Virtue

Laws, 626b–636e, 644b–645c, 653a–c, 660e–664a, 688a–689e, 696b–697c, 710a–b, 726a–734d, 782d–783a, 835c–836a, 963a–964a, 965c–e; Protagoras, 352a–360e; Gorgias, 466a–468e, 491c–508c; Republic, 427d–444e; Timaeus, 41d–44d, 69c–70d, 86b–87b

The divine goods which are the chief object of legislation correspond to the four virtues listed in the Republic, 427e ff. Other features of the opening pages of the Laws will also seem familiar to those acquainted with earlier dialogues. For example, the idea that the legislator should aim at virtue as a whole may recall the Socratic doctrine that virtue is one because it consists in knowing the good. Similarly, the suggestion that laws will need guardians, some using knowledge and some true belief, may remind us of the Republic, where the philosopher rulers alone have knowledge, though the lower classes may have true belief. But, as well as these points of similarity, there are also features of these early pages that are inconsistent with Plato's earlier moral philosophy, or at least suggest some confusion of thought. Consider, for example, the following:

(1)   At 630b the Athenian suggests that even mercenary soldiers, notoriously reckless and brutal characters, can exhibit courage. This implies that courage is separable from the other virtues and that virtue cannot therefore be one.

(2)   The same conclusion seems to follow from the Athenian's proposal at 632d–e to consider different institutions each designed to inculcate a different part of virtue.

(3)   The Athenian gives the four virtues different places in an order of priority, with wisdom first and courage emphatically last. This would be nonsense if the virtues were all one and therefore identical with one another. Even without the doctrine of the unity of virtue, this ranking of the particular virtues would require explanation.

(4)   Similarly, the assertion that justice results from a mingling of wisdom, temperance and courage is both obscure in itself and inconsistent with the claim that virtue is one.

(5)   When he first lists the four virtues (630a–b), the Athenian includes *sophrosune*, temperance, but when he repeats the list at 631c he refers instead to a 'temperate condition of the soul involving reason'. One would expect the choice of this phrase to have some significance, but it is by no means clear what that significance could be.

Some scholars have concluded that this whole section is radically incoherent, for, although Plato seems to be reaffirming some of the key doctrines of his earlier moral philosophy, much of what he says looks patently inconsistent with those earlier views (Gigon, 1954; cf. Müller, 1951). In this chapter, I shall adopt a more positive approach and shall try to make sense of these early pages in the light of the account of virtue as it develops through the dialogue.

1   *Moral psychology*

At 632e, after establishing that virtue is the main object of legislation, the Athenian turns to consider the Dorian institutions designed to inculcate courage. As the Cretan and Spartan understand it, courage consists in doing battle with fears and pains, but they readily agree with the Athenian when he suggests that it is equally important to struggle against desires and pleasures. Indeed it is the man who gives way to these who has really lost mastery over himself (632e–633e). The Athenian proposes the institution of drinking parties as a means of training the young to avoid this danger.

Implicit in this passage is a fairly simple kind of moral psychology. A man's 'true' or 'better' self is distinguished from his pleasures and pains, his desires and fears ('his passions' one might say). Virtue is that state of the soul in which the true self exercises its proper dominion over these 'lower' elements. We have already met this contrast between a better self which deserves to rule and a worse self which should obey (626d–e, see above, chapter 4, section 1) and similar motifs occur elsewhere (e.g. 689a–c, 726–728a). A passage at 863a–864c, where the Athenian distinguishes three kinds of injustice, is particularly important in this respect. The first kind of injustice is due to the domination of the soul by anger, the second to its domination by pleasure and the third to ignorance. The Athenian points out that we talk of people 'overcoming' or 'being overcome by' pleasure and anger but not of their 'overcoming' or 'being overcome' by their ignorance (863d). Given the Athenian's conception of the human personality, the reason for this is pretty obvious. A man's true self is identified with his cognitive capacities (i.e. that part of him which knows or believes).

Ignorance is a defect in this part of the personality, so the man who goes wrong through ignorance, unlike the man who goes wrong through anger or pleasure, has not been overwhelmed by something external to his 'true' self.

The suggestion (863b) that anger (and presumably pleasure) might be regarded as distinct parts of the soul is an obvious reference to the doctrine that the human soul has distinct reasoning, spirited and appetitive parts. This doctrine will be familiar to most readers of the *Republic* (435a–441c) but the parallel with the *Timaeus* may be more significant. In that dialogue Timaeus explains how human beings are each created with a small portion of divine 'soul-stuff'. The natural movement of this divine soul is the same uniform circular motion as is revealed by the heavens, and Timaeus identifies this movement with the activity of reason. But when the soul is implanted in the body it becomes subject to sensations and passions, giving rise to all kinds of irrational movements. The human being will have no rest until it brings these irrational forces into conformity with the uniform motion of reason (42e–44d). Later the passions are treated as forming a 'mortal' soul attached to the immortal element of reason. Timaeus distinguishes a spirited and an appetitive part within this 'mortal' or 'lower' part of the soul and assigns them to separate parts of the body (69d–70d). His doctrine thus corresponds to that of the *Republic* in that he treats the rational part of the soul as the true self and believes that virtue consists in domination by this rational element of the lower parts.

The *Laws* follows the *Timaeus* and the *Republic* in treating the reason as the only divine or immortal element within us (713e–714a). This is why the virtues which involve following the dictates of reason are divine goods, while goods of the body are merely human (631b–c, 697b, 728d–e, 743e). Similarly, in the prelude to the *Laws* (726a–734d), the first part, in which the legislator praises virtues for their own sake, is said to be spoken 'from the divine point of view', while the second part, in which he praises them as leading to a pleasant life, is spoken 'from the human viewpoint' (732d–e) — pleasures and pains are, of course, part of the 'mortal' soul.

In the *Timaeus* and the *Republic* the separation of reason from the lower elements of the soul is bound up with the distinction between knowledge and belief. The function of reason is to know the eternal Forms, so in obeying reason we are acting on our knowledge of the Forms. The *Laws*, in keeping with its more practical focus, treats right belief as an acceptable alternative to knowledge (632c, 689a–e, 864a). It is assumed in practice that the virtuous man will act, not on his own insight into the foundations of good and evil, but in accordance with law, which rests on the insight and wisdom of the old (see above, chapter 3). This is particularly evident in the prelude to the laws, where the legislator begins by insisting that the better elements within us must rule over the worse (726a) but then assumes that this is equivalent to saying that we must obey the law (728a). The same kind of consideration may explain why the word for 'wisdom' in the lists of virtues (630a–b, 631c) was *phronesis*, not *sophia* (the word used in the *Republic*). If Aristotle's usage (*Nicomachean Ethics*, VI, v & vii) is any guide, *phronesis* refers rather to the practical wisdom which expresses itself in the prudent conduct of one's public and private business, whereas *sophia* would suggest the theoretical wisdom of the philosopher.

2   *Moral responsibility*

The account of the soul and its way of functioning implicit in the *Laws* raises problems about responsibility. In so far as these problems concern the penal code they will be discussed in chapter 14, but they also have important implications for the general account of virtue in the *Laws*. The difficulty is most apparent in the 'prelude' to the legal code (726a–734d) which takes the form of an exhortation to 'honour the soul'. In this prelude the legislator for the most part addresses the citizens as responsible beings — it is up to them to be virtuous and they must not evade their responsibility by blaming others (727b). But he also suggests that, since no one is willingly unjust, criminals should be regarded with pity rather than anger, the implication here apparently being that they are not really responsible for their misdeeds. So the legislator appears to be adopting inconsistent attitudes to the question of individual responsibility. More generally one might argue that the emphasis throughout the *Laws* on the importance of education and law in making the citizens virtuous precludes any attempt to regard people as responsible for their own shortcomings. But later, when he discusses the divine government of the universe, the Athenian insists quite emphatically that our state of virtue or vice is the product of our own will (904c–d).

There is a parallel problem in the *Timaeus*. In that dialogue the demiurge or creator explicitly suggests that human beings can be a cause of evil to themselves, i.e. they are responsible for at least some of their mistakes (42e), but it is also said that we can bring the disorderly movements under the control of reason only if we have the right education and upbringing (44b–c). At 86b Timaeus gives a purely physiological account of certain 'diseases of the soul that are due to the disposition of the body'. Among these are almost all the cases commonly called 'incontinence with regard to pleasures'. No one voluntarily becomes bad — one becomes bad through a disorder of the body or bad upbringing, both of which are hateful to everyone and involuntary (86d–e). A few lines later Timaeus sums up his position. Those of us who are bad become so 'through two causes that are quite against our wills': through bad conditions of the soul which in turn result from bodily disorders or through being brought up in badly organized cities. The blame for these things must, he suggests, fall on parents and those who bring up children rather than on the children themselves. But Timaeus still seems to hold that it is up to us to look after the condition of our own souls 'a man must try in every way possible, by education, by the activities he pursues and by study to escape from evil and seize hold of its opposite' (87a–b).

On a superficial reading, it may look as though Timaeus is here represented as a determinist, that, in his view, all human acts are the result of physiology or environment and no one may therefore be held responsible for his misdeeds. But this conflicts not only with the claim at 42e that we may be the cause of evil to ourselves but also with the willingness Timaeus displays in this very passage to blame parents and educators and with his belief that we ourselves should try to escape from wickedness. So if Timaeus was a determinist he would be a very inconsistent one. The solution to the problem lies in the recognition that Timaeus does *not* suggest that all human acts are causally determined in all respects. His position seems to be that one's virtue or vice is the product of two factors (a) the strength of the disorderly movements of the lower soul and (b) the degree of effort the rational soul puts into controlling them. No doubt there are cases, as in children and those who have been very badly brought up, where the disorderly movements are so strong that no one could control them. In more normal cases they are controllable providing that we try hard enough. But even if our vice is due to a failure of effort on the part of the rational soul it is still not voluntary. The rational soul never *wants* vice even though it may be so feeble that it puts up very little stuggle.

The same solution can be applied to the problem of responsibility in the *Laws*. No one ever really wants to be vicious but we may become so if we are badly brought up or if we make insufficient effort to struggle against vice. In many cities the education given to the young may be so bad that it is practically impossible for people to become virtuous. The city of the *Laws* on the other hand will be well constituted with a proper system of education. One may therefore assume that any vice displayed by the citizens is largely their own fault.

Something like this position has to be adopted by anyone who wishes to maintain a belief in individual responsibility while acknowledging the importance of environmental causes: one has to argue that, while such causes may always influence action, only in unusual circumstances is this influence so powerful as to determine what the agent does (i.e. to give him no chance of behaving rightly).

3   *Self-control and the possibility of* akrasia

If virtue requires that our passions be guided by the judgements of reason as enshrined in law it follows that three kinds of vice are possible. The first would occur where our judgement is misguided as a result of intellectual error so that we honestly hold false opinions about what we ought to do. The Athenian takes this possibility seriously in his attack on atheism in Book X. The second kind of vice would be exhibited by a man who struggles unsuccessfully to overcome temptation. Here the judgement is correct but the passions push us too strongly in the opposite direction. This is what we call 'weakness of will' and what Aristotle calls *akrasia*. The third kind of vice is that displayed by a man whose passions are so dominant that they distort his judgement. His desire determines his conception of what is good and right. This is probably what Aristotle would call *akolasia* (*Nicomachean Ethics*, 1152a 4–6). Corresponding to the last two forms of vice are two forms of virtue. One may behave rightly either because one has wrongful desires but overcomes them or because one's desires have been brought into the harmony with the judgements of reason. Broadly speaking, Book I of the *Laws* concentrates on the first kind of virtue, that which consists in overcoming desires, while Book II concentrates on the second form, the harmonization of desire with right judgement.

As we have already seen, a main theme of Book I is the need to provide institutions which will train the young in resisting pleasures and desires as well as pains and fears. This point is developed at great length. Sometimes the speakers use military metaphors: we must fight against pleasure and pain; virtue consists in being victorious over them, but to be defeated is vice (633c–634b, 647c–d). In another passage the human being is represented as a puppet pulled in different directions by different strings; his task is to co-operate with the 'golden string' of reason or law while resisting pleasure and pain (644d–645c).

Drink makes us like bad men because it reduces our self-control (645e–646a), but drinking parties held under the right conditions are to be recommended because they can help train people to resist pleasures (646d–650b).

If people need training to help them exercise self-control it follows that the state of being unable to control one's passions must be relatively common. In other words people really must be subject to the condition called *akrasia*, weakness of will. This is made clear in Book III where the Athenian describes what he calls the 'greatest folly' or 'greatest stupidity':

> It is what we see in a man who hates, rather than loves, what he judges to be noble and good, while he loves and welcomes what seems unjust. This disharmony between one's feelings of pain and pleasure is, I maintain, the extreme of stupidity. . . . When the soul opposes forms of knowledge, opinion or reason that are naturally fitted to rule I call it folly; likewise when in a state the masses disobey the magistrates or laws and in an individual when rational judgements in the soul achieve nothing, or even worse than nothing. (689a–b)

The word *amathia*, which I have rendered 'stupidity' could also bear the translation 'ignorance'. But the point is not that those referred to in the passage lack knowledge: they know what is right, but, because their passions are not in harmony with their reason they fail to do it. It is fair, therefore, to take this passage as a description of *akrasia*.

This acceptance of *akrasia* may come as a surprise. Socrates notoriously had denied the possibility of *akrasia*. He had also argued that no one willingly does wrong. These two claims are so closely associated with one another that they are often treated as equivalents. Plato in the *Laws* still claims that no one willingly does wrong. How then can he allow the possibility of *akrasia*?

One might seek to explain this by the hypothesis that much of the argument of the *Laws* is directed to an unsophisticated audience. The idea of *akrasia* was apparently so well entrenched in ordinary thought that one can see why the Athenian would not wish to perplex the two Dorians by denying it. But this suggestion may not be needed. There are independent grounds for believing that Plato at this stage in his career would himself have accepted the possibility of *akrasia*. To understand how he could do this one has to see that the doctrines (a) that *akrasia* is impossible and (b) that no one willingly does wrong, although closely associated, are not in fact equivalent. This is clear if we consider the argument by which Socrates, in the *Protagoras* 352a–360e, attempts to show that no one willingly does wrong. The denial of *akrasia* play an essential part in that argument but only because Socrates apparently assumes that a wrongful act done as a result of *akrasia* would be voluntary. Thus in order to maintain that no one willingly does wrong he has to deny the reality of *akrasia*. But this is not the only way in which one could support the claim that all wrongdoing is involuntary. An alternative strategy would be to argue that acts done through *akrasia* are not voluntary in the full sense. A genuinely voluntary act, one might say, must accord with the wishes of the rational soul. In *akrasia* the rational soul is overwhelmed by the lower elements. So acts done through weakness of will are not genuinely voluntary. Thus we become unjust against our will. This is the position adopted by Timaeus at 86e where he argues that acts attributed to incontinence (*akrasia*) are really involuntary and by the Athenian in *Laws* 734b where he maintains that intemperance or self indulgence (*akolasia*) is involuntary because it results either from ignorance or *akrasia*.

These passages can be seen as the conclusion of a development which may have been going on through most of Plato's philosophical career. Socrates, as represented in the *Protagoras*, plays down the importance of the passions and insists that virtue is knowledge. The *Gorgias, Republic* and *Phaedrus* have much more to say about the 'lower' soul. The *Republic* even describes what seems to be a state of *akrasia* (439e–440a). It is not altogether surprising therefore that the *Timaeus* and the *Laws* should apparently accept the possibility of *akrasia* and should hold the correct training of the lower soul to be as important for virtue as is right judgment. But so long as Plato treats pleasures and pains as separate from the true soul he can continue to treat vice, a state in which the true soul is overwhelmed by external forces, as involuntary.

4   *The harmony of passion and judgement*

Those who do wrong through *akrasia* have correct beliefs about what is right but are overcome by pleasures or pains. But, of course, not all wrongdoing is of this kind. We often indulge our desires without seriously acknowledging that we ought to do otherwise. This could be due to intellectual error but it is more commonly the result of allowing one's desires to distort one's better judgement. Our desire to do something stops us attending to the more objectionable features of the proposed act. Or we manage to convince ourselves that what we desire to do is, after all, right. Conversely, we may behave rightly because we actually want to do what is morally required. Virtue, then, may consist in having desires that are habituated to accord with one's better judgement.

Plato's recognition of this point is clear from the beginning of Book II. The Athenian argues there that virtue and vice first enter a child's soul through the feelings of pleasure and pain. These feelings must be correctly trained in childhood, though only when the child reaches the age of reason will he be able to see for himself that the dispositions thus acquired harmonize with the judgements of his understanding. This harmony is virtue (653b–c). A few pages later the Athenian maintains that, since education aims to lead the children to accept the principles of law as confirmed by the wisdom of the old, the important thing is to accustom the children to having appropriate feelings of pleasure and pain (659d–e). The Athenian attaches great importance to music and dance as devices for reinforcing this educational process. It is therefore more important that the performer should have the right opinions and feelings that agree with them, than that he should have technical expertise (654b–d). The criterion of excellence in art is not pleasure as such but the pleasure felt by the good (658e–659c). In general the aim of education is not merely to encourage us to control our wayward passions, but to make us feel pleasure in virtue and find vice painful.

Of course it may not in practice be possible to draw a clear line between those who are virtuous through the exercise of self-control and those who have correctly trained passions. We may begin by having to struggle against our desires, inhibiting them through shame or fear of punishment (646e–647c), but come eventually to love the good life for its own sake. Conversely our first steps in vice may be due to weakness of will, but as we go on we may lose our awareness that what we are doing is wrong. There is a gentle slide from weakness into wickedness. This is presumably why the Athenian says (734b) that licentiousness, *akolasia*, may result from *akrasia*. He may have a similar point in mind when he describes those who, through a discrepancy between their natural character and their upbringing, enjoy music which they really know to be bad. They are like men who fall into bad company and find a certain pleasure in their evil acquaintances. They may rebuke their companions but they do not really mean what they say. They have only a dreamlike awareness of their own vice and, even if they are ashamed actually to praise those whose company they enjoy, they inevitably become like them (656a–b).

Self-indulgence can easily become self-deception. This seems to be an underlying theme of the prelude to the *Laws* in Book V, 727a–734e. The legislator exhorts the citizens to honour their souls, but one of his main points is that we deceive ourselves when we think that we honour our soul by indulging it or by trying to evade responsibility for our misdeeds (727a–b). A main cause of vice is self-love which, like all forms of love, blinds us to the true character of its object. So self-love distorts our perception of the just, the good and the noble, makes us take our own folly for wisdom and leads us to think we know everything, when, in fact, we know practically nothing (731e–732a).

The language here recalls the Socratic idea that the greatest evil is to think one has knowledge when one is, in reality, ignorant. No doubt the remedy for 'double ignorance', as it is called in Book IX, 863c, consists partly in the acquisition of a sounder knowledge of right and wrong. But since it is usually our own desire that blinds us to our ignorance, the correct habituation of the lower soul must also play its part. So the *Laws'* recipe for virtue combines the right instruction of the judgement with the correct training of the emotions.

5   Sophrosune: *the mainspring of the* Laws?

According to Barker (1960, p. 343) self-control is the 'principle' or 'mainspring' of the *Laws*. In one way this could be misleading. 'Self-control' may suggest the kind of virtue that consists in fighting against and overcoming the passions, whereas Plato is more concerned to produce a harmony between the passions and the judgements of reason. But, in fact, Barker seems to be using 'self-control' as the equivalent of Greek virtue of *sophrosune*. This meant much more to the Greeks than 'self-control' does to us. In Athens it was recognized as the characteristic virtue of the citizen in time of peace, expressing the 'all-embracing order and morality of restraint and limitation' required by the city-state (North, 1966, pp. 150–2). It could also describe the rather unimaginative self-discipline of the Spartans (North, 1966, pp. 102–4; cf. Thucydides, I, 68–9). In the *Charmides* it is successively defined as quietness (159b), respect (160e), doing one's own work (161b), self-knowledge (164d). All these definitions have a basis in popular thought, though in the *Charmides* they are rejected in favour of the Socratic claim that *sophrosune* is knowledge of good and evil. Another popular idea considered by Plato is that it consists in heeding the maxim 'nothing in excess', i.e. that *sophrosune* is moderation (*Philebus* 45d–e). According to the *Gorgias* (491d) the many regard *sophrosune* as a matter of controlling the appetites but in the same dialogue Socrates describes it as a state of order in the soul (506c–507a). The *Republic* cites the popular view of *sophrosune* as obedience to rulers and the control of one's appetites (389d–e) and then subsumes this definition in an account of it as a harmony of the different elements in the state (430d) and in the soul (442c–d).

The word *sophrosune* itself occurs infrequently in the *Laws*. When its meaning is explicit it generally refers to the capacity to restrain one's appetite, the popular virtue which the Athenian says is valueless in itself (696b–e). In these contexts 'self-control' is an adequate translation, but they do not justify the claim that self-control is the mainspring of the *Laws*. What does deserve this description is the wider ideal of *sophrosune* which embraces, not only self-control, but also order, harmony, moderation and self-knowledge. These ideas dominate much of the dialogue:

(1)   The idea that the aim of legislation should be the victory of the better elements in the state and in the soul is considered, but replaced by the ideal of harmony through law (626b–628b).

(2)   The institution of drinking parties is advocated on the grounds that they develop and test the young man's capacity to resist pleasures (633d–634c, 636e–650b, 671a–674b).

(3)   The long digression on education and the arts in Book II, 652–670e, develops the conception of virtue as a harmony of reason and emotion.

(4)   The failures of Argos and Messene are attributed to a discord between rational judgement and emotion. The suggested remedy is the acknowledgment of due measure or proportion in the distribution of power (686a–687e, 691b–d).

(5)   The successes of the Persian monarchy and of the Athenian democracy are attributed to their maintenance of a mean between freedom and despotism. Their failures are attributed to the abandonment of this moderation (693d–701e).

(6)   The prelude to the legal code begins within an attack on those who think they honour the soul when they are in fact yielding to their desires (726a–728c).

(7)   A few pages later self-love is said to blind us to what is really good and make us take our wisdom for folly (731d–732b).

(8)   The prelude ends with the praise of the temperate life with moderate pleasures and moderate pains (732b–734d).

Between them these passages touch explicitly or implicitly on almost all aspects of *sophrosune* in the widest sense. Fundamental to them all is the idea that virtue requires a right relation between reason and passion. Left to themselves the passions would lead us into all manner of excess and wickedness. We possess *sophrosune* if reason governs our passions and keeps us in the way of moderation. Understood in this wide sense, *sophrosune* is the *raison d'être* of the social and educational institutions described in the later books. It is as fundamental to the *Laws* as justice, *dikaiosune*, is to the *Republic*.

6 The unity of virtue

In Book XII the key task assigned to the nocturnal council is that of discerning the one end of all legislation, and for this they must understand how virtue is both one and many. It is easy enough, the Athenian there suggests, to see why we give particular virtues different names as though they were distinct from one another. For example, courage, which is concerned with fears, develops naturally in children and animals without any element of reason. But obviously there cannot be wisdom without reason (963e). The difficult task, which the Athenian leaves unexplained, is to see in what respects these virtues are one.

This passage immediately explains some of the peculiarities noticed at the beginning of this chapter. The courage that springs up naturally in children and animals is presumably the same as that evinced by the mercenaries of 630b. It is simply the capacity to resist immediate fears for the sake of some longer-term goal. One can see how the Dorian institutions might produce this form of courage in isolation from other virtues. There are other passages that seem to refer to a corresponding form of temperance (696b–e, 710a–b). But these unreasoned capacities cannot be what the Athenian generally understands by virtue, for virtue in his view requires that the passions be subordinate to right judgement. One cannot therefore be properly virtuous without knowledge or true belief about the good. This is presumably why the divine goods are said at 631d to look to reason as their leader and why the Athenian speaks in the same passage of 'a temperate condition of the soul involving reason'. Similarly at 696b–c he says that temperance is valueless in itself but that no other virtue is worthwhile without it. The point must be that both wisdom and the capacity to control one's passions are necessary to virtue. Self-control without wisdom could be used for the worst ends, but wisdom would be equally valueless if one lacked the self-control to put it into practice.

There is no explicit reference in the *Laws* to the kind of virtue which, according to the *Republic*, can be achieved only by the philosopher who apprehends the Form of the good. On the other hand the kind of virtue described in the *Laws* does bear a close resemblance to the kind of virtue that might be expected of the soldier or auxiliary class in the *Republic*. This virtue consists in the capacity to maintain, through all temptations, the principles which one has been taught in youth (412c–414a). It does not require knowledge, as such, but it does presuppose true belief which is acquired through right education.

It is possible that Plato withholds mention of the 'philosophical' form of virtue because he judges it to be out of place in a practically oriented dialogue like the *Laws*. We shall see in chapter 12 that there are similarities between the courses of study prescribed for the nocturnal council in the *Laws* and the philosopher–guardians in the *Republic*. We might take this as a hint that the *Republic*'s account of virtue is being presupposed without being stated. On the other hand, we have seen in this chapter a number of reasons for supposing that Plato might have changed his view. His various treatments of the Socratic paradoxes do seem to show an increasing doubt about the power of the rational soul to control its irrational elements. The underlying reasons for these doubts come to the surface in the moral psychology of the *Timaeus*, with which the *Laws* seems to be in agreement. According to this psychology, we have within us at least two elements, one divine and rational, the other mortal and irrational. Since the mortal element is by nature intractable, the rational element can never guarantee to control it. There cannot therefore be a form of knowledge that guarantees virtuous behaviour.

In the Socratic dialogues, virtue is held to be a unity because all virtues ultimately consist in a knowledge of what is good. In the last few pages of the *Laws*, the Athenian is made to insist that virtue is both one and many. It may therefore seem that the doctrine of virtue as knowledge is still lurking in the background. However the account of virtue just given suggests another way in which the thesis that virtue is both one and many might be supported. It might be one, not because it is identified with some kind of knowledge, but because it always involves the proper subordination of the passions to right judgement. The names given to the particular virtues draw attention to the different aspects or components of this harmony. 'Wisdom' points to the leading role of right judgement, 'temperance' and 'courage' to the need to control, respectively, pleasures and pains, 'justice' to the fact that this inner harmony leads to right action. One may even be able to make some sense of the ranking of the virtues. Wisdom comes first because rational judgement must be in control, temperance comes second because the main danger is that we will succumb to pleasure.

The difficulty is to see why justice comes between temperance and courage. If the account just suggested is correct it should really come into a different category since it is a result rather than a component of the soul's harmony. Perhaps the Athenian has been led astray by his desire to emphasize that physical courage is of comparatively minor importance. Of course this account is largely speculative but it is sufficient to show that the doctrine of the unity of virtue need not be inconsistent with the general account of virtue in the *Laws*. The charge of radical inconsistency in the opening section of the dialogue cannot, therefore, be upheld. The truth probably is that Plato would not want us to press the details of these passages. Unlike the Socrates of the early dialogues who would doubtless have pounced on the assumption that courage can be pursued in isolation from the other virtues, the Athenian treats his companions' views with a cautious respect. He leaves their presuppositions unchallenged while allowing his own account of virtue to reveal itself gradually as the dialogue progresses. One consequence of this technique is that one cannot treat the early parts of the dialogues as fully articulated expressions of Plato's considered doctrine. They have to be taken in the context of the dialogue as a whole.

6

Pleasure and the Good Life

Laws, 636d–e, 644c–645c, 653a–c, 660d–664a, 732d–734e; *Protagoras*, 351d–358d; *Gorgias*, 492d–500d; *Phaedo*, 68d–69c; *Republic*, 580c–588a; *Philebus*, especially 59c–67b

A central doctrine of the *Laws*, as of many other Platonic dialogues, is that it is in each individual's own interests to be virtuous. In the *Republic*, Plato had supported this thesis with three main arguments: (a) that since virtue is a healthy and harmonious state of the soul it is to be desired even more than bodily health; (b) that the virtuous life is more truly pleasant than any other; (c) that after death the virtuous will be rewarded and the wicked punished. All three arguments are present, at least by implication, in the *Laws*. It shares with the *Republic* the view of virtue as a harmonious state of the soul under the direction of reason. (See above, chapter 5.) The Athenian also maintains that the wicked will fare badly after death by being sent to a lower plane of existence along with their fellow sinners (903b–907c; cf. 728b). But, in so far as the Athenian argues explicitly for virtue, he pays most attention to the idea that it is pleasurable. This has puzzled many readers because it could be taken as a commitment to the hedonist view that the good after which we should all strive is simply pleasure.

Plato's attitude to hedonism seems to have varied over the years. In the *Protagoras* he apparently identifies pleasure with the good, but the *Gorgias* and the *Phaedo* are diametrically opposed to this. The *Republic*, too, maintains that pleasure is not the good, even though it argues that in fact the good life will be more pleasurable than any other. The *Philebus*, a dialogue that may be close in date to the *Laws*, treats pleasure as a constituent of the good life but argues that it is not the most important element nor the one that makes the life truly good.

The position in the *Laws* is very obscure. In Book I, pleasure appears primarily as something to be resisted and overcome. In Book II, the Athenian stresses the need to educate the young, so that they feel pleasure in the right things, and argues that the just life must be the pleasantest. A passage in Book V has been taken to claim that we can and should do only what seems pleasantest to us. None of these passages is clear in itself and jointly they can present an appearance of total confusion. One may well feel sympathy with Crombie's comment (1962-3, vol. I, p. 271) that Plato manages 'to sit on all the fences'.

1 Book I: pleasure and self-restraint

The purpose of the drinking parties which the Athenian advocates in Book I is to train the young to overcome pleasure and desire (633d-634c, 636a-650b, 671a-674c). On the face of it this suggests a strongly anti-hedonist doctrine. Of course, a hedonist can advocate a kind of self-control — he can advise us to resist immediate temptations in order to maximize our pleasures in the long term — but the Athenian's sweeping condemnations of pleasure (e.g. in 633d-634c) seem to apply to all alike. These passages have an almost ascetic ring.

Two passages in this book discuss at some length the role of pleasure and pain in human choice:

(1) The 'two springs' passage, 636d-e: here the Athenian maintains that any discussion of legislation must be almost entirely concerned with the roles of pleasure and pain. 'These flow like two springs sent forth by nature; a city, a private individual or any other creature that draws from them the right amount, in the right place at the right time, is happy; he that draws foolishly and at the wrong moment is miserable.'

(2) The 'puppet of the gods' passage, 644c-645c: according to this picturesque account of human choice, there are in each of us two mutually antagonistic advisers, pleasure and pain. We also have opinions about the future. The expectation of pleasure is hope; the expectation of pain is fear. In addition, there is within each of us a power of reasoning or calculation that tells which among these pleasures, pains, hopes and fears is better and which worse. When embodied in a decree of the city this reasoning is called 'law'. Then, in one of his more striking images, the Athenian invites his listeners to look on man as a puppet of the gods. We are each of us suspended, as it were, from three strings. The strings of pleasure and pain are hard as iron, but the golden string of reason and law is pliant and flexible; it needs help to overcome the other forces. Our task, then, is to co-operate with this golden string in resisting the others.

If one was determined at all costs to impose a hedonist reading of the Laws, one might conceivably be able to force the 'two springs' passage into that mould. The point would then have to be that we need to choose our pleasures and pains carefully in order to get the greatest possible pleasure in the long run. But, on the face of it, this interpretation is highly implausible. If a medical man argued, as Greek medical men often did, that the road to health lay in eating the right amount at the right time and place, one would not conclude that good health consisted in eating the greatest possible amount in the long run. Rather one would suppose that there was some independent criterion of health which might require one to curtail the intake of food. Similarly the natural reading of the 'two springs' passage is that there is some independent standard of good in the light of which one might need to restrict one's pleasures. Pleasure itself cannot, therefore, be the good.

The 'puppet of the gods' passage is more puzzling. There are at least three points that might prompt a hedonist interpretation. (a) If the expectation of pleasure is hope and the expectation of pain is fear, that suggests that pleasure is the only good and pain the only evil. (b) The image of the puppet might lead us to expect a deterministic model in which all human behaviour is regarded as the product of pleasures and pains. It would follow that we have no choice but to seek pleasure and avoid pain. (c) The description of the third string as '*logismos*', calculation, recalls the *Protagoras*, where the role of reason is to calculate the balance of pleasures and pains.

Against this we can set two other points. (a) The puppet, oddly enough, has a certain freedom: it can choose which of the three strings to co-operate with. If we take this seriously it suggests that the choosing self is distinct both from reason and from the passions, though Plato usually identifies the self with the reason. It is difficult to see how this model could be worked out coherently, but the implication appears to be that we can act in ways that do not simply maximize our pleasures and that we sometimes ought to do so. (b) The Athenian says both that the golden string of calculation judges pleasures and pains, hopes and fears, deciding which of them is better and which worse, and that, in co-operating with calculation we have to resist the pull of the other strings. The implication is surely that we judge which pleasures are to be pursued and which avoided in the light of some independent criterion of goodness and that this criterion is known to reason.

Overall it is difficult to avoid the conclusion that the Athenian has not thought through his account of choice in these passages. It looks as though he is trying to combine two possibly incompatible doctrines, that pleasure and pain are the main determinants of conduct, and that we ought to follow reason in resisting these feelings.

2   *Book II: pleasure and happiness*

The main theme of Book II is that the young must be educated to take pleasure in the right things. This, in itself, implies a more positive evaluation of pleasure than one might gather from Book I.

Part of the Athenian's educational doctrine is that poetry must be controlled. The leading theme of poetry must be that the virtuous are happy. Those things normally held good (e.g. wealth, fine physique, power, long life, etc.) are blessings to the good man but are positively bad for the unjust (660b–661d). The Cretan and the Spartan find this hard to accept: like some of Socrates' respondents in earlier dialogues, they can agree that the life of the unjust man is dishonourable, but not that he is unhappy or that his life is unpleasant or unprofitable to him (661d–662a, cf. *Crito*, 49b, *Gorgias*, 474c).

The Athenian replies by asserting his own complete faith that justice, happiness and pleasure coincide. As a lawgiver, he would impose severe penalties on anyone who said that a bad man could live a pleasant life or that there is a difference between what is just and what is profitable. He supports this view with a complex argument designed to show that anyone who advocates justice, be he a god, a lawgiver or a parent, must agree that the most just life is also the most pleasant (662c–663a).

The argument is a form of *reductio ad absurdum*: the Athenian claims that anyone who advocates justice while denying that the just life is the pleasantest will be committed to the obviously false conclusion that the happiest life is not the pleasantest. The key premise is at 662e. According to the Athenian those who urge the young to live a just life claim to want the happiness of their charges. They are thus committed to saying that the just life is the happiest. This means that if the just life was not the pleasantest these people would have to agree that the happiest life was not the pleasantest. But the Athenian thinks that this is absurd, for, he asks, 'What good could come to us unaccompanied by pleasure (663a)?' Thus the only sensible conclusion is that the just life is also the pleasantest.

This argument rests on two questionable assumptions. The first is that anyone who advocates justice is committed to maintaining that the just life is happiest. This is one of Plato's standing beliefs, but it is certainly not self-evident. In the present context he supports it only by showing that human legislators and parents urge the young to be just while claiming to want their happiness. The trouble with this argument is that, at most, it proves only that people often think and talk as though justice and happiness coincide, not that they coincide in reality.

The second dubious assumption is that the happiest life is pleasantest. The Athenian does not support this directly; instead he suggests in a series of rhetorical questions that the *just* life must be pleasantest. 'Is a good reputation among men and gods a fine thing but not pleasant?' 'Is it not pleasant to commit no acts of injustice and to have none done against oneself?' But, even if we were to agree with the Athenian in answering 'No' to these questions, we would be committed only to saying that the just life is *pleasant*, not that it is the *pleasantest*. Moreover the argument relies on the supposed consequences of justice. Plato rightly rejected such arguments in the *Republic*, since, even if justice generally produces pleasant consequences, it need not always do so. There is, regrettably, no guarantee that the just man will escape injury by others or that he will get a good reputation. So the Athenian has proved neither that the just life must be happy nor that it must be pleasantest.

In the passage that follows (663b–664c), the Athenian combines a disreputable argument with one that is suggestive and interesting, if not wholly convincing. The disreputable argument is that, whether true or not, it will be useful to propagate the idea that the just life is pleasantest, since no one would allow himself to be talked into an act unless it produces more pleasure than pain (663b). The interesting argument is that our perceptions may be clouded by our point of view. From the standpoint of the unjust man, unjust acts appear pleasant and just acts appear unpleasant. From the just man's standpoint the opposite is the case. But the good man's view is authoritative for truth. So it is the task of the legislator to correct these tricks of perspective.

There is an important point here. Different people take pleasure in different things. Someone wholly committed to justice (i.e. who wanted above all to be just) would presumably find his greatest pleasure in justice. So for those with just souls the just life will be pleasantest. But one cannot conclude from this that the life of the just will necessarily be pleasanter than that of the unjust. As Crombie (1962, p. 271) points out, it could be simply that justice is pleasant to those who have a taste for that kind of thing. The really unjust man could well find his greatest pleasure in behaving unjustly. There is, moreover, no reason why the just man's verdict should be regarded as peculiarly authoritative on this issue — that would prejudge the question. So, although the Athenian's arguments go some way towards showing that the just life can be *pleasant*, they certainly do not prove that it is the pleasantest kind of life.

Leaving aside the question whether the Athenian has succeeded in proving that the just life is pleasantest, we may complain that he has still not taken up a clear position on the fundamental issues. His insistence that justice, happiness and pleasure must all coincide may suggest that pleasure is the ultimate good and the claim at 663b that no one would willingly do an act that did not result in a balance of pleasure over pain might indicate a commitment to the psychological hedonist position that human beings can only seek pleasure. But his point could still be that, although the good life always happens to be pleasant, pleasure is not itself the good.

3 *Pleasure and the choice of lives*

Before we pass to Book V, it may be helpful to distinguish two conceptions of moral choice.

The first conception treats morality as primarily concerned with the choice of particular acts on particular occasions. The kind of question we have to answer is 'What shall I do here and now?' or 'What shall I do next Tuesday evening?' Since most of us know which kinds of things give us pleasure and which do not, it may make good sense to answer a question of this kind by saying, 'Do what will give you most pleasure.' Here the hedonist model of choice has definite attractions.

Plato, however, concerns himself not so much with the choice of acts as with the choice of character. The *Republic*, for example, sets out to show that we will be better off if we have just, rather than unjust, souls, and that a life of justice is therefore preferable to one of injustice. Just and unjust acts enter the picture only because they tend to shape the character — we become just by behaving justly and unjust by behaving unjustly (444c–e). The focus of the *Laws* is similar. The legislator sets out to make the citizens virtuous, not merely to secure external compliance with his edicts.

This view of morality does not necessarily imply the absurd idea that someone with an as yet unformed character might seriously sit down to decide what kind of person to be. One's character is, of course, to some extent formed before one is capable of taking conscious decisions of this kind. Plato's concern is to convince the ordinary man that it is worth struggling to retain one's moral integrity and to persuade parents and legislators that it is in their children's own interest to be brought up in the paths of virtue.

Clearly a choice of lives would be more complicated than a choice of acts. In particular one could not tell someone who was genuinely asking himself what kind of life to live that he should choose the life he would find most pleasurable. What gives us pleasure depends largely on our desires, wishes and interests. In choosing a life one would be choosing, *inter alia* what desires, wishes and interests to adopt. Thus an appeal to the distinctive pleasures of any life prejudges the issue in its favour. The Athenian's claim that the pleasures of the just life are more genuine because the decision of the just man is authoritative (663b–c, cf. *Republic*, 582a–583a) begs the question in precisely this way. One could retort that the just man finds pleasure in justice only because he has been conditioned to do so by his conventional upbringing and has therefore had his capacity to enjoy the pleasures of injustice blunted. So, while the Athenian is entitled to point out that justice has its own pleasures, he is not entitled to say that they are necessarily greater or more genuine than the pleasures involved in other kinds of life.

There are, however, other ways in which pleasure could be relevant to the decision which of two different kinds of life is to be preferred. Firstly there are some experiences, especially certain physical sensations, that almost everybody, whatever his interests, finds pleasant or painful. A life that involved a great deal of physical pain would, to that extent, seem undesirable to virtually everyone. Then there is the matter of external circumstances. One may desire things that are in short supply or difficult to come by, or one may want to do something that is possible only when conditions are particularly favourable. A life that includes many such desires is inherently more likely to result in frustration and disappointment. Lastly, we may notice that different lives contain different mixes of pleasure and pain. One life may contain periods of exhilaration mingled with times of despair; another may furnish an even-tenored contentment. One could have a preference for one pattern rather than another without being committed to any particular way of life.

Given these points, one can see that, although Plato is not entitled to maintain that the pleasures of justice are intrinsically preferable to those of injustice, he can legitimately refer to pleasure in his argument for the just life. He could claim that the pleasures of justice, unlike many others, carry no risk of physical pain, and that, because they do not depend on external circumstances, they are less likely to be frustrated or to be mixed with great disappointments. This is the strategy he follows in Book V.

4   *Book V: divine goods and human pleasures*

The Athenian returns to the subject of pleasure in his general 'prelude' or 'preamble' to the legal code (726–734e). The first six pages of this prelude consist of an exhortation to live virtuously and, in particular, to honour the soul as one's most divine possession. Then a change of direction is announced:

> Thus, as regards the right character of institutions and of individuals, we have now laid down practically all the rules that are of divine provenance. Those that are of human origin we have not, as yet, stated. But state them we must, for we are talking to men, not gods. By nature, pleasures, pains and desires are especially human; and from these, of necessity, every mortal creature, so to speak, depends and hangs by the strongest cords of influence. Thus one should commend the noblest life, not merely because of superiority in reputation, but also because, if a man consents to taste it and does not shun it in his youth, it is likewise superior in that which all men seek — an excess of joy and a deficiency of pain throughout one's whole life. (732d–733a, translation adapted from Bury)

The contrast here between the rules of divine provenance and those of human origin is of the greatest importance since it reveals the relationship between a number of distinct and superficially conflicting strands in the moral theory of the *Laws*.

From a very early stage in the dialogue the Athenian has argued that, since the soul is our most divine possession, virtue (the good of the soul) is to be preferred to all human goods. (See especially 631b–c, 697b, 726–728c). Within the soul it is the immortal element of reason, not the mortal elements (the passions and desires), that is supposed to be divine (644c–645c, 713e; cf. *Timaeus*, 42c–44d, 69d–e). Thus wisdom has first place among the divine goods and they look to reason as their leader (631c–d). One honours the soul by resisting the blandishments of pleasure and by enduring pain and fear (727c). Thus when he talks from the divine point of view the Athenian is anything but a hedonist. His rules of divine provenance bid us to struggle against pleasures in order to honour the reason and to subordinate ourselves to it.

If we were fully rational beings, like the gods, we would presumably conform without question to the dictates of reason. We would see what was good and do it without hesitation. But, as embodied beings, we are subject to irrational forces, to desires, to pleasures and pains, and to motions like anger and fear (644c–645c, 863b–c; cf. *Timaeus*, 42a–b). We are thus likely to be virtuous only if we can see that the virtuous life will be pleasant (663b). Fortunately, the Athenian believes, the virtuous life is pleasant, so the case for virtue can be made on the human, as well as on the divine, level. And, since the feelings of pleasure and pain have the strongest influence on human beings, it is this aspect that is most relevant to the practical work of the legislator (636d). That is why it is important to train the young to feel pleasures and pains in the right kind of way (635a–c, 659d–e). By right education the disorderly motions of the lower, mortal soul can be subordinated to those of reason (*Timaeus*, 44c, 87a–b). So in setting out the rules of human origin the Athenian is seeking to demonstrate not that pleasure is the good but that a creature subject to pleasures and pains can still be advised to pursue the same kind of virtuous life that would be recommended by the reason.

5   *Pleasure and choice*

The Athenian now proceeds to describe the rules of human origin (733a–d). He maintains that anyone who tastes the good life in the correct way will see that it is superior in respect of pleasure and pain. But what, he asks, is correctness here? To understand that we have to compare the pleasanter and more painful lives and see which is genuinely in accord with human nature. We will then find that:

(1)   We desire pleasure but do not choose or desire pain.

(2)   We do not desire a neutral state in place of pleasure, but we do desire it in place of pain.

(3)   We desire more pleasure with less pain; we do not desire less pleasure with more pain.

(4)   When two states contain equal proportions of pleasure and pain we cannot say which we would prefer. (An alternative translation would be: 'We cannot say whether we would desire a state in which pleasure and pain are equal'.)

In assessing these feelings we have to take into account their number, size, intensity and equality (or the opposite). Hence:

(5)   In the case of a life that contains feelings which are numerous, great and intense, we want it if pleasure predominates, but not if pain is predominant.

(6)   In the case of lives containing feelings that are few, small and weak, we do not want that in which pain predominates, but we do want that in which pleasure predominates.

(7) A life with an equal balance of pleasure and pain is to be regarded in the same light, i.e. we desire it in so far as it predominates in what we like, but we do not want it in so far as it predominates in what we do not like.

The conclusion is that our whole lives are bound up in the feelings of pleasure and pain and that we must therefore distinguish what kinds of life we by nature desire. Anyone who suggests that we may desire something apart from these is talking through ignorance or inexperience.

It is natural for a modern reader to see this passage as an anticipation of the Benthamite felicific calculus. The underlying assumption of such a calculus is that, whenever we have a choice between two or more courses of action, the various possible outcomes can, in principle at least, be ranked on a scale of pleasure and pain. If we are rational, we choose the course that will bring most pleasure and least pain. The Benthamite calculus thus carries an explicit commitment to hedonism. But before jumping to any hasty conclusions we should notice some important differences between Plato's calculus and Bentham's.

In the first place, Plato is concerned with a choice of lives rather than a choice of acts. As we saw above, such choices cannot be made simply on the principle of maximizing pleasures and minimizing pains, though pleasure and pain are not altogether irrelevant. The second point is that the present passage does not provide a method of ranking all lives in relation to one another. It explains how we will choose between certain pairs of alternatives but these by no means cover all possibilities of choice. In particular, nothing has been said about how we would choose between lives containing a predominance of difference kinds of pleasure. The upshot of this is that 733a–d lists a series of conditions which govern the choice of lives but which are insufficient to determine the choice in every respect. To put it another way, pleasures and pains may be constraints upon choice but they need not be the sole objects of choice.

In 733d–734e these considerations are applied to the choice of lives. The lives of temperance or self-restraint, wisdom, courage and health are opposed to those that are foolish, cowardly, licentious and diseased. It is argued that the man who really knows what he is doing will prefer the temperate life to the licentious. It is gentle both in its pleasures and in its pains and has an abundance of the former. The licentious life, on the other hand, is extreme in both pleasures and pains and has a balance of the latter. No one therefore will voluntarily be licentious. People become licentious through ignorance or inability to control themselves. Parallel arguments are used to recommend the brave, wise and healthy lives. The conclusion is that the life of moral and physical excellence is superior to that of vice in being pleasanter, as well as in beauty, rightness, virtue and reputation. It makes its possessor happier in every respect.

The argument here does not justify the Athenian's conclusions as they stand. We may grant that the temperate life probably is, on balance, pleasanter than one of unlimited self-indulgence, though this is not strictly proved. But one cannot conclude from this that virtue is pleasanter than vice in general. Nothing has been done, for example, to prove that a virtuous life is pleasanter than one of cool calculating villainy. But the Athenian does not need to prove such a strong conclusion. If, as he maintains, there are rational non-hedonistic grounds for pursuing virtue, all he needs to show is that it is within the capacity of human nature to choose the life of virtue, i.e. that the virtuous life can satisfy the constraints on choice described in 733a–d. For this he has to show only that the virtuous life has its own pleasures, that these generally exceed the pains, and that the vicious do not normally do better in this respect.

We are now in a position to answer most, though not all, of the problems raised earlier in this chapter. In particular, one can see how the Athenian might hope to reconcile the hedonistic and the non-hedonistic strands in his thought. He believes, it seems, that virtue is good in itself because it is the ordering of the soul in accordance with reason. In so far as we are rational, we will therefore require no further argument for virtue. But, since we are embodied beings, we shall be able to pursue the life of virtue only if it is pleasurable. Thus, although pleasure is not itself the good, it is a necessary condition of the good life for mankind. In this way the Athenian can, without inconsistency, maintain the propositions that are most central to the ethical doctrine of the *Laws*: (a) that the virtues are intrinsically of supreme value; (b) that virtue can require us to resist the temptations of pleasure; (c) that we can become truly virtuous only by learning to take pleasure in the right things; (d) that the good life is pleasurable. Virtue is valuable in itself because it is the life according to reason, but the virtuous life is possible for human beings only to the extent that they can take pleasure in virtue.

This interpretation aligns the *Laws* quite closely with the *Republic* and the *Philebus*. In the *Republic* Socrates is first made to argue that justice is intrinsically preferable to injustice (444e–445b) and later that the life of the just man is more truly pleasant (580c–587c). In the *Philebus* he concedes that pleasure is an essential ingredient of the good life but argues that it is by no means the most important ingredient nor the one which really makes the life good (20c–23a, 64b–67b). Both dialogues apparently accept that no one would deliberately choose a life known to be less pleasant, but that does not commit them to the view that the good consists in pleasure.

7

Political Analysis

Laws, 676a–702a; *Republic*, 543a–580a; *Statesman*, 291c–293e, 302b–303d

At first sight the long historical digression which occupies almost the whole of Book III looks irrelevant to the main themes of the *Laws*. But its purpose becomes obvious on a closer view: it sets out the principles which, according to the Athenian, should govern both our assessment of existing states and the construction of the new Cretan city. So, in many ways, it parallels the passages in the *Republic* and the *Statesman* in which Plato classifies and analyses existing constitutional forms.

1 The origin of states

The book begins with an account of the development of human society from an imaginary time in the remote past when natural disasters had destroyed all previous civilizations (676a–682e). This account is notable for its sense of the enormous lengths of time which have preceded the present epoch and for its reliance on rational reconstruction rather than myth. It establishes a number of points significant for political theory:

(1) Although it is not automatic or innate for man to live in society, states develop naturally over a long period of time. At first there are only family groups, these coalesce into larger units until, eventually, cities are established. Plato implicitly rejects doctrines like those he put into the mouths of Protagoras (*Protagoras*, 320d–322d) and Glaucon (*Republic*, 358b–359b) which represent political life as unnatural, the result of divine intervention or of human agreement.

(2) The primitive shepherds who lived scattered apart on the hills were lacking equally in virtue and vice (677b, 678b). In other words the *Laws* assumes that life in a civilized community is the normal goal of human development. (In the *Republic*, 372e, Socrates at least

pretends that the primitive life is ideal.)

(3)   Paternal government was originally the norm. When family groups joined together, lawgivers had to be appointed to choose among the customs of the different groups and to select rulers (681c–d). Thus lawgiving is a deliberate human activity, though it rests on a natural development.

2   Peloponnesian history

Attention next shifts to the history of the three Dorian states of the Peloponnese: Sparta, Messene, and Argos (682e–689e). This, largely fictitious, account establishes two points of fundamental importance to the political philosophy of the *Laws*: (a) the political importance of *sophrosune*, and (b) the need for a mixed constitution.

According to the Athenian, the Dorians, on their arrival in the Peloponnese, established three linked states. Within each of these the kings and the people bound themselves by oaths not to infringe each other's rights. Each state also swore to come to the aid of the others if either of them was threatened with destruction. This arrangement should have meant that the Dorians would obey their laws, but in fact it came to nothing (682e–686b). The reason, according to the Athenian, is that, although human institutions, used correctly, can give great power to those who have them, they can be positively harmful to those who do not know how to use them correctly. If we judge wrongly in determining the ends for which powerful instruments are used, they will lead to disaster, like that encountered by the foolish man whose foolish prayers are answered. The trouble with the Dorians is that they were subject to the 'greatest folly', i.e. to a disagreement between their feelings of pleasure and pain and their rational judgements (see above chapter 5, section 3). This 'folly' affects the state when the people are unwilling to obey their rulers or the laws. In the case of an individual, it means that the rational principles a man possesses, so far from doing good, may actually be harmful. No one in this condition should hold any office. The lawgiver must therefore strive to drive out this folly and implant the wisdom which consists in inner harmony (686b–689e).

This brings us back to the themes of Books I and II, the fundamental importance of *sophrosune* and the failure of the Dorian institutions to foster it. The earlier books showed that *sophrosune* cannot exist without the right kind of political institutions. Now we learn that even the best institutions are doomed to failure if the citizens lack *sophrosune*. Neither can exist without the other. So the legislator's work is incomplete unless he inculcates a proper self-discipline.

Underlying this there is a more general point: no constitution can survive unless the people accept it and are willing to follow it, even when they find this uncongenial. It is not enough simply to suggest good constitutional forms; one must also secure a match between the constitution and the character and aspiratons of those who live under it.

3 *Seven claims to rule*

At 690a–691a there is a digression in which the Athenian considers seven 'claims to rule' in cities and in households. (Saunders' translation, 'seven titles to authority', may convey too strong a suggestion of legitimacy.) The claims are those (a) of parents over their children, (b) of noble birth, (c) of age, (d) of masters over slaves, (e) of the stronger to rule the weak, (f) of the wise to rule the ignorant and, (g) of those selected by lot (which is taken as a sign of divine favour).

It is not at all clear on what principle this classification is based. Any interpretation produces seemingly insoluble difficulties:

(1) Are the claims to rule claims which are actually made, whether justified or not, or are they claims which the Athenian endorses as justified? If the list is intended to cover all those claims actually made by Plato's contemporaries, why is the claim of wealth not mentioned? If, on the other hand, it is a list of claims endorsed by the Athenian himself, it ought not to include the claim of strength which he later explicitly rejects (714b–e).

(2) Grote (1888, p. 309) and Strauss (1975, p. 47) note that claims (e) and (f) receive most emphasis. Claim (e), the claim of strength, prevails among the animals and is called natural by Pindar but the Athenian himself prefers (f) the claim of wisdom. Significantly he calls it 'the natural rule of law over willing subjects'. Strauss, recalling the *Gorgias*, 488d, where the many are said to be strong, identifies the rule of the strong with democracy and that of the wise with kingship. This would link the present passage to one a few pages later where democracy and monarchy are named as the two mother constitutions (693d–e) but it has no other support in the text and probably rests on a misunderstanding of the kind of classification that is now being offered. The Athenian insists that in any state there must be rulers and ruled (689e) and that the claims to rule apply to households as well as to states (690a). It seems, therefore, that he is concerned not so much

with constitutional forms as with the claims of individuals to be rulers. There is no need to mention a claim of the many because the many cannot all be magistrates, but the Athenian does mention the claim of those selected by lot, the democratic states' way of choosing officials. Similarly nothing is said about monarchy as such, presumably because the claim of any individual to rule as monarch might be based on a number of different grounds. Monarchy has in fact been defenced on grounds of wisdom, strength, noble birth and paternal authority.

(3)   The claims of the master to rule his slave and the parent to rule his child apply in the first place to households. The others all apply in the first place to states. To list them side by side is, to say the least, confusing (cf. Aristotle, *Politics*, I.i, 1252a 9–17).

(4)   At least one of the claims, that of lot, indicates a definite mechanism by which rulers can be selected. The claims of noble birth and age also suggest procedures for deciding who should rule and they correspond to known constitutional forms. The claim of wisdom, on the other hand, suggests no particular procedures. How are we to decide who is wisest?

It is difficult to avoid the conclusion that Plato has not thought out at all clearly what he is trying to do with the classification of claims to rule. At 690d the Athenian suggests that conflict between the different claims is an important cause of dissension, but in fact he attributes the failure of the Dorian states not to this but to failures of character. Otherwise, apart from rather casual references at 692a and 714e, he ignores the classification altogether. This is a pity, because his fundamental idea may be a good one. In Plato's day, at least, supporters of different constitutional forms differed fundamentally on the question, 'What considerations are relevant in deciding who should exercise power?' As long as such disagreements persisted there would always be a danger of civil strife. So it made sense to devise a constitution which took account of as many of the different claims as possible. To a considerable extent, Plato achieves this in the constitution he proposes for the Cretan city.

4   *Sparta and the mixed constitution*

Argos and Messene failed because their kings, corrupted by luxurious living, transgressed the very laws they had sworn to obey. The legislator should see that in all things one must respect due measure (otherwise 'proportion' or 'moderation'). Just as ships cannot bear sails that are too large or bodies too much food, so a man cannot bear more than a due measure of power. A young man who wields great power unchecked is bound to be overcome by folly (691c–d). Of the three Dorian states, Sparta alone survived in good order. This happened because it developed a system in which there were (a) two kings, rather than one, (b) a council of elders and (c) powerful officials called ephors, chosen by a method close to that of lot. All of these could act as a check on one another. Thus it survived by becoming a mixture of different elements and acquiring 'due measure' (691d–692a). The original founders of the Peloponnesian states sought in vain to impose moderation by means of oaths. Now, in the light of the Spartan experience, we can see what really should have been done (692b–c). To found a state which will be free, wise and in friendship with itself, the legislator must avoid establishing any office with great or unmixed power (693b).

This introduces another of Plato's key principles, that of the moderate or mixed constitution. (The word *metron* means 'measure' in the sense of 'that by which something is measured' but it also has the sense 'due measure', 'limit' or 'proportion'. The corresponding adjective, *metrios*, means literally 'measured' but is usually translated 'moderate'.)

There is, of course, nothing particularly original in the praise of moderation. Sayings like 'Nothing in excess' or 'The half is better than the whole' were commonplace. Even the application of these ideas to constitutional theory is not new. The constitutions of Solon and Theramenes, for example, had both been called 'moderate' or 'measured'. But an appeal to 'moderation' or 'due measure' could mean many different things. As applied to Solon's constitution it meant a balance between the claims of the rich and the poor. As applied to that of Theramenes it referred to a moderate oligarchy which was supposed to come midway between extreme oligarchy and democracy. In the present context Plato is emphasizing the need to restrict the power of individuals. The power of the Spartan monarchy is restrained by dividing it between two kings and by combining it with other kinds of authority. This idea that moderation can be secured through a constitution in which different elements act as a check on one another is of immense historical importance. It is, perhaps, the major contribution of the *Laws* to political theory. But there is more than this to Plato's conception of the mixed or moderate constitution, as becomes apparent in the pages that follow.

5   *Persia and Athens*

At 693d the Athenian proposes to describe two 'mother constitutions' (Taylor: 'matrices of constitutions'), monarchy and democracy. He regards all other constitutions as combinations of these. The extreme of monarchy is represented by the Persians, that of democracy by Athens. The success of the Spartans and Cretans is attributed to their avoidance of these extremes. On the Athenian's account the Persians have experienced alternating periods of success and disaster. At first, under Cyrus, they kept a balance between slavery and freedom. As a result they were not only free themselves but became masters of others. Because the rulers granted their subjects a degree of freedom and equality the soldiers were well disposed to their commanders and willing to encounter dangers. Because there was freedom of speech, any man was able to add his wisdom to the common stock. Thus everything went well because of their freedom, their friendly feelings, and their ability to share their powers of reason (694b–c).

After the death of Cyrus disaster overtook the Persians, because Cyrus' sons who had been brought up by the womenfolk when their father was away on campaign were, as we would say, 'hopelessly spoilt' (694c–695b). After Darius seized the throne the process repeated itself. Darius enacted laws which gave a degree of equality and limited his financial exactions. Thus, by money and gifts, he won over the Persians, aroused feelings of friendship and community and gained the good will of his army (695c–d). After his death disaster struck again because his successor, Xerxes, had had the same bad upbringing as the sons of Cyrus (695d–e).

The Persians failed through an excess of slavery and despotism. The Athenian experience, by contrast, shows that liberty without authority is vastly inferior to a moderate form of control. The success of Athens at the time of the Persian wars is attributed to fear of the laws which they were accustomed to serve as slaves do a master. This fear of the laws is called *aidōs*: 'respect', 'reverence' or 'awe' (Saunders' 'modesty' is too weak). Such attitudes together with their fear of the invaders created feelings of friendship and community (698b–c, 699c). This voluntary slavery to the laws was especially evident in the case of laws governing music (700a). People used to submit willingly to discipline in these matters, but now they consider only what gives pleasure; the applause of the multitude has replaced the judgement of those who really know what is good or bad. From music this disorder can spread to affect the whole life of the community. People begin to think they know everything and to behave lawlessly. Through confidence in their own wisdom they become fearless, and this fearlessness breeds a kind of shamelessness — a disregard, through excess of liberty, of the opinion of one's betters. There follows an unwillingness to serve the authorities and a contempt for parents, for law and even for the sanctity of oaths (700a–701d).

6   The politics of due measure

There is no doubt that Plato is unfair to Athenian democracy. Law and order did not break down even though there was a substantial degree of personal freedom. Plato's account of Persian history may be equally inadequate. But Persia and Athens are introduced into the argument not for their own interest but as examples of extreme monarchy and extreme democracy. They function as ideal types. So what really matters is not whether the picture of these two states is historically accurate but whether Plato is right in suggesting that a well ordered state must be a mean between the two extremes as he describes them.

It is natural to suppose that in discussing monarchy and democracy Plato is concerned with constitutional forms, that monarchy represents the unchecked rule of a single individual and democracy the rule of the many. Thus Taylor suggests that the Athenian is demanding a balance between personal rule and popular control (1960a, p. xxvii). But in fact the Athenian says nothing about institutions as such; he concentrates entirely on the need for a balance between freedom and despotism. A balance of this kind was apparently achieved both by the Persians under Cyrus and Darius and by the Athenians at the time of Marathon and Salamis, even though the Persians had no democratic institutions and the Athenians no monarch. This is what one would expect in the light of the *Statesman*, where Plato argues that it does not matter whether there are few or many rulers. What really matters is whether the ruler(s) possess the science of ruling (292c). If such an expert ruler is not available, what matters is not primarily the number of rulers but whether they rule in accordance with law (302b–303b).

What is meant by freedom and despotism in this context? The freedom Plato attacks is an absence of restrictions, a situation in which individuals may do as they please. One would therefore expect its converse, despotism, to be a situation in which this personal liberty is very restricted. But, if this were so, then the Athenians when they were 'slaves to the law' would probably have been living under a greater despotism than the Persians ever experienced. As Mill saw, democracies may threaten individual liberties more than monarchies. In fact, the trouble with the Persians in their more decadent periods seems to be that they were subject to arbitrary exploitation by their rulers. The kings used their subjects for their own purposes without any consideration of what was right or good for the subjects themselves. The better monarchs, on the other hand, sought the good of their subjects and listened to what they had to say. So the subjects willingly accepted their rule in the same way as the Athenians willingly enslaved themselves to the laws. The balance to be sought between monarchy and democracy is not a midway point between having many restrictions on personal liberty and having none. It is a condition in which restrictions are accepted willingly because they are recognized to be good. This is brought out clearly in Book IV, 712e ff.: most existing forms of rule do not deserve the title 'constitution' because they require some citizens to live in subjection to others like slaves (712e–713a). The true constitution will involve subjection to laws that aim at the good of the whole community (715a–d).

Plato's theory of the moderate or measured constitution is the political counterpart of a doctrine prominent in his later metaphysics. In the *Statesman* (283c–284b), he distinguishes two kinds of measurement. One kind concerns itself with the greatness or smallness of its objects relative to one another; the other is concerned with their greatness or smallness relative to 'due measure' or 'the right standard'. Plato suggests that the arts and crafts produce good and beautiful results by maintaining due measure. In the *Philebus* (23c–26d), all reality is divided into the unlimited, the limit, the mixture of these two, and the cause of this mixture. The unlimited includes qualities capable of being more or less, for example, hotter and colder; the limiting factors are measure, proportion and ratio. The imposition of the limit on the unlimited produces order and harmony, so health, music and good weather, for example, are all thought of as mixtures of the limit and the unlimited. The good life involves the imposition of law and order, which involve the limit, on our pleasures and appetites. In the universe at large these orderly mixtures are created by the divine reason of which our human reason is a small fragment. The parallels between these passages and the doctrine of the moderate constitution are obvious. Despotism and freedom form an indefinite continuum like the hot and the cold. In a well ordered state these extremes are reconciled by law. Law in its turn is a product of reason which governs the universe. God is the measure of all things (716c).

The theory of the limit and the unlimited presumably has its origin in Pythagorean musical theory. It fits music well. If one stops a vibrating string so that the ratio of the two parts is, say, 1:1, there will be a concord; if one stops it so that the ratio of the parts is, say, 5:2, there will be a discord: it will sound as though the two parts are in conflict with one another. Thus one can think of musical harmonies both as midpoints between extremes, and as reconciling conflicting elements. One may be able to apply such notions to health, since health does depend on maintaining the right temperature and the right ratios among the chemical constituents of one's body. But they offer no guidance when applied to the soul or to political systems. No doubt the virtue and the well-being of a state depends on the acceptance of some form of law and order, but forms of political order cannot be expressed in numerical ratios, and in any case there is no one form of order which is objectively right, laid down in the nature of things. Thus in politics and ethics, the doctrine of measure lacks the scientific status it has elsewhere. In practice it boils down to the claim that a good constitution must avoid extremes, impose checks on individual power and reconcile conflicting claims.

8

The Sovereignty of Law

Laws, 627e–628a, 656c–657b, 691c–692c, 698b–c, 699c, 700a, 712b–715d, 769a–771b, 772a–d, 822e–823a; *Statesman*, 300a–301a

1   *In what sense can law be sovereign?*

The fine scheme of the Peloponnesian states collapsed because their rulers, lacking self-control and subject to no external constraints, failed to obey the laws. The Athenians, likewise, prospered when they were slaves to their laws and declined when they abandoned them. The assumption which underlies these accounts, that in a well run state law will be supreme, is brought to the surface in Book IV, 712b–715d. At 712d–e, Megillus professes himself unable to classify the Spartan constitution according to the conventional categories of political thought. It is not exactly tyranny, aristocracy, democracy or kingship, though it has elements of all these kinds. The Athenian attributes Megillus' difficulty to the fact that Sparta has a genuine constitution: what pass for constitutions elsewhere are simply arrangements by which one section of the community enslaves another (712e–713a).

There follows a digression on the age of Cronos, the imaginary time in the remote past when divine beings ruled directly over men (713a–e). The conclusion is that we should run households and cities in accordance with the small element we possess of immortality, i.e. in accordance with reason. We call the form of order created by reason 'law' (713e–714a). The Athenian then attacks existing states whose so-called laws simply enforce the interest of the stronger party: genuine laws must be directed to the good of the city as a whole (715b). Rulers must be chosen, not for their wealth, strength, physique or any such thing but for their willingness to be slaves to the laws.

> I see destruction threatening any city where the laws are overruled and lack authority; but where law is master of the rulers and the rulers are its slaves, I see salvation and the promise of every blessing that the gods bestow on cities. (715d)

This claim that law should have ultimate authority can be interpreted in a number of different ways:

(1)   There is a sense in which any state in which there is a recognizable government must acknowledge the authority of law. There must, at very least, be a rule which says who is in charge. An absolute monarchy, for example, might be run according to one basic law, 'Obey the king'. But in a state of this kind one could not say that the ruler was the servant or slave of the laws, since the law gives him unlimited power.

(2)   A state may be said to be governed in accordance with law if the government recognizes the so-called 'rule of law', i.e. the government acts in accordance with general rules; these rules apply to all alike and are made public in some way; disputes are settled by some non-arbitrary procedure. Observance of the rule of law, understood in this sense, certainly restrains governments and may prevent some of the worst injustices. But if the government can change the law at will, it can hardly be said to be the servant of the laws.

(3)   To make sense of the notion that rulers may be servants of the law we need to add at least two further conditions. (a) The laws must be sufficiently specific to act as genuine restraints on government action. (b) The government must not be able to alter the law at will.

2   *How can the sovereignty of law be ensured?*

A good many of the Athenian's proposals could be seen as promoting the sovereignty of law: in particular every official in the proposed Cretan city would be subject to some kind of judicial control. The Athenian would thus put into practice the lesson he drew from his discussion of Spartan history — that no one should be given unrestrained power (691c–d, 693b). His doctrine here is the ancestor of modern theories of constitutional checks and balances, including Montesquieu's celebrated separation of powers. But Plato does not distinguish judicial and executive power. Most of the officials in his state would possess both. Instead the constitution is so arranged that each body of officials is responsible to some other organ of state. Thus no one should be able to get away with any illegality.

Plato sees clearly that talk of the supremacy of law becomes meaningless if the dominant parties in the state can change the law at will. At 713c–715d he contrasts the sovereignty of law with political systems in which so-called 'laws' are used by factions for their own purposes. Genuine laws are designed to promote the good of the whole community, not to satisfy the greed of the dominant party. To guard against this kind of abuse the Athenian envisages that a detailed legal code will be laid down in advance by a single legislator or legislative commission. This code will be very difficult to change and the citizens will be educated so that they become slaves to the law, not only in the sense that they respect the legislator's explicit provisions, but also in the sense that they strive to embody his ideal of virtue (822e–823a).

Some scholars might challenge this claim that law, in the Athenian's view, should be very difficult to change (Hall, 1981, pp. 98–100). There are certainly a number of passages where he suggests that the legislation proposed for the Cretan city is incomplete. It will be left to the officials of the new state (principally the guardians of the laws) to fill in the details 772a–c, 818e, 828b, 835a, 843e, 846b–c, 957a–b, 968c). In at least one case he admits that his measures may need alteration (not merely supplementation) in the light of exprience (840e). In 769a–d he compares the task of legislation with that of an artist who constantly retouches his picture, always improving it, but never reaching perfection. One might draw from this the impression that the Athenian sees legislation as a continuing process. This would, I believe, be a mistake. In many of the passages where the Athenian mentions the need for legislative supplementation he stresses that this is to be concerned with matters of detail, the kind of thing that any competent person could handle or for which existing codes of law provide adequate guidance (772a–c, 843e, 846b, 957a). He does not, it seems, anticipate significant innovations. Moreover he expects the period during which supplementation will be needed to be strictly limited. In the case of the regulations for religious festivals there should be a ten year period during which the various boards of officials (acting with the original legislator if he is still alive) should report omissions in their own departments to the guardians of the laws and should suggest improvements. The regulations will then be declared unalterable and enforced along with the measures established by the legislator. Thereafter the details of the festivals may be altered only of necessity with the consent of the whole people, all the officials and all the oracles (772b–d). There is a similar, though less explicit, treatment for the details of legal procedure (957a–b). The implication of this is that once the state is properly established, the law will be very difficult to change — precisely what one would expect from the Athenian's reverence for the long-established codes of Crete and Sparta, his general hostility to change, and his belief that law embodies principles of the eternal reason.

3 *Is the sovereignty of law realistic?*

One possible objection to the Athenian's conception of the sovereignty of law is that his ideal is not a practical possibility. In the work of any human legislator there are bound to be imperfections that need to be remedied in the light of experience. More importantly he fails to recognize that law must change itself to meet changing social and economic conditions. A system as rigid as that described in the *Laws* would be doomed to collapse; so the ideal of the sovereignty of law, it might be said, is no more realistic than the ideal of the philosopher king.

Against this it could be argued that a degree of fixity in law is obviously desirable. Otherwise there will be nothing to prevent constitutional rulers from turning themselves into tyrants by (e.g.) prolonging their own terms of office or proclaiming that all opposition is henceforth illegal. And, since most people obey the law out of force of habit, it is unlikely that a code which constantly changed would command the respect of the population at large — it might even be difficult for them to remember what the law is. Any civilized way must therefore presuppose some kind of compromise between Plato's ideal of an unchanging code and a system in which rulers can alter the law at will.

In practice most of the states we now regard as having constitutional governments have effected such a compromise by distinguishing different kinds of law. Besides the ordinary rules by which the citizens are supposed to govern their daily lives, there are certain rules which determine what is to count as a valid law and how legal disputes are to be adjudicated. Rules of this latter kind, or at least the most important of them, may be thought of as forming the constitution. The constitution may also include other elements, particularly rules to render void any legislation which would infringe basic rights of the citizens. One of the essential features of constitutional government is that these fundamental rules should not be subject to frequent or arbitrary change. This does not mean that the constitution must be unchangeable: merely that in practice it must be difficult to effect constitutional change. Where, as in the United States, there is a written constitution, this stability is ensured by the requirement that special procedures must be adopted before constitutional changes can be brought into effect. Many believe tht the absence of this kind of constraint is the main weakness of parliamentary democracy as it has evolved in Great Britain. But even here there are some constraints on legislation. The members of Parliament cannot simply change the law at will. Their decisions are law only if certain rather complex procedures have been followed.

To some extent Plato is aware of the distinction between constitutional and other laws. Book VI, 751a–768e, describes what we would call the constitution of the proposed Cretan state, and the transition to the substantive legislation is noticed (768e). But Plato shows no awareness that constitutional law could be given any special status. In general it is assumed that talk of a state's laws, *nomoi*, and of its constitution, *politeia*, are one and the same thing. Equally he makes legislative change so difficult as to be virtually impossible. In doing so he pitches the requirements of the sovereignty of law impossibly high. Stability need not mean total rigidity.

A second objection to the ideal of the sovereignty of law is that any legal system is bound to enshrine the interests of the dominant classes. Thus those who appeal to the sovereignty of law are, it is alleged, in fact seeking to perpetuate class rule. This pattern of criticism, which has resurfaced in Marxist theory, was familiar to Plato (712e–713a, 714b–715a; cf. *Republic*, 338c–339a). Plato's reply to this objection is clear enough: genuine law seeks the good of the whole state (715b) and is the product of reason (713e–714a). So while it may be true that so-called constitutions of existing states reflect class interests this would not be true of a state with a genuine constitution.

As it stands this reply is unconvincing because it assumes that there are absolute standards of right and that human legislators may know what these are — points that would be denied by Plato's critics. But Plato could fall back on the doctrine of the *Statesman*, 297e–303b. Even when legislators have been imperfect, a state governed by law is better off than one subject to the arbitrary rule of an individual tyrant or of a faction. One does not need to believe that there ever could be a state with a completely rational code of legislation in order to maintain that the rule of law offers the best hope for mankind.

4   Sophrosune *and the sovereignty of law*

The doctrine of the sovereignty of law embraces most of the key political ideas expounded in the *Laws*. From the beginning, one view of the legislator's role is that he has to produce internal peace as well as security from external dangers. This is best done through reconciliation by means of laws (627e–628a). In 715a–d the Athenian argues, in effect, that this can only come about if the rulers are servants of the law. Similarly the discussion of Athenian and Persian history shows that a state can only prosper where the constitution is measured, i.e. where voluntarily accepted laws impose an order or structure upon it. And the experience of the Peloponnesians shows that this law-abidingness can be achieved only where political power is divided among different office-holders.

But the sovereignty of law is not simply a political slogan. It is the counterpart of the other main theme developed in these early books, the theme of *sophrosune*, self-control. At the beginning, it is argued that the greatest victory is that over oneself, i.e. the victory of the better elements in the soul over the worse. But the political parallel suggests that even such a victory is inferior to a genuine harmony, a condition where our conflicting passions and motives have been reconciled by the internalization of law. Most of Books I and II are devoted to showing how the institutions of the state can be designed to promote this inner harmony. Book III, on the other hand, argues that the institutions of the state themselves depend on an underlying *sophrosune*, the ability to abide willingly by the rules. Since, in practice, no human being possesses this virtue to a sufficient degree, the constitution must be arranged so that external constraints supplement our self-control.

Plato sees a two-way relationship between the sovereignty of law and *sophrosune*. Law can be truly sovereign only where the people possess self-control, but they can acquire this virtue only by being brought up under the right institutions. There is obviously a good deal in this view. Laws by their very nature are constraints upon what we do. Obedience to law requires us to act against our own desires, at least on occasion; so voluntary obedience requires a measure of self-control. Of course, a state can survive if some of its members obey the law only to the extent that they are coerced. But if no one obeyed the law voluntarily there would be no one to exercise this coercion; we cannot all coerce each other all the time. Thus self-control is essential to life in a community. On the other hand, it seems that human beings cannot acquire self-control if left to themselves. We acquire it by internalizing rules laid down by parents, teachers and society at large. So *sophrosune* and the sovereignty of law are mutually interdependent; we cannot have one without the other.

In this respect the argument of the *Laws* is much more powerful than that of the *Republic*. The key virtue in the *Republic* is justice both in the state and in the individual. One major difficulty in the *Republic* is that the relationship between the just individual and the just state is purely analogical. The state is just when the three classes which comprise it are properly related to one another. The soul of the individual is likewise just when its three parts exhibit the correct kind of order. On this account there is no obvious reason why the just state, rather than states of other kinds, should be inhabited by just individuals. In the *Laws* there is also a parallel between the state and the soul, but the connection between the good state and the good soul is much more obvious. One can see why the sovereignty of law should flourish only where the citizens possess *sophrosune* and also how recognition of the sovereignty of law might itself promote that virtue.

9

Towards the Ideal State

Laws, 702a–e, 704a–712a, 734e, 739a–e, 745e–746d, 747d–e; *Republic*, especially 473c–474b, 499a–502c, 592b

The *Laws*, like the *Republic*, has often been described as utopian (e.g. Saunders, 1970a, p. 13). If this description means simply that the *Laws* depicts an imaginary society, no one could take exception to it. But the term 'utopian' has more than one sense. According to the dictionaries, it can be applied to anything which would be ideally perfect but is not, as a matter of fact, a practical proposition. In political philosophy it is generally applied to schemes of reform which envisage the abolition of existing forms of society and their replacement by brand new models. Thus there are two questions which need to be answered before the *Laws* is characterized as utopian:

(1)   In what sense is the city described in the *Laws* an ideal?

(2)   What part does the description of the ideal state play in Plato's political theory?

1   *Ideal states and utopias*

Aristotle (*Politics*, IV.i) rightly observes that, although political theory is always concerned with the ideal or best constitution, what constitutes the ideal will vary according to the precise circumstances we envisage. The point here is really a logical one. 'Best' means 'best possible' and possibility is always relative to assumed background conditions. The best constitution achievable by us in the next five years will not be the same as the best constitution that could be achieved by people who were more rational or more benevolent than ourselves, by ones who lived in a kinder natural environment or by ones who had inherited a different set of customs and institutions. Confusion on this point is the source of many criticisms of utopian theory. In discussing a proposed ideal society we have to be clear whether it is envisaged as having an immediate application or merely as what would be best if circumstances were more favourable than they actually are.

Just as there are different varieties of ideal so the description of an ideal can play different parts in political theory. Talk of utopianism generally brings to mind schemes such as those of the levellers or of the early socialists who were attacked by Marx and Engels. They aimed 'to discover a new and more perfect social order and to impose this on society from without by propagánda and wherever possible by model experiments' (Engels, 1972, p. 609). Their schemes were intended as blueprints for immediate action. It is entirely appropriate, therefore, to object to such schemes on the grounds that they could not possibly be put into practice in the social and economic conditions of the time. This does not mean that such utopian schemes are entirely valueless. They could still help to focus the discontents of the underprivileged and to define the principles by which a better life could be sought.

At the other extreme there are descriptions of ideal societies whose authors do not claim that they could, even in principle, be put into practice by real men in the real world. Plato's descriptions of the age of Cronos (*Laws*, 713a–714a; *Statesman*, 269c–275a) would come into this category. At that time the gods ruled directly over men, and trouble and misfortune were unknown. Plato, like Hume after him (*Treatise*, III, II, ii), mentions such stories, not because he believes that the golden age could ever become a reality, but to contrast it with the real world in which we live. In order to survive in these more difficult conditions we have to create peace and harmony by means of law rather than by relying on divine rulers.

Between these two extremes there are many different possibilities. More's *Utopia*, for example, describes a community whose inhabitants are fully human and whose natural environment is not very different from our own. The difference is that they operate consistently at a level of rationality which we achieve only rarely. No one with any sense would expect to make this Utopia a reality, but the contrast between Utopia and our own society throws into relief our own folly and greed. Speaking more generally, the description of an ideal society which is not a practical proposition can give a more concrete expression to abstract political and moral principles. Instead of merely asserting the principles of (e.g.) liberty, equality and fraternity, one can attempt to describe a society in which these principles are fully instantiated. Although such a society will never come about, it may be something towards which one can aspire, a direction in which one can move. And it may be comprehensible to those who would not be able to grasp the principles in the abstract. In the same way some people may find it easier to take the life of Christ as a model, rather than to achieve intellectual mastery of the principles of Christian ethics.

Seen in this light there may not be much difference between some utopians and other kinds of social reformers, between the politics of aspiration and the politics of principle. Bentham, for example, was a systematic social reformer. He did not seek to remodel society from without but to suggest the principles by which society might reform itself from within. He could perhaps have done this by describing a perfect utilitarian society. If he had done this with any skill he might have escaped the charges of aridity which are often levelled against him. His theories would have had more appeal to the imagination. The danger would be that readers might have been distracted by the peripheral details of his account and might therefore have lost sight of the underlying principles.

2   The Cretan colony

The transition from the meandering discussions of the early book to the account of the imaginary city begins at 702a. The Athenian summarizes what has been achieved so far. The object of the discussion has been to discover how a city might best be run and how an individual might best manage his life. But some test is needed to discover whether all this has been worthwhile. Conveniently Cleinias, the Cretan, announces that he has been appointed to a legislative commission established with the object of drawing up a legal code for a new Cretan colony. The commission may take their laws from any source, native or foreign, providing only that they choose the best. The Cretan suggests, therefore, that he and his companions should select from the topics they have discussed so far and 'establish a city in words, founding it, so to speak, from the very beginning'. This will give the Athenian the kind of enquiry he is seeking while Cleinias may be able to put what they say to practical use when he engages in his own legislative activity (702b–d).

There are several clues here to Plato's purpose in describing the city of the *Laws*:

(1)   The reason the Athenian gives for describing the city is to test the principles which have been expounded in the earlier books, presumably by demonstrating how they might work out in practice. So Plato seems to think of himself as proceeding from the discovery of basic principles to their instantiation in the constitution of the city. He

does not first paint an attractive picture and then try to deduce from it a political programme: the principles have priority.

(2)   The foundation of the new Cretan city provides the occasion for expounding a constitution, but the constitution the Athenian suggests is not supposed to be the constitution for that city. Though the Athenian shows interest in the particular circumstances of the city and even addresses the subjects of his imaginary legislation as 'Magnesians', Cleinias does not ask him to do his legislative work for him; he merely hopes that he will be able to make some use of the Athenian's suggestions. It looks as though there is good reason for this. The Athenian believes, no doubt rightly, that constitutions must be adapted to the particular circumstances of each city. But to explore in great detail the exact circumstances of the new city would involve Plato in discussion of a great deal of material quite irrelevant to the needs of other cities and to the interests of most readers. He therefore offers us something of a compromise. Although the proposed constitution suits the general situation of the new Cretan city, the Athenian does not investigate its applicability in detail. Indeed he sometimes indicates that adaptations will have to be made to suit prevailing conditions (745e–746d, cf. 737c–d).

(3)   The Cretan legislative commission is not expected to be particularly original in the laws it proposes. It is to select what seems best from Crete and elsewhere. To a considerable extent this is what the Athenian himself does: most of his suggestions have some basis in existing Greek practice; such originality as he shows lies chiefly in his manner of incorporating and codifying these elements into a new constitution. Thus Plato is not proposing to engage in pure speculation but to build upon the experience of real men in real cities.

3   The conditions for legislation

The Athenian's first reaction, on being invited to propose a constitution, is to make enquiries about the situation and circumstances of the new city. These are described in sufficient detail to suggest that Plato has a quite specific region of Crete in mind (704b–c, 705c; Morrow, 1960, pp. 50–1, 95; Saunders, 1970a, p. 15). Later it is given a name, Magnesia. The geography of the proposed site turns out to be perfect in the Athenian's eyes, largely because there will be little temptation for the citizens to engage in foreign trade or to establish a navy. The fact that the colonists will be drawn from many different cities will make it easier for them to accept a completely new code of legislation, though it will make it more difficult to make them feel as one (708a-d). The Athenian goes on to emphasize the importance of what we might call contingent factors in legislation. Accident, war, poverty and disease are the universal legislators. God is the supreme ruler and under him comes chance. But there is also need for the skill of the human legislator who knows how to use opportunities offered (708e-709c).

The skilled legislator would know what circumstances to pray for in order to further his work, i.e. he would know what is the most propitious situation for the introduction of a really good legal code (709d-e). This turns out to be when a wise legislator can co-operate with a young but naturally self-disciplined tyrant. Among other kinds of state the most suitable will be a constitutional monarchy followed by some form of democracy. Oligarchies will be especially difficult to reform because in them the largest number of individuals have entrenched power (709e-711a). Tyranny offers the best opportunity for carrying through reforms because those who possess power are strongest and fewest in number. Not only is a tyrant best able to force through legislation, he can also exercise the greatest moral influence over the character and behaviour of his people. Thus the fundamental requirement is to create a desire for temperate and just institutions among those who exercise power, whatever the basis of that power. Although this great blessing has come only rarely to men, when it does occur states can easily and quickly be transformed.

There are a number of puzzling features here. One is the contrast between the realism the Athenian shows at the beginning of the passage and the optimism evinced at the end. He begins by asserting the importance of geographical, social and other factors which lie outside human control; the legislator's skill lies in making best use of these. He thus rejects, quite explicitly, the kind of utopianism which rests on the supposition that human planning can end all social evils. At the end of the passage, on the other hand, he suggests, quite unrealistically, that a tyrant acting under wise guidance could easily change the habits of an entire city.

A second source of difficulty lies in the sudden switch from problems about the foundation of a new city to problems about the reform of an existing one. The Athenian has been asked to 'found a city in words' and his enquiries about the geography and citizen body of the new Cretan city relate to this request. But in talking about the tyrant who co-operates with the wise legislator he is really asking what conditions facilitate the reform of an existing state. This is the more puzzling because the situation in which Cleinias and his colleagues have been asked to legislate looks more favourable than could ever be found in an established city. They have *carte blanche* in their legislation and have to overcome no resistance from entrenched interests.

A third surprise is the sudden suggestion that there should be *both* a wise legislator *and* a young but disciplined tyrant. In the rest of the *Laws* Plato writes as though the wisdom needed to discern what laws are right and the political power needed to put them into effect will both be embodied in one man. He talks of the legislator as though he were all-powerful. Now he suddenly separates the two, but not for long. In 711d–712a he suggests that wisdom and power may sometimes be combined in the same man. Thereafter the young tyrant disappears as quickly as he arrived. Charitably, one might suppose that he was introduced in order to make the point that wisdom and power are not the same; or perhaps Plato believes that, while a young monarch will usually be too immature for wisdom, an old one will be set in his ways. But neither of these points is made in the text.

It is difficult to escape the conclusion that Plato is here recycling material from an earlier period. The passage reeks of the Syracusan affair with Plato himself cast in the role of the wise legislator and Dionysius as the young tyrant. In its context it is largely irrelevant, though it does make one or two important points, particularly the suggestions (a) that the fewer centres of power there are in a city the easier it is to reform, and (b) that power is in fact most widely distributed, not in democracies, but in oligarchies.

4   *The second-best state*

In 712b–715d attention shifts from the conditions necessary for successful legislation to the form of constitution which should be established. It is here, as we have seen, that Plato affirms most strongly his doctrine of the sovereignty of law. It is devotion to the law on the part of the rulers that distinguishes a true constitution from a mere faction state. Law is itself the embodiment of reason, the immortal element within us, a point which is reinforced by the story of the age of Cronos.

This assertion of the primacy of reason demonstrates that, so far as their most fundamental principles are concerned, there is not much difference between the *Republic* and the *Laws*. In each the ultimate goal to which any constitution-maker must aspire is unity and harmony under the control of reason. In the *Republic* this reason is embodied in the persons of the guardians, but the *Laws* reinforces the point made in the *Statesman*: there is no possibility in practice of obtaining wise rulers among men. The direct rule of fully rational beings would be attainable only in another age where conditions are quite different from those we know. Wisdom must therefore be embodied in law. But even the city of the *Laws* can be brought into being only where circumstances are especially propitious: it requires, among other things a wise legislator who somehow possesses the power to get his proposals put into practice.

At 739a–e there is what looks like a more explicit discussion of the relation between the *Republic* and the *Laws*. The context is a discussion of the choice of citizens, the distribution of land and of restrictions on the holding of private property. The Athenian remarks that the state which he and his companions are now describing can have only a second-best constitution. He expects this claim to come as a surprise, though reason and experience will demonstrate its inevitability (739a). The best city would be one in which all things are held in common. This would be possible only among gods or children of gods but it is still the paradigm, or standard, of a constitution. The constitution now under consideration will be closest to the paradigm in immortality and second in merit. We may also go on to consider the third best constitution (739a–e; cf. 853c). Since in the city of the *Republic* the guardians practise complete community of property, it looks as though we are here being told that that city is an ideal but not a serious possibility for ordinary human beings.

Although the promise to describe the third best constitution remains unfulfilled, it is not difficult to see why such a constitution might be required. In founding his imaginary state the Athenian assumes the best conditions likely to occur on earth but he is conscious that most legislators will not be so lucky. Founders of brand new cities are fortunate in that they do not encounter quarrels over land or property. Those legislating in different conditions will have to be content with gradual change (736c–d). If the population of a city becomes depleted by war or disease, there may be no alternative but to take in ill-trained citizens from elsewhere (741a). It would be desirable for all citizens to arrive with equal property, but this is impossible in practice. The Athenian's suggestions for the numerical division of the citizens can be observed only so far as possible (747e). The general position is summarized in an important passage at 745e–746d. One must not suppose that a legislator will ever encounter such favourable circumstances that all the proposed arrangements can be applied in all their details. For example, they presuppose that the citizens will willingly accept the proposed restrictions on property and arrangements for the distribution of land, they will also require the right topography for the city and surrounding countryside. Does this mean that the Athenian's proposals are as unrealistic as dreams or models made from wax? The reply the Athenian offers on behalf of his legislator is significant: 'In considering programmes for future action it is only right to omit nothing of what is truest and best. Where one of these suggestions turns out to be incapable of realization one need not attempt to put it into practice. Instead one should try to bring about whichever of the remaining possibilities is most closely related to the model' (746b–c).

5   Plato's purposes

We have seen that, according to the *Laws*, neither the direct rule of philosopher kings nor community of property are possible among men as they actually are. Thus the ideal state of the *Republic* could never in practice be attainable. This may mean that Plato has changed his mind in the direction of greater realism, but it is equally possible that the *Republic* and the *Laws* represent different kinds of ideal. The citizens of the *Republic* are recognizably human and live in a world like our own. But their rulers are much more rational than we could ever be, and the lower classes exhibit a quite unrealistic willingness to follow the guidance of their betters. So in the *Republic* we are presented with a picture of how men would live if they were capable of organizing their lives with total rationality. In practice, no human community has this capacity, but that does not mean that the *Republic* lacks any practical relevance. We can aspire to the sort of political harmony it exhibits even if we know that we can never reach that level. This seems to be recognized in the *Laws*. We can imitate the rule of divine reason by submitting to the rule of law (713e–714a); we can try as hard as we can to find a form of society which resembles the complete community of the first best city (739d–e).

The city of the *Laws* is much more closely related to practical experience than that of the *Republic*, but even it is not a blueprint for political action. As we have seen, the Athenian acknowledges that it will not be possible to enforce his recommendations to the letter. It is more accurate to regard the imaginary city as a model based on the assumption that the conditions of its foundation are as favourable as any likely to be found on earth. Since no human legislator is likely to encounter conditions which are completely favourable in every respect, it is unlikely that the proposed constitution could ever be put into effect in all its details. But this does not prevent the *Laws* being a practical guide to legislation. In teaching any kind of technique we usually begin with illustrations, often imaginary ones, in which everything goes right. In reality things seldom go completely to plan. We have to use our judgement in adapting the models we have learnt to the vicissitudes of ordinary life. But this does not prevent the use of the model as a guide to action. Plato seems to have seen the city of the *Laws* in this light, as a model, not a blueprint. Whether it is a good model is, of course, open to dispute, but it does seem fitted for the role in the sense that most of its features could be adapted to the conditions prevailing in real cities. Many of them in practice have been.

Popper (1966, ch. 9) contrasts Plato as a utopian with what he calls the 'piecemeal social engineer.' So far as the *Laws* is concerned this charge is unfair; its approach is neither clearly utopian nor clearly piecemeal. It is not, as Popper (p. 157) claims, a blueprint to be imposed on society; it leaves room for adaptation to the different needs of different communities and stresses the need for the legislator to use his judgement in dealing with the particular situation confronting him; it recognizes that on many occasion small-scale changes will be the only possibility. On the other hand, Plato would not think that piecemeal engineering was sufficient in itself. He stressed in 630d–632d that the legislator must direct his activities systematically to a single goal. Certainly he overdoes this: a reformer does not need a complete programme worked out in every detail. But he does need some kind of overall view of what he is trying to achieve. Without this he would have no way of deciding his priorities or of ensuring that different parts of his legislation did not counteract one another. For example, there would be no point in a government's reforming housing law in order to promote home ownership if its taxation policy made this more difficult.

Attacks on utopian social engineering rest, in part, on the belief that large-scale schemes are liable to be misdirected or to collapse under the weight of the bureaucracies they generate. This may well be true if we think of attempts to transform radically a modern nation state. But, of course, Plato is concerned with the politics and institutions of city states which would seem tiny by our standards. In the Greek world the opportunities for making a fresh start and for doing so successfully were much greater than in our own. The situation envisaged in the *Laws*, where a brand new state is to be founded, would by no means have been unique. On occasion, established states also would adopt new constitutions. There is a tradition that Plato himself was invited to propose laws for the newly founded city of Megalopolis. There are some parallels between the circumstances of this foundation and those envisaged in the *Laws*. A number of other Greek cities are also said to have sought legislative assistance from the Academy (Morrow, 1960, p. 8, n. 11). The *Laws* might well be intended as a handbook for such activities. One should not assume that it should be regarded in the same light as a modern utopian's dream of the future.

Popper compares Plato with Marx, not only because he sees both as advocates of large-scale social engineering, but also because he regards them as historicists, i.e. as believing that history has its own laws which govern human development. In Plato's case this charge has to be based on the *Republic*, Books VIII and XI, which describe a progression of constitutions. Most scholars regard this section as metaphorical. In the *Laws*, Book III, there is a general account of world history but there is no attempt to extrapolate from the past to the future. The new city will be the outcome, not of a process of historical development, but of deliberate human intervention. It is a product of skill operating on chance factors under the general guidance of God. Plato is not in the business of predicting the future course of history.

10

Society

1 The problem

The driving force of Plato's social philosophy is his conviction that Athens in his day was a sick society and that its malaise could be cured only by a radical transformation of the social fabric. In the *Laws*, as in the *Republic*, he stresses his view of Athenian democracy as lawless and devoid of moral restraint (700a–701d; cf. *Republic*, 555b–561e). In the *Laws* this condition is attributed, at least in part, to the lack of control over music. Whereas in its golden days Athens adhered to strict rules of music, now anything which earns the applause of the multitude is praised; this lawlessness is liable to infiltrate all other areas of the city's life. The aim of the *Laws* is to re-establish respect for law as a fundamental requirement of a healthy society.

The lawlessness which troubles Plato is not only a matter of external behaviour; it permeates the soul of the democratic man who is driven this way and that by his unregulated desires (*Republic*, 560e–561e). Similarly, the *Gorgias* contrasts Callicles' ideal of the man who seeks to gratify his appetites without restriction with the law and order enshrined in Socrates' conception of the just man (491c–495b, 503d–508c). As we have seen, the same emphasis dominates the early books of the *Laws*: lack of self-control is the root problem for all existing communities, including the Persians, the Athenians and even some of the Dorians. The first principle enunciated by the legislator in his prelude is the requirement to honour one's soul, not by the indulgence of desire, but by obedience to law (726a–728c). This is the goal of the laboriously discussed drinking parties and the rest of the educational system.

Plato connects the lawlessness and self-indulgence of contemporary Athens with economic causes. The simple city of the *Republic* becomes 'fevered' when new trades are introduced to pamper the desires of the citizens (372e–373e). Most of the social and economic changes described in the *Republic*, VIII and IX, are instigated by economic factors. Money and desires go together: indeed Plato calls the appetites the 'money-loving' element in the soul (580e). Thus there is a sharp opposition between the love of money and Plato's own ideal of lawfulness: 'it is impossible to honour riches and at the same time to have adequate self-discipline (*sophrosune*) among the citizens' (555c–d). The *Laws* also attributes much of the contemporary malaise to the desire for gain (705a–b, 714a, 727e–728e). But Plato's belief in the economic basis of social disorder is most clearly indicated by his proposed remedies; he places severe restraints on the capacity of the citizens to own property and accumulate money.

Associated with the supposed lawlessness of contemporary society is its disunity. The purpose of the community of property and abolition of the family among the *Republic's* guardians is to make them feel as one, for disunity is the greatest evil the state can encounter (461e–466d). We have seen how this concern for internal peace, unity and harmony forms one of the guiding principles of the *Laws*.

It is hard to know how much justice there is in Plato's criticisms of Athenian society. But the picture he paints has much in common with what many people have felt about modern societies in which there is a high degree of personal freedom. They say that there is a lack of firm, generally accepted standards, that people live only for the pleasure of the moment, that they value financial gain above everything else, that there is no sense of belonging to one another, no sense of common responsibilities or of common concerns. One might dismiss these complaints as reflecting the conservatism of middle age or the cowardice of those who, unable to live with freedom, seek the security of a paternalist authority. But perhaps there is more to it than that; thinkers of more than one political persuasion have diagnosed the condition of modern man as one of alienation. It is worth exploring the parallels between these ideas and Plato's complaints about contemporary Athens.

Marx's concept of alienation is rooted in his analysis of the capitalist mode of production; it would be anachronistic, therefore, to see Plato's analysis of the ills of Athens as foreshadowing Marx. On the other hand there may be parallels between some of the phenomena which Marx saw as symptoms of alienation and some of the features of contemporary society that troubled Plato. In particular, both complain of the lack of a sense of community and of the preference for individualistic and competitive, rather than for co-operative modes of activity. Perhaps we should also consider here Plato's idea that manual labour and trade are degrading, *banausic*. Plato is totally unsympathetic to the manual worker, but he shares with the Marxists a belief that to labour for wages is incompatible with the true dignity and self-fulfilment of a human being.

There may be a closer parallel with Durkheim's conception of *anomie*. According to Durkheim, men in a state of anomie lack any feeling of constraint upon their desires. The growth of individualism has replaced the *conscience collective*, that corpus of common sentiments and shared beliefs which was characteristic of earlier societies. Men no longer have a sense of belonging, of being integrated into the community. Plato's picture too is of individuals left without any guidance, external or internal, apart from their own desires, having no firm standards and no sense of belonging to a larger whole. It looks very much as though Durkheim detected in nineteenth-century France some of the features which Plato thought he saw in fourth-century Greece. This condition of anomie can be painful: it is hard to go without the security and sense of certainty which our forefathers apparently knew. But it is not clear how we should react to it. Durkheim looked to the development of *organic solidarity*, i.e. a system of functional interdependence based on the differentiation of social roles. At times Plato seems to have wanted simply to put the clock back. But perhaps we should regard anomie as the price we have to pay for freedom. After all, the modern individual is free precisely because he is not bound by traditional constraint.

2 *Plato's remedies*

The city of the *Laws* is intended to remedy the defects of contemporary society by creating unity under the control of a firmly accepted code of law and morals. This purpose will be met in part by the adoption of a new legal system and new style of lawgiving and by the creation of an elaborate educational system. These are discussed elsewhere. The other remedies suggested by the Athenian include: (a) population controls, (b) the selection of the right physical environment for the new city, (c) controls over economic life, as well as (d) measures designed to foster feelings of unity and friendship through the family and other social groups.

Population controls

In view of the allegations that Plato is a racialist or advocate of a caste system, one might expect a close attention to the genetic make-up of the citizen body, but, in fact, there is surprisingly little on this point. The new Cretan colony will draw its inhabitants from all over Greece, although Dorians will be particularly welcome. The Athenian comments that this will be a disadvantage from one point of view but an advantage from another. Colonists drawn from different cities will not have the same unity of feeling that colonists from the same city would have had; on the other hand, it will be easier to impose new customs on them than it would be if they all came from the same background sharing a common tradition (707e–708d). Later he draws a comparison between the legislator and a stock breeder who must purge his herds of inferior stock if they are to prosper (735b–c), but the purges he proposes are less drastic than one might expect: sentences of death or exile for the most serious criminals and the sending out of new colonies when the competition for scarce resources threatens to cause civil strife (735d–736a). In the case of the new Cretan city, of course, such measures will not be necessary; we have to select citizens from different sources and mingle them as we might waters from different springs aiming to keep the mixture as pure as possible (736b–c). How and on what criteria this selection is to be done is not entirely clear: Saunders translates the relevant passage (freely but intelligibly), 'when we have screened the bad candidates over a suitable period and given them every chance to be converted, we can refuse their application to enter and become citizens of the state; but we should greet the good ones with all possible courtesy and kindness.' Whatever this means, it seems that the selection is on moral rather than on racial grounds and that dubious candidates are to be given the chance to make good (736b–c).

The Athenian is more concerned about the size of the population. The ideal number of households is 5040. This number is chosen because it is divisible by all numbers between 1 and 12 except 11 and is therefore a very convenient number if one wants to divide the state into groups of different sizes for different purposes (737e–738a). But presumably these mathematical considerations are not the only ones Plato has in mind. He must believe that around five thousand households will produce a state small enough to have a real sense of unity and to permit decisions to be made and officers to be appointed on the basis of a real personal knowledge and at the same time large enough to bestow the full benefits of civilized life (738a–e). Various devices are available to maintain the population at a constant level; these seem to consist largely of measures to persuade citizens to maintain a suitable rate of reproduction. If these fail it may be necessary to send out a colony to get rid of excess citizens (740b–741a). It is worth noting that no mention is made of the practice of exposing infants (Plato's apparent acceptance of this in the *Republic* has been the source of a good deal of modern criticism).

Geography

The Athenian is concerned about the geography of the new colony. He would have preferred it to be far from the sea, or at least to have no harbours; at any rate the city should not be established on the coast. It is a good thing that the countryside will produce all that is necessary for daily life, but not in such abundance as to leave a surplus for foreign trade; it is also fortunate that the prerequisites for shipbuilding are not abundant (704a–705c).

The key points here are Plato's hostility to trade and to sea power. The trouble with trade is that 'it fills the land with wholesaling and retailing, breeds shifty and deceitful habits in a man's soul and makes the citizens distrustful and hostile, not only among themselves but also in their dealings with the world outside' (705a, trans. Saunders). Presumably the point is that those who are in market relations to one another act out of concern for cash values rather than for law and morality and see one another as competitors or as objects for exploitation rather than as fellow citizens or brothers. Elsewhere the Athenian seeks to limit contacts with other states on the grounds that they introduce undesirable foreign habits (949e–950a). The objection to naval supremacy is that those who fight at sea see nothing wrong with retreating rather than bravely facing the enemy. Sea power has a bad effect on character because it relies on cunning and stratagem rather than on the virtues of courage, endurance and self-control. Moreover, the credit for naval victories goes not to the bravest soldier but to the skill of sailors who include men of all kinds with no particularly commendable qualities. There is an echo here of the oligarchic idea that Athens' maritime success put political power into the hands of the poorest classes, which furnished the oarsmen, but that idea is given a new twist, in that naval tactics themselves are seen as the source of moral corruption (706a–707d).

Economic organization

Agricultural land is to be divided into lots of equal value so that there is one lot per household (763d–737d, 739e–741a). The lots and the equipment needed to work them will be inalienable (741a-e), and the property held by any citizen will be limited to a value four times that of the lot. The citizen body will be divided into four classes, the lowest owning only the lot and its equipment, the higher classes having respectively two, three and four times this amount (744b-745a; see Saunders, 1961). Family law is directed to ensuring (a) that there will always be a male heir (adopted if necessary) for each lot, and (b) that no male citizen will be left without a lot.

These measures ensure that citizens of the new state will all basically be farmers. What is not clear is whether they will work the land themselves or whether they will entrust it entirely to slaves. At first sight, 806d looks decisive for the latter view: the Athenian describes the leisured life of the citizens who have given their farm work out to slaves. There are, however, a number of considerations pointing in the opposite direction: (a) there is no express prohibition of agriculture by citizens; (b) the agricultural laws of 842b-846a are explicitly (842d) designed for citizens who will themselves be engaging in agricultural labour (Morrow 1960, pp. 531-2); (c) the measures for the election of the Council (756b-e) apparently presuppose that frequent attendance at the assembly will be especially burdensome to the lower classes, presumably because they have to work; (d) as Aristotle (*Politics*, 1265a 15) points out, an enormous territory would be needed to support 5040 unproductive families. It seems likely therefore that the majority of the citizens are expected to be working farmers, and that most citizens will be more like prosperous peasants than landed aristocrats.

Citizens will be excluded from taking any part in trade or manufacture (846d-847b, 915d-920c); they will be prohibited from doing so even indirectly through their slaves. Essential manufactured goods will be provided by resident aliens (849b-d, 919c-920c) whose period of residence will normally be limited to twenty years (850a-b). Lending at interest will be prohibited, as will the holding of gold, silver and 'hard' currency, though there will be a local currency for use within the city (742a-c). The import of luxuries is prohibited, though the state will see to the import of essential military supplies (847b-d).

The effect of these regulations is to keep the commercial activity of the city to an absolute minimum and to see that, at all costs, citizens take no part in it. The reasons for Plato's disapproval of trade are not very explicit. In part, no doubt, it reflects a general Greek attitude — a number of states did prohibit citizens from engaging in trade or manufacture, and it was generally regarded as undignified and unworthy of a free man (919d-e). Athens was unusually tolerant of these pursuits. Plato's main objection seems to be that commerce makes possible the unlimited pursuit of gain (736e, 741e, 847d, 918d). He is not against all gainful pursuits; external goods do have a value though they come below those of mind and body. Even farming can be pursued for gain, though the amount a citizen could make from his lot would obviously be limited. Presumably the greed which commerce permits can make us forgetful of more valuable things and, no doubt, it appeals to the less rational elements in the soul, thus destroying the discipline on which Plato places such a high value. But it is not only wealth that can corrupt, but also poverty, since that forces us into shameless and unworthy ways of life (919b-c): Plato thus recognizes that commerce which permits relative wealth must also permit relative poverty.

The fullest account of Plato's attitude to trade is at 918a-920c. There the Athenian argues that trade, properly understood as the redistribution of goods where they are needed, is a laudable thing. But it is abused because few can resist opportunities for excessive money-making. For example, innkeepers who set up in remote areas treat travellers as prisoners to be held to ransom, rather than as honoured guests. The objection here seems to be as much to the exploitation of one's fellows as to excessive profit-making.

The family and other social groups

In the *Republic* the existence of distinct social groups within the state is seen as a threat to its unity; this is why the family is abolished. The *Laws* follows the opposite policy. The state is seen as a union of households, not as a collection of individuals (Morrow 1960, p. 118). Men are required to marry between the ages of thirty and thirty-five, and much legislation is designed to strengthen the family bond and to ensure that families do not die out. There are family shrines and family courts. The homicide legislation is based on the principle that the dead man's relatives must see that he is avenged. Crimes against parents are punished with particular severity.

The citizen body is divided into twelve tribes, each with its own territory (745b-d). There will apparently be twelve local subdivisions in each tribe, corresponding to the Attic demes (771b; cf. 746d). Each tribe and subdivision will have its own monthly religious festival. These have a social purpose: they enable the citizens to get to know each other well (738d-e, 771d; cf. 828a-d). There is a passing reference to phratrys, which in Athens were groups of associated clans (746d).

The Athenian takes it for granted that the citizens of the new state will continue the Cretan and Spartan practice of eating common meals. He also proposes their extension to women (780e–781d). The desirability of this institution is taken so much for granted that the Athenian sees no need to argue for it in the case of men. The reason for extending it to women is to promote respect for law and custom in what we might normally regard as private life. Its purpose seems to be partly to indoctrinate the citizens by promoting a common ethos and partly to emphasize the social being of the citizens rather than their lives as individuals.

The common meals are, of course, a feature of the *Republic* as well as of the *Laws*, but the acceptance of the family and of tribal organization is a new departure for Plato. It is clear that they are not merely tolerated as unavoidable evils but welcomed and encouraged as things of great value. No explicit reason is given for this but implicitly Plato seems to be acknowledging a point made in more recent times by Durkheim and others. The more closely individuals are integrated into social groupings, the less they are likely to suffer from the feeling of rootlessness and lack of constraint which Durkheim calls *anomie*. Membership of smaller social groups mediates our loyalty to and respect for the state. Part of what belonging to a a country means to us is our membership of smaller groups within a larger whole. The proposal in the *Republic* to promote unity by abolishing these smaller groups is superficially attractive but quite misguided, given men as they actually are. It is not clear whether the recognition of this in the *Laws* is due to a new awareness on Plato's part or whether it is simply a corollary of the decision to legislate for men as they actually are in the real world rather than for those in ideal circumstances.

3   *The position of women*

One of the more notorious proposals of the *Republic* is that, so far as the guardians, at least, are concerned, women should be treated equally with men. This proposal had a corollary in the suggestion for the abolition of the family. The positive emphasis given to the family and the generally more cautious tone of the *Laws* preclude such drastic proposals. The Athenian still wants to give women a more prominent role than they could normally play in fourth-century Athens, but it is not clear how far he is prepared to go in this direction.

Since the new city will be composed of families rather than of separate individuals, it is assumed that marriage will be the vocation of all women, though, as an innovation, men will also be required to marry between the ages of thirty and thirty-five (721b–d; but see

722d). As in Athens an unmarried woman will be legally under the guardianship of her father or nearest male relative, a married one under that of her husband. But there are some small moves towards recognizing the legal personality of women. Those over forty will be able to act as witnesses in courts, and widows or divorcees will be able to initiate legal actions in their own right (937a). Divorce law is also more favourable to women than in Athens (929e–930b), and it is envisaged that in certain very limited circumstances an heiress may be able to choose her own husband (925a–c).

These measures would, at best, constitute modest improvements in the status of women. More striking proposals are that they should bear arms on behalf of the city and should receive the same education as men. The argument here is that a state which fails to assign its women any military function is gratuitously weakening itself, since women constitute half the population. But if women are to serve in the army they must also receive military training and take part in athletic contests (804d–806d, 833c–d). Women also have an important effect on the moral ethos of the state. They should therefore receive the same moral training as men and should have their own common meals (780c–781d). This last suggestion would be an innovation: even in Crete and Sparta, the common meals were confined to men. In making these proposals the Athenian assumes that women are in general inferior to men in respect of virtue, but he gives them special credit for orderliness and moderation (802e). Since these virtues are central to the moral doctrine of the laws, his attitude here seems barely consistent.

It is not clear what political rights will be granted to women. At 785b it is suggested that women should be eligible for office from the age of forty (the corresponding age for men is thirty). Membership of the assembly is open to those who have borne arms (753b). It looks therefore as though older women, at least, would be eligible for the full range of political offices. This is what one would expect in the light of the argument for women's participation in the army. It would, one supposes, be just as serious a waste of human resources to exclude women from office as it would be to exclude them from bearing arms. Against this one may point to the fact that the Athenian nowhere explicitly mentions female holders of the main offices of state. (This may not be very significant, since, in Greek, masculine grammatical forms can 'embrace the female'.) He does, however, refer occasionally to women who will act as supervisors of marriage and family life (784a, 930a). It could be these he has in mind when he speaks of women being eligible for office from the age of forty.

It is difficult to see how one could decide between these two interpretations. It is possible that the ambiguity is deliberate. Plato may realize that his arguments commit him to the equal treatment of women and yet be reluctant to suggest openly such a bold change. But even if one supposes that he does want women to hold political office, it would be wrong to classify him as an early exponent of women's liberation. The truth is that he was not interested in liberating anyone, male or female; liberty, in the sense of the opportunity for individuals to choose their own way of life, is not one of his values. The fundamental aim of the proposals for the position of women in both the *Republic* and the *Laws* is the full utilization of their abilities for the good of the state as a whole. Since women constitute half the population, to neglect the education of women is to risk the corruption of the whole community. To exclude them from bearing arms is to reduce substantially the military strength of the city. It follows that women must be educated and receive military training.

4 Slaves and aliens

Since most forms of economic activity are forbidden to citizens, the new city will depend heavily on the labour of slaves and of resident aliens or *metics* as they are generally known. Of these, the slaves will be used in three main capacities: (a) as the domestic or agricultural servants of citizen households; (b) as slaves of metics engaged in trade or manufacture; (c) as public slaves of the city used (e.g.) in the maintenance of public works.

It has sometimes been supposed that the agricultural slaves will really be in a condition of serfdom like that of the Spartan Helots, a subject people held in permanent subjection tied to the land. The evidence for this view is at 806d where the Athenian describes the leisured life of citizens whose 'farms have been given over to slaves'. Taylor translates this 'their farms let out to villeins', but there is nothing to justify this writing of the feudal system into Plato's text. As we have seen, it is likely that the citizens would themselves be running their own farms using slaves as servants. The Athenian himself is highly critical of the Spartan system of Helotage (776c). The objection is, apparently, that the Helots, because they formed a coherent class with a common language, offered a permanent threat of rebellion. The Athenian advises that so far as possible slaves should come from different countries and speak different languages (777c–d).

In general, the Athenian regards slaves as simply a form of property (776b, 777c), as things to be used. Man is a particularly difficult kind of animal to handle; one should, therefore, avoid treating slaves harshly, because that will make them more troublesome. On the other hand citizens should not live on familiar terms with slaves or attempt to argue with them. One must always use the language of command (777d–778a). This attitude is borne out in the detailed legal provisions, particularly of the penal code. In most cases they are liable to different penalties from those imposed on free men, usually some form of capital or corporal punishment. The Athenian's main concern seems to be to stamp on any act of insubordination which might threaten the privileged status of the citizens. For example, a citizen who kills a slave in anger is required only to purify himself for the pollution he has incurred and to compensate the slave's owner for his loss. By contrast, a slave who kills a citizen in anger will be handed over to the relatives of the dead man; they may treat him in any way they wish, provided that they do not leave him alive (868a–c). A free man who kills in self-defence will undergo no penalties; a slave who kills a free man in self-defence will be executed as though guilty of parricide (869c–d). Morrow (1939, 1960) has shown that where Plato's proposals differ from contemporary Athenian practice they almost always do so in the direction of greater severity towards the slave. Penalties are more severe, and slaves are deprived of almost all legal protection against wrongs and assaults suffered at the hands of citizens.

One might try to excuse Plato by arguing that, living in a slave society, he took the existence of slavery for granted. Perhaps, one might say, future generations will feel as horrified by (e.g.) our practice of eating meat as we are by the institution of slavery. And no doubt those who were born or sold into slavery quickly acquired servile habits; it must have been easy, therefore, to believe that they were by nature inferior. Popper (1966, pp. 222, 224, 236) counters this defence by claiming that some of Plato's contemporaries saw that slavery was unjustified and advocated its abolition. There is very little evidence for this. One of the few passages which Popper cites in support of his claim is Euripides, *Ion*, 854, where it is said that a loyal slave can be as good as a free man. Plato himself recognizes this in 776d–777a, though he balances this admission with a reference to those who say that slaves are inherently inferior. In any case he does not question or attempt to mitigate the rigours of slavery; rather he attempts to strengthen the institution.

What strikes us most in Plato's treatment of slavery is his lack of humanitarian principles. This is in line with his general attitude. He does not see the fact of a shared humanity as creating any demand for respect or sympathy. The slave is not an end in himself but a means, and Plato consistently treats him as such. To concede him political or legal rights would be inconsistent with this perspective. So there is a ruthless logic about Plato's proposals. Even so, one might expect him to have rather more doubts about slavery than he actually shows. One of the guiding principles of the *Republic* is that people should be used in the role for which they are best suited by nature. This principle is still evident in the treatment of women in the *Laws*. It follows that if one is to justify using freemen and slaves in radically different ways, one should show that they have radically different natures. Plato does not attempt to do this.

By comparison with his attitude to slaves, the Athenian's treatment of the metics, or resident aliens, seems very favourable. The presence of these people in the new city would not be unusual. Metics played an important part in the life of most Greek cities, with the notable exception of Sparta. They were particularly prominent at Athens, the main commercial centre of Greece. The Athenian proposes that their residence in the new city will be subject to two main restrictions: (a) they will not be able to stay longer than twenty years unless they receive special permission (850b–c); (b) they will not be able to accumulate wealth in excess of that held by the third property class (915b–c). In these respects they would be worse off than the metics of Athens, some of whose families had been resident for several generations and many of whom were wealthy. The Athenian's aim is clearly to prevent the development of a class of non-citizens who were, nevertheless, permanent residents and regarded the city as their home. The restrictions on wealth would prevent them acquiring great political or social importance as well as preserving the status of the citizens. On the other hand the metics will be exempt from military service and taxation (850b–c). They will enjoy full protection of the law. Overall their situation will not be at all undesirable. In many ways they will be the freest group within the population. This is not due to an unwonted access of liberalism on Plato's part. The city needs the metics and they have to be persuaded to come voluntarily, so their position has to be reasonably attractive.

5 *Class distinctions and the division of labour*

The principle that different kinds of task should be undertaken by different kinds of people is fundamental to the *Republic* where it gives rise to the threefold class system of guardians, auxiliaries and farmers/artisans. In the *Laws* this principle is applied in two main ways. Firstly it is the basis on which citizens are prohibited from engaging in manufacture or trade; the craft of the citizen, to maintain the good order of the state, is a full-time occupation (846d). Secondly it requires that the metics who work as artisans should be forbidden from practicing two different trades.

Some modern critics have taken the sharp distinction between the citizens on the one hand and the slaves and metics on the other as evidence that the city of the *Laws* will be based on class divisions. Two different lines of argument are possible here.

(1) Saunders (1962) has argued that there are close parallels between the *Republic* and the *Laws*. The guardians of the laws, he claims, correspond to the guardians in the *Republic*, the bulk of the citizens to the auxiliaries and the slaves, and metics to the farmer/artisan class. But although there are some resemblances here, the differences are at least as striking. In the *Republic*, fighting and ruling are seen as distinct tasks and both are marked off sharply from farming as well as from trade and manufacture. Farming here includes not only agricultural labour but also the ownership of land. The guardians are forbidden to own property because then they would become farmers and householders. By contrast the citizens of the *Laws* share in all three kinds of function. They have a part in government, they must serve in the army and they must own land.

It is possible that the difference between the *Republic* and the *Laws* is due simply to the fact that the *Laws* is more closely tied to practicalities. Plato recognizes that the sharp divisions proposed in the *Republic* could never become a reality, and therefore compromises by treating the position of citizen–farmer as a single role. But the differences in the social structure of the two states could also reflect different views of human nature. The *Republic* is based on the assumption that human beings come in three varieties, depending on whether reason, spirit or appetite predominates in the soul. Different social roles require different capacities and so each man must be given only that role for which he is suited. Since the citizens of the *Laws* are allowed, indeed required, to operate in all three capacities, it would seem that this doctrine of different kinds of men has disappeared.

There is a corresponding difference in the way in which the two states are supposed to hold together. The *Republic* exhibits an organic unity. The different elements are like the different parts of an organism or a machine such as a clock. The parts have quite different characteristics but by interacting with one another promote the end for which the organism or machine is designed. The citizens of the *Laws*, on the other hand, do not differ in their nature or function. It seems to be their very similarity, their common tasks, their shared customs and traditions which will hold them together.

The class divisions of the *Republic* can be criticized not only because they restrict individual choice and create unequal privileges but because they expropriate part of the individual personality. While it is not true that human beings come neatly packaged in three varieties, it is almost certainly the case that if human beings were subjected to the kind of division of labour envisaged in the *Republic* they would develop three distinct kinds of character. Each person would be able to develop only a small part of his human capacities. He would not be a full man. This would not be the case with the citizens of the *Laws*; it would be possible for them to live a fully rounded existence. So, while there is little trace of *humanitarianism* in the *Laws*, it is a more *human* work than the *Republic*.

(2)   It has been argued more generally that in the *Laws* Plato seeks to perpetuate and reinforce the position of the aristocratic class to which he himself belonged. He therefore advocates a system in which an hereditary landowning aristocracy (the citizens) rule over slaves and aliens who lack both land and political rights (Wood and Wood, 1978). This class system is, if anything, more firmly fixed that that of the *Republic*, since each individual's position will be permanently fixed by birth rather than by the rulers' estimate of his abilities. On this view, then, the *Laws* is a straightforward product of aristocratic reaction. Plato, an aristocrat himself, looks for a state in which the powers and privileges of his class will be unshakeably guaranteed.

There are two main difficulties with this interpretation:

(1)   Much of the evidence suggests that the citizens will be small farmers rather than aristocrats. There are supposed to be 5040 citizen households in a relatively small and infertile area. Even if we suppose they will not actually engage in agricultural labour, they will certainly need to supervise their farms. They will not be rich and there will be rather a lot of them. This does not fit the conventional picture of an aristocrat.

(2)   Neither the metics nor the slaves are intended to form permanent classes within the state. The limitation on their period of residence would prevent metics from coming to regard the new city as a permanent home and from becoming linked with one another by ties of birth or kinship. Similarly the provision that slaves should, if possible, be of different origin and speak different languages implies that the majority of them will be purchased from abroad rather than home bred. And, if it is true that most citizens will work or at least supervise their own farms, most slaves will presumably live as adjuncts

to citizen households rather than have homes of their own. The Athenian's comments on the Spartan system of Helotage make it clear that he seeks to prevent the development of the slaves into a distinct social class.

There are more general reasons why it may be misleading to think of the city of the laws as a state based on class distinctions. In the *Republic* the members of the lower classes are nevertheless part of the state. The city is seen as an organism in which each element has its own function. For the city to do well, all parts must perform their own task and no class has a special claim to happiness. In the *Laws*, on the other hand, the aliens and slaves are specifically excluded from membership of the state; they do not have even an inferior brand of citizenship and have no right of permanent residence. One cannot, therefore, say that the state is composed of three classes. Rather it consists of a single citizen class which relies on the labour of individuals who themselves stand outside the state. Thus, whereas the classes in the *Republic* may be compared to the parts of the body, the role of the slaves and metics in the *Laws* would be more like that of tools or possessions which are not part of the man but are needed by him to further his purposes. If they fare badly, that does not, in itself, mean that the state has been harmed. Conversely, in seeking the good of the whole, the legislator is not essentially concerned with the good of these supporting groups.

The difference here might not be very important in practice. If you are a member of an underprivileged group, it may not matter much to you whether you are officially a member of the state. But this point can be important when we try to understand the basic patterns of Plato's political thought. As we have seen, he is not given to humanitarianism. It is not the function of his legislator to secure the salvation of mankind. But he does have an obligation to secure the welfare of the city. From this point of view, it counts very much whether a particular social group is seen as part of the city, and therefore as falling within the scope of the legislator's concern, or as something external which may be used or discarded as suits the interest of the city proper.

Seen in this perspective, Plato is not erecting a state dominated by class divisions but seeking to abolish such distinctions by excluding from the state all those who cannot live the life he judges worthy of citizens. His ideal is one which has appealed to many generations in political thought, the ideal of an agrarian community in which every citizen is a farmer. Unfortunately this could only be achieved by a sleight of hand. The excluded groups are smuggled in again as slaves and metics.

11

The System of Government

Laws, 751a–768e, 855c–856a, 875d–876e, 945b–948b, 951c–952b, 961a–962e

After considering the social and economic conditions of the new city, the Athenian turns, at the beginning of Book VI, to consider what we would call its 'constitution'. The plan he apparently intends to follow is set out at 751a: we must first establish political offices and then lay down laws for the holders of these offices to administer. Most of the main offices of state are described between 751a and 768e and the carefully marked transition at 768e to the substantive legislation suggests that the Athenian regards the first phase, the establishment of offices, as completed by this point. It may come as something of a surprise, therefore, that two new offices, the scrutineers (otherwise 'examiners' or 'auditors') and the nocturnal council, are introduced in Book XII. It has sometimes been supposed that these offices must be an afterthought. But as early as 632c there was a hint that some special body would be needed to give the state its intellectual underpinning, and 818a–d seems to prefigure the nocturnal council's programme of study. The introduction of the council at the very end of the *Laws* enables the dialogue to end on a suitable note of solemnity. The tidy-minded may feel that, with the introduction of the scrutineers and the nocturnal council, the top of the political pyramid becomes dangerously overcrowded, but there is no inconsistency either at the theoretical or at the practical level.

Most of the offices and institutions proposed in the *Laws* have precedents somewhere in the Greek world, usually at Athens; so classical scholars have rightly expended effort in exploring the relationship between Plato's proposals and the practice of real Greek cities (see especially Morrow, 1960, chapters V and VI). These studies are important for the light they cast on Plato's method of working, but, for philosophical purposes, it is more important to consider the underlying principles than the detailed provisions of the constitution. Its most important features are outlined in the Appendix.

1   *Magisterial power*

The new state's most striking departure from the practice of fourth-century Athens will be in the power bestowed on the magistrates (i.e. on those elected to the principal offices of state). In the Athens of Plato's day, ultimate authority rested with the Assembly and the large popular juries, though conservatives pined for the days when the Areopagus (a council of ex-magistrates) had been the dominant influence. In the new city the guardians of the laws will be pre-eminent. As their title suggests, their main task is to guard the laws (754d–755b). This apparently amounts to overseeing the other organs of state and initiating prosecutions of those magistrates who step outside established law. They are to act as legislators by filling in details omitted by the original lawgiver and by initiating changes in the legal code on the rare occasions when this will be necessary (770a–771a, 772a–d). The large number of more specific duties mentioned as the dialogue progresses, taken together, give them a general power of supervision over every area of the common life, including social, commercial, religious and domestic matters, as well as what we would call political affairs (Morrow, 1960, pp. 198–204).

The same shift of power from the popular institutions to the magistracies is evident in the proposals for the administration of justice. The competence of magistrates to dispose of minor cases is increased and the senior magistracies are involved closely in important cases: the 'select judges' will be the ultimate court of appeal in civil disputes (767c–e) and, together with the guardians of the laws, they will form a special court to hear capital cases (855c–856a); three senior magistrates will be responsible for the second of the three stages in the trial of public cases (768a).

Why would Plato transfer power to the magistrates? The immediate answer is that power must be exercised by those best qualified in terms of family background, character and training (751c–d). But what exactly are the relevant qualifications? In the *Republic* Plato had assigned supreme power to the guardians on the grounds that they alone would have the requisite philosophical understanding. To some extent the same line of thought is evident in the *Laws*: the nocturnal council, the membership of which overlaps extensively with the guardians of the laws and the other senior magistracies, will devote itself to philosophical and theological matters. But throughout most of the work the emphasis is on correct moral training rather than on philosophy. The guardians of the laws and the scrutineers will have the advantage of age, since they must be at least fifty years old, and in practice will probably have had a good deal of administrative experience. (The offices of the country wardens and their assistants may be designed as a kind of training ground, and promising young men will have attended the nocturnal council.) But, although the citizens are enjoined to elect the best men, there are no institutional guarantees that only those who have proved themselves in this way will be elected. As Plato himself sees, the system will in the last resort depend on having citizens sufficiently well educated to make the right choices (751c–d).

But there is more to Plato's preference for magisterial power than the wish that decisions should be taken by those best qualified for the job. He believed that the institutions of Greek democracy were inherently irrational (*Republic*, 487b–497a, 557a–558c; *Statesman*, 296a–297c). In the *Laws* this belief is most evident in the discussions of judicial procedure. The Athenian complains, explicitly or implicitly, about the uproar in democratic courts, the inability of jurymen to question litigants and witnesses, the lack of time available for trials, and the secrecy of voting when the jury gave the verdict (766d–767a, 855c–856a, 876a–e). Plato's ideal court is one in which a relatively small number of judges examine the issues in a calm and unhurried way; they are able to question witnesses fully and when the decision is taken each judge takes personal responsibility for his vote. The Athenian departs from this ideal to the extent of giving a role to 'tribal' courts, apparently chosen by lot from the whole people, but he seems to regard this as a concession made to give all the citizens a sense that they really are members of the state (768b).

These points which the Athenian makes about the courts could equally be applied to the political process. Where large numbers of people are involved, as in democratic assemblies, it will be difficult to achieve the careful, responsible deliberation Plato seeks. But he is equally hostile to bestowing power on single individuals. The Athenian generally talks as though the guardians of the laws are to act jointly as a group. The same goes for most of the other magistracies. In other words, the magistrates in the new city will be more like members of a committee than executive officers. We are not told how these committees will conduct their deliberations, but presumably Plato believes that if they discuss matters in a sufficiently calm and unhurried way they will eventually reach some kind of consensus.

The *Republic* has often been criticized for its assumption that there are experts in politics to whom all power should be entrusted. The *Laws* shares the view of politics as a rational pursuit but interprets it more realistically by suggesting that good government can be achieved where a well-educated citizenry elects experienced officials and leaves them to pool their wisdom in taking decisions. For much the same reasons, most modern states and most institutions and associations within the state now govern themselves through elected committees.

2 Checks and balances

In discussing Peloponnesian history, the Athenian argued that no individual should be allowed great or unmixed power (693b: Saunders translates 'powerful or extreme authority'), and that the success of Sparta was due to the development of a system in which different organs of state, owing their authority to different sources, acted as constraints on one another (691b–693c). He then advocated a moderate state combining monarchic and democratic elements (693c–702e). As one would expect, these arguments are reflected in the constitution proposed for the new city.

In the constitution there are a number of devices for restricting the power of individual politicians:

(1)   All officials on election will undergo *dokimasia*, an examination of their fitness (753d–e, 755d–e, 756e, 759c–d, 760a, 763e, 765b–c, 766b, 767d). Presumably this examination would in most cases be conducted by the guardians of the laws; it is not clear who would examine the guardians (753d).

(2)   At the end of their term all officials will undergo *euthuna* (variously translated 'examination', 'audit' or 'scrutiny' (946d–e). The importance of the officials ('scrutineers') who conduct these examinations is emphasized by the extraordinary honours bestowed on them (945b–948b).

(3)   All officials will be liable to prosecution for maladministration or giving corrupt verdicts (762a–b, 767e, 846b).

(4)   All public acts will be subject to the general supervision of the guardians of the laws.

(5)   The requirement that boards of officials act jointly should restrict the excesses of individuals.

(6)   There is a system of appeal against judicial decisions (766d–767d).

This list would be impressive were it not that all the items, apart from the supervisory role of the guardians of the laws and the system of appeals, had some kind of parallel in fourth-century Athens. Yet Plato professes to consider the Athenian state lawless and unrestrained. The point must be that in democratic Athens there was no restraint on the powers of the assembly and the popular courts. But then one might object that in the new city there will be few restraints on the guardians of the laws as a group, though there would, no doubt, be adequate sanctions to deal with an individual guardian who stepped out of line. Morrow (1960, pp. 549–51) suggests that the guardians of the laws, the scrutineers and the select judges are intended to act as restraints on one another. This may be so, but in view of the very similar background and membership of the three bodies they would be unlikely to check each other very effectively. So, while the power of individual magistrates is severely restricted, the Athenian is prepared to give almost unlimited authority to what could be a clique of elderly men. No doubt they would be scrupulously law abiding, but life would be distinctly bleak for any Magnesian with deviant or reformist tendencies.

In Book III the Athenian distinguished seven claims to rule (689e–690c) and appeared to attribute the success of Sparta, not only to the restrictions which it imposed on individual power, but also to the existence, alongside the two kings, of a council owing its authority to age and of a quasi-democratic body of ephors (691d–692a). One might draw from this the lesson that in a successful state there must be different organs of government, able to restrain one another, and owing their authority to different sources. Polybius (VI, XI, 11–12) interpreted the point in this way and he was followed by Montesquieu when he argued for the separation of the legislative, executive and judicial powers. Plato, on the other hand, does not make any clear separation between different parts of the government, though, as we shall see in a moment, he does take some account of the different claims to authority. The result is a state which, for all its safeguards against the tyranny of a single official, offers little protection to an individual or group who falls out with the authorities as a whole.

3   A mixed constitution

Since the proposed constitution lacks distinct monarchic, oligarchic and democratic *organs*, it is clear that in demanding a mixed constitution, the Athenian is seeking to combine different kinds of political *principle* within the same governmental structures. This is confirmed when, after describing the complex elections to the council, the Athenian remarks, 'The election made in this way will be a mean between a monarchic and a democratic constitution — and the constitution always should be midway between these' (756e). Here democracy and monarchy are apparently combined in the process of electing a single set of officials. The Athenian then goes on to compare two types of equality. One is 'the equality of number, weight and measure' which can readily be achieved by the use of the lot (757a–b). This is apparently what Aristotle calls 'arithmetical' equality (*Politics*, 1301b29–1302a8; cf. *Nicomachean Ethics*, 1131b25–1133b28). It is a matter of treating everyone alike. The Athenian's second kind of equality apparently corresponds to Aristotle's 'geometrical equality'. It consists in giving 'due measure to each according to his nature', i.e. more to the greater and less to the lesser. It requires us to give a greater share of honours and offices to those pre-eminent in virtue and education. This is the true form of equality and constitutes justice. It needs the wisdom and judgement of Zeus and brings great blessings to a city. But in practice, in order to avoid dissension, it is sometimes necessary to use the other form of equality, that embodied in the lot (757e–758a).

The distinction between these two types of equality has been central to most subsequent discussions of justice. It is commonplace to say that justice consists, not in treating all men alike, but in giving equal consideration to everyone's claims. Those with equal claims are to be treated equally, while those whose claims are not equal may be treated differently. The difficulty with such a doctrine is that it does not tell us what kinds of claims are to count nor how different claims are to be assessed. It is thus compatible with a wide variety of competing political and social outlooks. In the present passage, the Athenian affirms that the main claim is that of virtue or goodness. But it is not at all clear what this has to do with the election to the council.

One line of interpretation stems from Aristotle (*Politics*, 1266a5–28). He complains that the constitution is not, as Plato seems to suppose, a mixture of democracy and monarchy, but a mixture of democracy and oligarchy. Aristotle says this because of the attention paid to property classification, particularly in the elections to the council. He interprets these as oligarchic provisions designed to extend the influence of the wealthy. Barker (1960, pp. 388–90) follows this line of interpretation and therefore assumes that, when Plato advocates his second 'true' kind of equality, he has in mind the fact that greater power will be given to those of greater wealth. He then, quite properly, complains that, since virtue and wealth do not coincide, Plato should not describe his sytem as bestowing greater honours on those of greater virtue.

In an obscure passage (744a–c), the Athenian claims that property classes will be necessary because of 'the equality of opportunities in the city'. They will enable offices, taxation and distributions of public revenue to be assigned not only in accordance with the virtue of an individual or of his ancestors or in accordance with his physical attributes, but also in accordance with his possession (or use) of wealth or his poverty. This unequal, though proportional, distribution will prevent dissension. Some commentators have taken this to mean that an individual's possession of wealth is to be treated as a sign of his personal virtue. Saunders (1972, pp. 31–2) suggests that it is rather the *use* of wealth that indicates virtue. Neither of these interpretations pays sufficient attention to the fact that the Athenian's language in 744b–c suggests a contrast between virtue, on the one hand, and wealth or poverty on the other. The possession or use of wealth thus seems to be an additional criterion to that of virtue, not merely an index of it. So the point seems to be that wealth needs to be taken into account in the organization of the state, even though it may be independent of virtue. This makes it very unlikely that the account of the two kinds of equality in 756e–758a really involves the kind of confusion between wealth and virtue that is required by Barker's interpretation.

It is not clear that the constitution attaches as much importance to wealth as Aristotle (and Barker) suppose. The property classes enter into the election of the council in two ways: there are equal numbers of council members from each class and the lower classes are exempt from attending the later stages of the nomination process. The first of these points would increase the power of the wealthier classes only if they were numerically smaller than the lower classes. This would be a fair assumption in most states but not necessarily in one with maximum and minimum limits on the holding of wealth. The exemption of the lower classes from the later stages of nomination seems primarily intended to ease the economic burden of participation in public life. Its effect is difficult to judge but presumably it would tend to increase the influence of the wealthy. The same might be said of the provision that the lower classes will not normally be compelled to attend the Assembly (764a). A few of the less important magistracies are also restricted to the wealthier classes. But, in general, it is surprising how little use is made of the property classes. The privileges of the wealthy are very limited; in particular it is notable that the property classes play no special part in the courts of law or in the election of the most important officers of state, the guardians of the laws and the scrutineers, though Saunders (1972, p. 35) has read oligarchic intentions into the hint at 753d that participation in the final stage of the election for the guardians of the laws will be optional and will involve some kind of sacrifice. (There is some support for this in the *Republic*, 378a, where it is suggested that the knowledge of those myths which are of doubtful moral tendency could be restricted by the requirement that they be revealed only to those who have offered a large and expensive sacrifice.) On the whole, the function of the classes seems very much that suggested at 744c; Plato believes that there will be dissension unless the constitution takes some (albeit small) account of differences in wealth.

If the 'true' equality of 756e–758a is not a matter of giving greater power to the wealthy, what is it? Perhaps the first point to notice here is that, according to the Athenian, the simple 'arithmetical' equality is characterized by the use of the lot. He also says that it will in practice be necessary to combine both kinds of equality. We may therefore expect the method of electing the council to involve the true equality in one way or another. These elections are, in fact, peculiarly complicated. After an elaborate nomination process, twice the required number of candidates from each class is chosen by election and half of these are then chosen by the lot. Thus the process as a whole combines the lot with the vote. The natural inference is that the use of the vote is supposed to contribute the true equality by assigning greater honour to those of greater worth. This may seem strange to us because we regard the choice of officials by election as characteristic of democracies. But the Greeks thought differently. In their view the democratic method was to choose officials by lot while elections were, if anything, an oligarchic procedure (759b; cf. Aristotle, *Politics*, 1294b8–13). It is not difficult to see why they thought this: if all men really are equal, then all are equally deserving of office, and it does not really matter whom you choose: so why not choose at random? Putting it round the other way, in holding an election you are asking the citizens to say who is most suitable to hold office and this implies that some are better qualified than others. We tend to miss this point because we think in terms of choosing representatives. But the Greeks did not have representative democracies.

The Athenian clearly shares this view of elections as a method of choosing the candidates best qualified for office (751c–d, 945b–946c). Thus the most likely interpretation of his talk of two kinds of equality seems to be this. He thinks that the ideal would be to ensure that honours and offices go to the virtuous and that in a well-ordered state this can be achieved by elections. But even here he thinks it desirable to make some concession to egalitarian sentiment by incorporating an element of lot (756e–757a, 759b). Thus Barker (1960, p. 397) is quite wrong to assume that Plato cannot have supposed that the people would be qualified to choose its own rulers and that his proposals for elections are simply concessions to the masses. It is the lot, not the vote, which is used 'to avoid the discontent of the people'.

This leaves us with the problem of explaining how in 756e the Athenian can describe the election to the council as coming midway between democracy and monarchy. There is no element in the council or elsewhere that could clearly be called monarchic — nothing like the Spartan kings for example. The problem is similar to that raised in Book III, 693d–761d, where both the Athenian and the Persian states in their prime are said to have come midway between monarchy and democracy, even though Athens had no clearly monarchic element and Persia no clear element of democracy. As we saw (chapter 7, section 6), the only way to make sense of that passage is to suppose that the Athenian is asking for a state which blends liberty with respect for authority. The same would seem to be true of the present passage. 'Monarchy', it seems, does not mean 'kingship' but is applied to any system in which the citizens are expected to show respect for their rulers.

4   *Democracy*

It is sometimes said that the *Laws* shows greater sympathy for the ideals of democracy than does the *Republic*. To evaluate this claim we need to know what is meant by the 'ideals of democracy'.

From one point of view, no Greek state could claim to be democratic. In all of them the women and slaves who made up a large part of the population lacked significant political rights. The city of the *Laws* would be no exception in this respect, since, even if women are enfranchised, slaves and aliens will still be excluded from the political process. But, quite apart from this, there are other important differences between the Greek and the modern conceptions of democracy. In the Greek view, democratic constitutions were characterized by the following features: all adult male citizens had the right to serve on juries and vote in the assembly, ultimate political power rested with these popular institutions and magistrates were generally chosen by lot. On the modern view a democratic constitution is one where the government is chosen by elections in which all adult citizens have a right to vote.

The constitution proposed for the city of the *Laws* contains certain features which a Greek would recognize as democratic: all citizens have right to serve on juries and there is a (very limited) use of the lot in elections. But since ultimate power rests with the magistrates and since these are chosen chiefly by election, it would hardly count as a democracy in the Greek sense. On the other hand, because its rulers are elected, it would be much more like a democracy in the modern sense.

In addition to considering the outward forms of the constitution we should also ask what principles underlie it. Here again it is necessary to distinguish different views of democracy. Some democratic theorists have advocated democracy on the grounds that everyone has an equal right to participate in government. From this point of view the direct democracy of the Greeks might be seen as ideal, while a system in which the citizens elect representatives may be regarded as a way of avoiding the practical obstacles to direct democracy in a large modern state. We may call those who advocate democracy on these grounds *democratic idealists.* Such thinkers may believe that democratic processes will result in decisions taken for the common good, but they are not primarily interested in questions of efficiency. They emphasize the right to participate or the need to express the general will rather than the importance of wise government.

The second group of democratic theorists includes all those who advocate the choice of rulers by election on the grounds that this is the form of constitution most likely to produce good government. They are not primarily concerned to ensure that government decisions reflect the general will. They may even believe that the ideal ruler would be an enlightened despot. They would merely insist that there is no means of guaranteeing that a despot will be enlightened. They may be equally dubious about the political competence of the average voter. But they will still maintain that a system in which all citizens have the vote gives us the best chance of achieving a tolerable government and avoiding the excesses of tyranny. On the whole, they believe, the electorate will vote, not for men exactly like themselves, but for those with some degree of expertise and knowledge of political matters. Once a government is in power, the fear of losing office at the next election gives it a powerful incentive to consider the interests of the people at large. Moreover, an electoral system gives the citizens a sense of 'belonging' and helps them to identify with their government. Theories of this kind have been called 'democratic elitism' because they acknowledge that government will in practice be in the hands of an elite and confine the role of the electorate to choosing rulers from among this elite.

It hardly needs saying that Plato is no democratic idealist; he does not think that all men have an equal claim to participate in politics and he has no real respect for the will of the people. On the other hand, he does have a good deal in common with the democratic elitists. His primary concern is to bring about good government in a stable, peaceful community. He sees elections as a means of ensuring that political offices are held by properly qualified candidates whose character and education enable them to do what is right. The 'checks and balances' in the constitution will restrain any magistrate with tyrannical leanings, while the combination of democratic and non-democratic elements in the constitution will give the citizens a sense of solidarity (756e–757a, 759b).

12

Education and the Arts

Laws, 632–641d, 643a–650b, 652a–661d, 663d–674c, 700a–701c, 764c–766b, 788a–823a, 950d–952d, 960b–969d; *Republic*, 376c–412b, 521c–534e, 595a–608b; *Timaeus*, 47c–e, 80b, 88b–c, 90d

Education, as Plato conceives it, is a matter of training the young citizens in the forms of goodness or virtue they will require as adults (643d–e; cf. 641–c). We have already seen that the inculcation of virtue is also the main aim of the legal code as a whole (chapter 4 above). It follows therefore that education, in Plato's eyes, is not just one among many functions of the state but in some sense embraces all the other functions. This educational focus is apparent from the beginning of the dialogue, which starts from a criticism of the institutions by which the Cretans and Spartans tried to instill their own ethos into their young. The meanderings of Books I and II serve mainly to show how virtue may be taught. These ideas influence every aspect of the constitution proposed for the Cretan city but are picked up especially in Book VII which is largely concerned with the education of the young.

1 The aims of education

Speaking generally, education may be defined as a matter of training the young to be good at whatever pursuits they will have to follow as adults (643b). Thus, if a child is to be a craftsman, one will give him toy tools; if he is to be a soldier he will be taught riding and the like; in other words, children learn through play (643b–c). Of course, Plato, as we would now expect, despises such 'technical' training as 'illiberal' and 'banausic' (643e–644a), but he believes that the same principles apply to genuine education. One must encourage in children a passionate desire to be good citizens and to know how to rule and be ruled in accordance with justice. This kind of education is the greatest of gifts that can be bestowed on good men (644b). Since virtue consists in having our desires adjusted to whatever reason judges to be right, this citizen's education will involve so training a child's feelings of pleasure and pain that, even before his reason can grasp the nature of virtue, he loves what ought to be loved and hates what ought to be hated (653a–c). The judgements of reason are embodied in law (645a) which rests on the wisdom and experience of the old. So in saying that children should be habituated to feel pleasure and pain in accordance with law the Athenian is suggesting that their pleasures and pains should coincide with those of wise old men (659c–d).

Books I and II suggest two devices for achieving this kind of education. The first is the much maligned drinking party. The Athenian believes that, properly directed, such parties will provide ways of both testing and training the young men's powers of self-control (641a–d, 649d–650b; cf. 634a–b).

Since those who are mildly intoxicated often reveal what they would normally take care to conceal, it is easy enough to see why the Athenian should regard drinking parties as a means of testing a young man's character. It is less easy to see how these parties could actually help one to develop self-control. The Athenian's argument seems to be this: the Dorians (and others) train the young to resist pain by placing them in painful situations while encouraging them through fear of disgrace not to give in; drink intensifies pleasures; so one may train people to resist pleasures by giving them drink and at the same time encouraging them to resist temptation through a sense of shame (645d–650b; cf. 634a–b). The flaw in this argument is the assumption that drink is a means of intensifying pleasures. It may be that, but it is more obviously a means of lessening one's power of self-control (649a–b). So the proposal to strengthen self-control by drinking parties is not genuinely parallel to the practice of strengthening someone's physical courage by subjecting him to pain. There is therefore no reason why drinking parties should help the young to overcome pleasures in general. On the other hand, it is probably true that one cannot learn to resist the specific temptations of drink without having experienced them. So, submerged in the discussion of drinking parties, there may be a good point: one does not encourage a person to develop genuine self-control by protecting him from all temptations. This might be a sound criticism of the more restrictive aspects of the Spartan regime, as it would be of (e.g.) Calvinist Scotland.

The second educational device is the chorus. To understand the Athenian's comments on this, one needs to realize that the Greek chorus performed dance movements while singing in unison. Three choruses are envisaged, one of children, the second of young men and the third of older men. The age of the third chorus seems to increase as the dialogue goes on until it is very definitely a chorus of the old (664d, 665b, 670a–b, 671d–e, 812b–c). It soon becomes apparent that the Athenian is interested in the third chorus primarily because it will set the standards by which the choral singing and dancing of the young is to be judged (666d–671a, esp. 670c–671a). Thus music and dance will be the chief device for bringing the characters of the young into accord with the judgements of the old. Music and education are inseparable (642a).

2 Music

In 653c–654d the Athenian offers two explanations of why the chorus is needed. According to the first account it is needed to reinforce the education the citizens have received from childhood. Education consists in the correct discipline of pleasures and pains; but this discipline grows slack as we get older; so the gods have given us festivals (involving the chorus) as a means of recreation and to restore the habits in which we were brought up (653c–d). The second argument treats music as a way of creating order within us. Children resemble other young animals in being unable to keep still or quiet, but human beings are unique in having a sense of order in movement. We call this rhythm and melody (or 'harmony': there is no exact equivalent of the Greek *harmonia*) and it is a gift of those gods who lead us in singing and dancing. So a really educated man must sing and dance well (654b; cf. *Timaeus*, 47c–e). But this is not simply a matter of technical proficiency. One man may be able to express accurately what he imagines to be good without actually loving the good or hating the bad; another may have the right feelings of pleasure and pain without being able to express what he has in mind correctly in all respects. It is the latter, the one with the correct feelings, who is to be preferred (654c–d). In other words, the Athenian seems to be insisting that the success of the performer in conveying what is good does not matter so much as the sincerity and conviction with which he does it.

Since music and dance are so important for education, it follows that in order to tell who is genuinely educated we need to know the criterion of excellence in music and dancing (654d–e). The immediate answer is that there are tunes and dance forms associated with different kinds of character; those associated with goodness of soul or body are good and those associated with evil are bad (654e–655b). Thus, contrary to common opinion, what is good does not vary from person to person. If we believe that it does so vary, that is because we falsely imagine that goodness consists simply in giving pleasure and because we find most pleasure in whatever happens to accord with our own character. Those who take pleasure in performances they really know to be bad are in special danger because they will tend to grow more like the things they enjoy (655e–656b). The point seems to be that if we allow ourselves to enjoy music and dance appropriate to bad characters we will eventually acquire bad characters ourselves.

Since music and dance can have this corrupting effect it follows, according to the Athenian, that they cannot be left uncontrolled. So he praises the Egyptians who long ago established rigid norms of music based on what is naturally right. We likewise should try to establish a code of permitted musical forms and should consecrate them to make them as permanent as possible. We must resist the love of novelty (656d–657b). This means that we can no longer treat musical festivals as simple contests in giving pleasure. It is, rather, the pleasure of the old and wise that is the criterion of education. So the judges in musical contests must resist the applause of the masses and try to teach them what is right (657c–660a). The same principles apply to poetry. The content must be correct and, in particular, poets must teach that justice and happiness coincide (660a–664d).

The Athenian returns to the topic of correctness in music and dance while professing to give directions to the chorus of Dionysus (i.e. the chorus of inebriated old men). He treats these arts as imitative (mimetic). The excellence of such arts, as of everything else, depends either on the pleasure they bring, or on some kind of correctness or on their usefulness (667b–c). (This seems to be a good general point, though of course, some philosophers, notably the utilitarians, would try to assimilate the different criteria of value). Some harmless pleasures may be judged simply as pleasures, but, in the case of the imitative arts, the important thing is that they should possess 'equality of quantity and quality' (667d). Music must therefore be judged according to whether it exhibits 'similarity in its imitation of the beautiful' (668a–b). The point seems to be that anything which seeks to imitate or portray something must accurately represent its proportions. So, the Athenian argues, in judging an artistic creation we must understand its essential nature, which, apparently, amounts to knowing the intention with which it is represented and what it is supposed to represent. This point is illustrated with a discussion of visual representations which leads to the conclusion that in assessing any kind of representation we need to know (a) what is represented, (b) how correctly the representation is done, and (c) whether the manner of representation is a good thing (668d–669b). The point of this difficult passage seems to be that accuracy of representation is essential but is not enough in itself: the work of art must have moral as well as technical excellence.

The Athenian now launches into an attack on poets who are indiscriminate in their use of words, melodies, rhythms and dance movements. They do not make these consistent with one another or assign them appropriately to the characters they supposedly represent (669b–670c). So the third chorus will have to have sufficient understanding of musical matters to choose a correct style for their own characters and to set an example to others (670d–671a).

There is no doubt that Plato took seriously his claim that art (especially music) can be morally corrupting and must therefore be strictly controlled. There are corresponding arguments in the *Republic* (376e–403e, 605a–608b, esp. 395b–396e, 605c–606d). He ascribes the supposed moral decline of Athens to lawlessness in music (700a–701c), and he shows how these ideas could be put into practice in the new Cretan city (798e–802e, 812a–813a, 814d–816d).

In his description of Athens, the Athenian appears to be claiming as a matter of observed fact that disorder in music leads to a more general lawlessness. Of course, it is obvious enough that there are correlations between musical and social change — it is no accident that 'punk rockers' do not dance minuets or Viennese waltzes — and Plato is no doubt right in supposing that there was a connection between changes in music and the move towards a more permissive society in Athens. We know also that music can help to spread ideas and attitudes — this is why people write patriotic or revolutionary songs, for example. But presumably music can have this effect only when social conditions are ready for it. So, although music may have a peripheral role in changing people's attitudes, it is natural to see changes of musical style as symptoms rather than as causes of changes in society.

Of course Plato's argument against innovation in music does not rest primarily on observed correlations between music and social change. He has a theoretical argument that music is naturally associated with character and that in performing or taking pleasure in music we assimilate our own characters to that associated with the music. This argument rests on Plato's concept of *mimesis*.

As Plato sees them, music and dance are imitative or *mimetic* arts (655d, 668a, 795e, 798d, 814e; cf. *Cratylus*, 423c–d, *Republic*, 393a–c, 401a, *Statesman*, 306d), but, as everyone who has read the *Republic* knows, Plato's concept of *mimesis*, or imitation, is very obscure. When it is introduced in the *Republic*, *mimesis* is defined as 'making oneself like some other thing in voice or appearance' (393c). In that passage Socrates distinguishes between mimetic poetry, which purports to give us the words of the characters represented in the poem, and purely narrative poetry, where the poet speaks in his own person (392d–394c). He proposes to abolish from the ideal state all mimetic poetry apart from that which involves the imitation of the most admirable characters (394c–398c). He uses different senses of *mimesis* a few pages later when he describes different musical modes as 'imitating' different kinds of character in different circumstances (399a–b) and suggests that architecture, as well as painting and sculpture, can provide images of the virtues and vices (401b). The picture is further complicated in Book X, where Socrates attacks all mimetic art. Some of his arguments there seem to assume that the art in question is like a *trompe-l'oeil* painting designed to make us take appearance for reality (596a–598d, 602c–603b), while others would seem to apply to all art (598d–602b, 603b–606d). In these contexts it looks as though Plato is confusing a more general sense of *mimesis*, in which it applies to all arts, with a more specific sense in which *mimesis* involves the attempt to recreate the appearance of a thing.

The importance of *mimesis* is not confined to aesthetic contexts. Plato also uses it in the following ways (among others):

(1)   The particulars of everyday life stand in the same relation to the Forms as images do to originals (*Republic*, 509d–511e). This kind of language is particularly prominent in the *Timaeus*, where the demiurge (i.e. the creator) is said to make the visible universe in imitation of the eternal Forms (*Timaeus*, 27d–29d).

(2)   In the *Cratylus*, Socrates argues that words imitate the things they stand for. He tries to demonstrate this by showing that the elements out of which words are composed are standardly correlated with elements in the things they represent (422b–427d).

(3)   Law imitates the rule of reason (*Statesman*, 300c–301b, *Laws* 713b–714b).

It is obvious that, in these contexts, imitation cannot consist in recreating the appearance of a thing. The Forms, for example, are not in time and space and therefore in themselves have no visible appearance. It looks as though what Plato means is that the Forms systematically determine the characteristics of the particulars that fall under them, so that we can fully understand why the particulars are as they are only by reference to the Forms. An analogy might be the relationship of a barometric chart to the variations in atmospheric pressures that it represents. The chart does not literally imitate the pressure system, but the pressure system determines the form of the chart and gives it its meaning and significance. We could capture this wider meaning of *mimesis* by translating it as 'representation' or even as 'expression'.

If this interpretation of *mimesis* is correct we can make sense of the notion that music is a mimetic art. It can represent certain characters, not in the sense that it literally resembles them, but in the sense that it exhibits in a different medium the same fundamental patterns of order or disorder. The music associated with bad character is thus intrinsically bad because it fails to reveal the right kind of order and bad in its results because in performing and enjoying it we take its character into our souls. There would be something especially wrong with a choral work in which the words, rhythm, melody and dance movements were inconsistent with one another in the sense that they expressed different kinds of character. Such music would be symptomatic of some kind of moral disintegration and would be especially abhorrent to anyone like Plato who saw the state as having a single overriding moral purpose. So there is a standard of correctness in music (657a, 667b–668d, 700e) which does not consist simply in pictorial accuracy. Neither is it purely intrinsic to the work of art. Music is 'correct' when it aims to embody forms of order characteristic of good soul and when it does this successfully.

The most obvious difficulty with this theory is that of seeing how the character of a human being could possibly exhibit the same kinds of order as a musical composition. A score will reveal with some precision the elements out of which a piece of music is composed and the ways in which they are related to one another: these are expressible in numerical terms. Psychology offers us nothing like this. Of course there is evidence of correlations between musical structures and particular human emotions or moods. Twentieth-century music has been criticized for neglecting these correlations and so losing the power to express any coherent pattern of feelings. There may be parallels between these criticisms and Plato's complaints of incoherence in music, though the reflection that similar complaints were made about (e.g.) Beethoven should discourage us from accepting them too readily.

At a less sophisticated level it is clear enough that music can help to create a mood. Consider, for example, the stirring effect of martial music and the use of music to create atmosphere in films. A choral work would be incoherent if the emotions created by its musical elements were quite different from those demanded by the words. But there appears to be no evidence that music has a lasting effect on character.

We know very little about Greek music but it is clear that there had been elaborate theorizing about the emotional significance of particular modes. In the *Republic* (398c–400c) Plato proposes to exclude those modes he judges to be inappropriate. In the *Laws* he is less precise and leaves the matter to the judgement of the third chorus (802a–e, 811b–c). This looks like a recipe for simple conservatism.

3   Education and play

Plato makes use of a punning association between *paideia*, education, and *paidia*, play, to suggest that education is or involves play (643b–c, 653c–654a, 803c–804b). He also uses the contrast between *paidia* and *spoude* which suggests seriousness, effort or zeal. This contrast works in two ways: (a) play as something enjoyable can be contrasted with what is irksome or involves effort and (b) play as something which has no value beyond the enjoyment it brings may be contrasted with serious activities undertaken for an end. Using these associations Plato can establish the paradox that *paidia*, play, is *spoude*, a serious matter. It is so partly because the education of children through play is a most important matter and partly because the most serious work of adults is a kind of divinely inspired play.

The most obvious application of these ideas is in the suggestion that children are to be educated through play. We have already met the idea that children should play at the activities they are to undertake as adults (643b–644a). Accordingly, the educational programmes of the new city should provide for careful control over children's games. In particular innovation in children's games is to be prohibited because it encourages a dangerous desire for change (797a–798e). A similar idea is applied to adults when it is suggested that religious festivals are given, not only as a means of recreation, but also to reinforce and restore their education (653c–d). But the notion of play also works in another way. The ideas that man is a puppet or plaything of the gods and that gods lead the celebrations in religious festivals (653e) are combined in 803c–804b. Human affairs are not of any real importance — only God really counts — and as man is the plaything of the gods he ought to live in a way appropriate to that role, engaging in the noblest kind of play. The purport of the obscure sentences at 803d seems to be this: we now think that work or effort should be performed for the sake of play; so the 'serious' work of war is undertaken for the sake of peace; but play or education is really the most important and serious thing and this will be found only in peace; so man's true vocation is to live in peace and to spend his time in forms of play, namely sacrificing, singing and dancing. These ideas are echoed in 806d–807e which describes the citizen's vocation to a life of serious leisure and, most strikingly, in 817a–d, where the Athenian describes legislators as poets who produce the finest drama. At least, the new state is intended as an expression or imitation (*mimesis*) of the noblest and best life which is supposed to be the truest poetry. (The word here is literally 'tragedy' but does not carry the implications of unhappiness involved in the English word.)

These passages show an interweaving of religious, political, ethical and aesthetic ideas. As we shall see (chapter 15), the order of the universe demonstrates the existence of a god or gods, and true religion requires an understanding of this cosmic order. The same patterns of order when transferred to the human sphere become law, which should shape both the city and the character of the individual (967e, see above, chapter 3, section 3). Music and dance are also forms of order which help to 'harmonize' the soul (653c–654a; cf. *Timaeus*, 47c–e, 80b). So the same forms of order are expressed in the heavens, the well-constituted city, the character of the good man, and in the finest music (cf. *Timaeus*, 88c–d). The appreciation of this point casts light on Plato's theory both of politics and of art as they are expressed in the *Laws*.

Plato's attitude to art has often seemed paradoxical. He is himself a great artist, yet, it may seem, the censorship he imposes on the arts would reduce poets, musicians and painters to the role of party hacks serving the purposes of the state. Part of the trouble here is that we are apt to see true art as consisting in self-expression, while Plato sees its essence in the expression of the order which underlies the universe, and the moral life alike. His position therefore has much more in common with the religious artists of the pre-Romantic era who saw their work, not primarily as expressing their own emotions, but as an expression of the divine truth. Although this perspective imposes limitations on the subject matter and style of art, it is certainly not incompatible with genuine artistic excellence. Similarly, on the political plane, one might compare the state, as Plato conceives it, with a monastic community seeking to glorify God in the order of its daily life and in the beauty of its liturgy. While there is a good deal to be said for this comparison there is at least one important difference between the two kinds of community. The members of a religious order accept their vocations voluntarily and willingly give up their freedom. Plato also expects the citizens of his state to live willingly, and perhaps joyously, within the bounds set for them, but this will be out of conditioning rather than free choice.

4 Organization and curriculum

The system of education proposed for the new city in general follows the principles laid down in the earlier books. Education will be the responsibility of the state and all children, male and female, will be required to attend school (804d-e). The system will be under the direction of a minister of education chosen from among the guardians of the laws by a vote of all the magistrates (apart from the members of the council and its executive committee). Since this will be the most important office of state, the electors must choose for it the citizen who seems most excellent in every respect (765a-766b; cf. 809a). To assist him he will have officers to take charge of schools and gymnasia and to act as judges in musical and gymnastic contests (764c-765d, 813c). The teachers themselves will be salaried foreigners (804d, 813e) — the Greeks seem generally to have held the job of a schoolmaster in low esteem.

The Athenian is concerned with the treatment children will receive from their earliest years. Small children and even the unborn must experience plenty of movement (790c-791c). They should be neither 'spoilt' nor repressed by undue strictness — the general aim is to avoid excesses of either pleasure or pain (791d-793a). From the age of three they will attend 'play groups' where they will be supervised by one of the female officials (793e-794d). Formal education will begin for both sexes at the age of six and will comprise music, dance, literature, gymnastics and military exercises as well as some arithmetic and the elements of reading and writing (809a-810a; cf. 794d-796d on gymnastics and military exercises; 810b-812a on literature, 814e-816d on dance; and 812a-813a on music). The Athenian appears to suggest a timetable whereby the years ten to thirteen will be devoted to literature and thirteen to sixteen to playing the lyre. But presumably he cannot mean that these years will be devoted exclusively to those pursuits. It is not clear how young citizens between sixteen and twenty-five years old would spend their time. One would expect a period of military service like the Athenian ephebate, but this is not mentioned explicitly. The office of assistant to the country wardens seems intended as a military and political training but this is left surprisingly late — the minimum age is twenty-five (760c).

Within this programme most attention is paid to music (812a-813a;

cf. 799a–802e) and literature (810b–812a). As we would expect, both are to be strictly regulated. In the case of literature the basic text will be the Laws itself — the Athenian seems to have in mind particularly the preambles to the laws. Teachers will learn these by heart, and the Minister of Education will use them as a guide in deciding what other forms of literature are to be taught (811c–812a).

5 Higher things

Everyone, the Athenian believes, should know the essentials of arithmetic, geometry and astronomy, though it is not necesssary for the population at large to study these subjects in great detail (818a; cf. 747a–b, 809c–d). There is emphasis on the practical value of these studies (809d; cf. 747a, 818c) but it is also made clear from the beginning that they are an essential preparation for more exalted forms of inquiry (747b, 809d, 818c–d). The Athenian bewails the ignorance of the Greeks in these matters compared with the Egyptians (819a–b). In particular he criticizes his contemporaries for failing to acknowledge the existence of incommensurables (819d–820d), and for believing that the planets 'wander' instead of following a fixed circular path (822a–c). It becomes obvious later why he is so concerned about this latter error, since the supposedly rational movements of the heavens play a vital role in the argument for the existence of God (897b–898e).

Only at the end of the dialogue, in the account of the nocturnal council, do we learn about the select few who will study mathematics and astronomy in depth. This council, which owes its sinister-sounding name simply to the fact that it meets in the small hours of the morning, is mentioned briefly at 908a and 909a, reappears at 951d–952c, and is discussed at length from 961a onwards. There are slightly different accounts of its membership but it is clearly intended to include the most distinguished members of the state including the ten oldest guardians of the laws (951e, 961a). These 'senior members' will each bring with them one young man aged between thirty and forty, though their choice will be subject to the approval of the council as a whole.

The first task assigned to the council is that of re-educating atheists (909a). At 951d–952a it is described as 'the council of those who oversee the laws ' and the main topic of investigation is given as 'the laws of their own city plus anything significant about these matters that can be learned from elsewhere'. In this capacity the council hears the reports of the 'observers' — citizens aged between fifty and sixty who have been allowed to go abroad to see if anything can be learned from other cities (951a–952d, 961a). The longer account of the council in 961a ff. is prefaced by a passage dealing with the need for some body to keep the laws safe from change (960b–e). One might think that this function had already been assigned to the guardians of the laws and the Athenian is very vague about the relationship between these two bodies — at 966b he seems to lose sight of any distinction between them. In view of the overlap in the membership of the two bodies this is not a serious error. The point seems to be that the guardians protect the laws by overseeing their day to day operation while the nocturnal council preserves their intellectual basis. It studies the laws but leaves to others the task of putting its discoveries into practice. So the older members can be seen as the reason of the state while the younger members are the senses which provide the information that reason requires (964e–965a; cf. 961d).

In discharging this function the council will have to consider firstly what is the aim of the state, then the means by which this aim is to be attained, and finally what laws or men give good advice (962b). The ensuing passage reiterates the need for legislation to be directed to a single goal, namely virtue (962c–963a). This leads into the problem of the unity of virtue. In talking of four virtues — courage, wisdom, justice and temperance — we imply that they are distinct but also in some sense the same. One duty of the council is to understand this unity (963a–964a, 965b–e). In doing so they will need not merely to know the names of things but also to give a definition or account of them (964a–b). This knowledge will especially qualify the council to educate the state in virtue (either by instruction or by punishment) (964b–c). As true guardians of the laws they must know in what sense good is many and in what sense one, they must know the true nature of the laws and must be able to teach and live their own lives accordingly (966a–b). To fulfil this task an essential requirement will be a complete mastery of the two doctrines by which the Athenian would prove the existence of a god or gods — the doctrines that soul is prior to anything else and that the movements of the heavens are rational. They will need to have completed the essential preliminary studies, to understand what these have in common, to apply their knowledge in framing appropriate moral and legal rules, and to be capable of giving a rational account of these matters where that is possible (966c–968a).

There is an interesting ambiguity in the Greek text of 967e. If we take the passage literally, it looks as though the Athenian is saying that the members of the council must be able to connect their other studies with their knowledge of music. Most translators take it in this way. But Cherniss (1953, p 377) who is followed by Saunders (1972, pp 9–10) points out that Plato sometimes says 'music' when he means 'philosophy'. In the present passage the ambiguity may be deliberate. It is presumably philosophy that enables the nocturnal council to unify its studies, but music, too, can reflect the fundamental order of the universe.

The Athenian refuses to describe in detail the course of study that will be followed by the nocturnal council, ostensibly because only those who have participated in such a course could understand the reasoning behind it (968d–e). There are some obvious parallels with the curriculum laid down for the guardians in the *Republic*. Like the members of the nocturnal council, the guardians of the *Republic* would begin their higher education with the study of mathematics (521c–531d), but would eventually achieve a wider insight into the relationship between the one and the many (531e–534e; cf. *Laws*, 965b). They would undergo their first period of philosophical training between the ages of thirty and thirty-five and would return to their studies at the age of fifty. At this stage they would finally achieve a grasp of the Forms (539e–540a). These ages correspond to those of the junior and senior members of the nocturnal council (951a–e, 961a–b).

Against this one has to acknowledge that there are discrepancies between the account of the nocturnal council and the description of the philosophic training in the *Republic*. In that dialogue Plato not only demands that the philosopher should be able to understand what the many particular instances of a certain kind have in common but talks as though the one Form of (e.g.) the beautiful or the just is distinct from the particulars that fall under it. The Form truly *is* while the particulars come between being and not being (475e–480a). The Forms belong to an 'intelligible' world, not to the visible world of everyday experience (508b–c, 509d, 517b–c). Nothing in the *Laws* suggests this kind of separation of Forms and particulars. The need is simply to show how we can talk of the virtues as one (963d–e), and this merely requires us to discern something that is the same in all of them (965c–d). In the *Republic* the knowledge of the good provides the means of understanding all reality (505a–509c), while in the *Laws* it is apparently reduced to the more obvious role of enabling the nocturnal council to give moral and political guidance. The guardians of the *Republic* have to turn away from the everyday world of becoming towards the 'true' being of the Forms (518a–519b, 521c–d); the nocturnal council needs the factual information provided by its younger members and is concerned with the practical problems of legislation (962b, 964e–965a). The *Republic* despises observational astronomy and seeks to replace it with a purely theoretical study (529a–530c); the *Laws*, on the other hand, requires a study of the visible heavens since it is their regularity and order that proves the existence of God (966e–967a).

These differences between the *Republic* and the *Laws* would not be particularly significant if there were strong independent grounds for holding that Plato maintained to the end of his life the theory of Forms as expounded in the *Republic*. After all, the discrepancies are mainly due to absence from the *Laws* of points made in the *Republic*. These omissions might have been made for the sake of simplicity. But it is notable that the *Parmenides* offers some convincing arguments against the theory of Forms so conceived, and that later dialogues (with the exception of the *Timaeus* whose dating is disputed) no longer use language that suggests a separation of Forms and particulars. On the other hand they show a strong interest in the problem of the one and the many. The *Sophist*, for example, shows how to define a 'sophist' by progressively dividing the category of an art or skill. This method would show how many different species could all be grouped under one general kind. The Athenian's brief remarks on the differentiation of courage and wisdom (963d–e) would fit this pattern. So there are grounds for holding that, in spite of superficial similarities between the *Republic* and the *Laws*, the *Sophist* and the *Statesman* give us a better idea of what the nocturnal council would actually do. We may find further evidence for this in 630e–631a, where the Athenian, in language recalling the *Sophist*, maintains that the true legislator would pursue his task systematically, setting out his laws in their various classes. Presumably his own legislative proposals are intended to illustrate this method. A concern for system is particularly apparent in Books IX and X, where there are systematic classifications of the causes of injustice, of homicides and woundings and of the various kinds of impiety (see below, chapters 14 and 15). It is not unduly fanciful to suppose that Plato sees this as an application of the method which he advocates in the *Sophist* and the *Statesman* and that he would wish the nocturnal council to adopt the same approach.

13

Punishment

Laws, 728b–c, 731b–d, 735d–e, 853a–882c, 908e–910d, 933e–934c, 941b–942a, 957e–958a; *Protagoras*, 323c–326e; Gorgias, 472d–480b, 507c–508b, 525b–c; *Republic*, 380a–b, 409e–410a, 591a–b

The Athenian takes it for granted that, as well as having persuasive preambles, laws also require sanctions to give them their force or necessity (722b); so laws embody a kind of threat (722e). It follows that the entire legislative code is to some extent concerned with punishment, though the more important pronouncements on the theory of punishment mostly come in Book IX where the Athenian describes what we would call the 'criminal' law of the new state.

1 The penalties

The penalties that the Athenian proposes differ considerably from those available to most modern courts. The chief penalties suggested are as follows.

Death

Capital punishment is prescribed for a wide range of offences including deliberate murder (871d), wounding a parent, brother or sister with intent to kill (877b–c), persistent atheism (909a), serious acts of impiety (910c–d), theft from temples (854e), theft of public property (942a), harbouring exiles (955b), waging private war (955c), taking bribes (955d) and obstructing the judgment of a court (958c). It looks as though these proposals would extend the use of capital punishment beyond what was current in Athens. The offences against the state discussed in Book XII are handled with notable ferocity.

Monetary penalties

These take a variety of forms. In some cases, for example, failure to marry by the approved age (774a), the amount of the fine varies according to the offender's property class: the wealthier citizens pay more. For offences which involve damage to the interests of, or injury to, another person, the general principle is that those convicted should pay compensation plus an additional sum by way of punishment. Thus in the case of theft all offenders are required to give double compensation (857a–b), a provision borrowed from Athenian practice. The chief innovation is the stipulation that no one shall be fined so heavily that he cannot afford to keep the equipment necessary for running his farm and that no one is to be subjected to complete confiscation of property (855a–c), measures that are essential if the full number of households is to be maintained.

Imprisonment

So far as we know, Greek states did not generally impose imprisonment as a penalty in its own right, though one could be detained while awaiting trial or sentence. Plato introduces it as a penalty for several kinds of offender including those who strike someone more than twenty years their senior (880b–c), citizens who engage in retail trade (919e–920a) and those who prevent witnesses or litigants attending a court (954e–955a). Imprisonment of a rather special kind is imposed on atheists (908e–909b). In some cases imprisonment seems to be envisaged as an alternative penalty for those who cannot or will not pay fines (855b, 857a).

Dishonour and deprivation of rights

Greek cities used a wide range of penalties under the general heading of *atimia* (literally dishonour) . In Athens this generally meant the suspension of civic rights, sometimes including the loss of citizenship. Elsewhere it could be some kind of public disgrace. In the code of the *Laws*, *atimia* sometimes involves minor deprivations of rights (754e–755a, 784d) but generally means having one's name posted or being in some other way publicly branded as a bad character (755a, 762c, 774c, 784d). It is stipulated that no one is ever to forfeit his citizen rights completely for a single crime (855c).

Exile

Sentences of exile were common in Greek states. The Athenian uses them for aliens, but in the case of citizens he would, with rare exceptions, restrict their use to cases of homicide where the underlying assumption is that the continued presence of the killer will lead to religious pollution (864e, 867c–868e).

Corporal punishment

This was rarely, if at all, applied to the citizens of Greek states, though it would, one assumes, have been used widely on slaves. The Athenian proposes that citizens should be beaten for physical assaults on their parents (881d). In a few cases he would allow third parties to beat offenders with impunity (762c, 784d, 845c). Corporal punishment is to be used more extensively for slaves and foreigners (854d, 879e, 881c, 882b, 917c–e).

2   The aims of punishment

Plato's views on the purposes of punishment need to be seen in the light of what we know about the views of his contemporaries. So far as can be gathered from our main source, the speeches of the Athenian orators, popular thought recognized three main aims that punishment might accomplish:

(1)   An orator will sometimes ask that a penalty be imposed as an example to stop the criminal himself from repeating his crimes and to discourage others from emulating them. This is, of course, the idea embodied in the modern concept of deterrence.

(2)   Sometimes courts were asked to penalize criminals to 'restrain' them or 'bring them to their senses'. While this can sound like the modern concept of reform it probably refers to more primitive notions — something like the demand that criminals be given a 'short, sharp shock'.

(3)   The orators make frequent use of the concept of *timoria*. This has certain analogies with the modern concept of retribution, though it is clear that the orators were not espousing a retributive theory of punishment as that would now be understood. Modern retributive theorists have been careful to distinguish the impartial requirement of retribution from demands for personal vengeance. Retribution is impersonal and is based simply on the idea that it is right for those who

have done wrong to suffer. The Greek orators, on the other hand, often make it clear that they are bringing prosecutions out of private resentment and they call upon juries to share their anger.

The *Laws* is by no means the first dialogue in which Plato discusses the problem of punishment. He puts a particularly notable account into the mouth of the sophist Protagoras: 'No one', say the sophist, 'punishes simply for the sake of the past; that would be to exact blind vengeance (*timōria*) like a beast. A rational man punishes to prevent the criminal himself and those who are aware of his punishment from doing wrong in future' (*Protagoras* 324a–c). There are two important points here:

(1)   Protagoras dismisses mere *timōria* and he does so in terms that would commit him to rejecting not only punishment as personal vengeance but also the kinds of supposedly impersonal retribution demanded by modern retributive theorists.

(2)   For *timōria*, Protagoras would substitute a preventive view of punishment, which seems to rely largely on deterrence, though it could leave room for elements of reform.

Elsewhere in the same speech Protagoras allows that cities may, by penalties of death or exile, rid themselves of those evil characters who are incapable of acquiring justice (322d, 325a–b). He also describes the punishment of children which he likens to the process of straightening a warped plank by blows (325d–e). Overall, Protagoras's attitude is that punishment ensures that people will conform to social rules; it thus secures the good of the community as a whole. In the *Gorgias* and the *Republic* the focus is rather different. The key doctrine in both dialogues is that injustice is bad, not only for society, but also for the unjust man himself. The unjust man is therefore like the sick man and punishment benefits him by curing his sickness. The emphasis here is on individual, rather than social, good. Of course, the two approaches are compatible: it could be that punishment does good both to the individual, by curing him of injustice, and also to society by enforcing social rules.

In the *Laws*, the Athenian's attitude to punishment becomes apparent in the prelude to the legal code (726–734d). Having exhorted the citizens to honour their souls, the Athenian's imaginary legislator goes on to describe what some, he thinks, might call the greatest 'judgment' (*dikē*) on those who behave badly. This judgment consists in their becoming like the wicked and so cutting themselves off from the company of the good (728b). The Athenian then corrects himself:

Now this kind of suffering is not a judgment, for justice and judgment are fine things. This is rather punishment [or 'retribution': the word is *timōria*], a form of suffering consequent on injustice. Both the person who has experienced this and the one who does not are wretched. The one is not cured; the other is destroyed that many may be saved. (728c)

The fundamental point is clear enough here: the Athenian is distinguishing between a genuine judgment that does good and the mere infliction of suffering which may do no good at all. What is not clear is why both those who undergo this suffering and those who do not are supposed to be wretched. The most plausible explanation is suggested by Saunders: the person who undergoes suffering is said to be wretched because that experience does nothing for his soul, while the person who avoids it is equally wretched because, as he continues his life of crime, he will eventually be executed.

A few pages later the legislator advises the citizens on how they should deal with the injustice of others. They should be gentle with and pity those whose unjust deeds can be cured. After all, no one is voluntarily a wrongdoer, for no one willingly accepts the greatest of evils into his soul. But when we come across someone who is thoroughly wicked, then we should give vent to our anger.

The emphasis here is strongly on doing good to the criminal by curing him of his injustice. Only when he is beyond cure should other considerations come into play. There are many other passages where the Athenian expresses the same fundamental attitude to punishment — that it must do good primarily by curing the criminal. (See, e.g., 735e, 843d, 854d–855b, 862d–863c, 933e–934c, 941d, 957e.) The underlying principles are discussed in detail in Book IX. Three passages in particular seem to offer a full and explicit account:

(1) In 854c–855a the Athenian is discussing the treatment to be given to those who have stolen from temples (a particularly horrendous crime). Slaves and foreigners are to be branded, whipped and cast naked out of the land. The Athenian hopes that this penalty will bring the criminal to his senses and make him a better man, for, he says, penalties are not imposed by law to do harm; they make the criminal more virtuous or less wicked. Citizens who steal from temples must be put to death since if they commit such a crime after the upbringing they have received they may be deemed incurable. For these people death will be the least of evils and they will benefit others by serving as an example to them.

(2) In 862e–863c some new elements are added to this penology.

Anyone who has done damage will be required to compensate those he has injured. But when the act results from injustice in the agent there will need to be additional measures in order to cure him of this 'disease' in his soul. The Athenian goes on to explain how this should be done:

> . . . whenever any man commits any unjust act, great or small, the law shall instruct him for the future either never willingly to dare to do such a deed, or else to do it ever so much less often, in addition to paying for the injury. To effect this whether by action or speech, by means of pleasures and pains, honours and dishonours, money-fines and money gifts, and in general by whatsoever means one can employ to make men hate injustice and love (or at any rate not hate) justice — this is precisely the task of laws most noble. But for all those whom he perceives to be incurable in respect of these matters, what penalty shall the lawgiver enact, and what law? The lawgiver will realize that in all such cases not only is it better for the sinners themselves to live no longer, but also that they will prove of a double benefit to others by quitting life — and thus he will of necessity inflict death as the chastisement for their sins, in cases of this kind, and of this kind only. (862d–863a, trans. Bury)

The difficulty here lies in the contention that the legislator may use any method in handling criminals. Reading this in the light of modern penal theory we may credit Plato with the insight that curing or reforming a criminal need not involve doing anything unpleasant to him. It is even conceivable that one could reform him by rewards or honours. This interpretation is the most natural one if the passage is taken by itself, and Saunders writes it into his translation. But throughout the *Laws* the Athenian takes it for granted that unpleasant penalties should be imposed on wrongdoers. The only other method is in the case of honest atheists who, while undergoing detention, will be 're-educated' by members of the nocturnal council (909a). The *Gorgias*, 478a–e, 525b, and the *Republic*, 380a, 591a–b, likewise assume that injustice can be cured only by the infliction of pain. A less 'progressive' reading of the present passage would thus fit better into the dialogue as a whole. The Athenian would not be denying that all criminals should be punished. Rather he would be asserting that, in addition to the punishment of criminals, all the other mechanisms of the state must be geared towards the promotion of justice. This will be done by words in the case of the preambles to the laws and many of the educational provisions. It will be done by deeds, not only when the wicked are punished, but also when the just receive rewards and honours. Thus the citizens in general will be steered into the paths of virtue and criminals will be given an incentive to reform.

(3)   In 933e–934c there appears perhaps the clearest summary of Plato's penology. The Athenian insists first that those who have injured others by theft or violence should pay a penalty proportionate to the amount of damage in order to restore the loss. (The word here is literally 'cure'.) Then the criminal must pay an additional penalty to bring him to his senses. This penalty should be less for those who, because of their youth, or for some similar reason, have succumbed to the influence of others. It should be greater for those who have gone wrong as a result of their folly or lack of self-control. They must pay the penalty not for the sake of their wrongdoing (what has happened cannot be undone) but for the sake of the future. The object is that they themselves and those who see their punishment should come to hate injustice or at least show some recovery from that 'disease'. The Athenian goes on to emphasize the need for care and precision in choosing the penalty for each offender.

The foundation of Plato's penology, as it emerges in these passages, is the claim that injustice is bad for us and may therefore be likened to a disease. The primary aim of the penal system must be to cure this disease but, particularly in the case of the incurable, there is room for other considerations such as deterrence and the need to rid the city of evil men. Superficially, at least, such a system may seem sophisticated and rational —Saunders has laid particular emphasis on its advanced 'scientific' character (1972, pp. 18–20; 1973a and b, 1976, 1981). There are certain analogies with the modern 'progressive'idea that criminals should be treated by psychiatric or similar methods — an idea defended by Lady Wootton (1963) and popular among some psychiatrists and social theorists. It is important for us to consider whether the formidable practical and theoretical objections that have been raised against these modern treatment theories would also serve to undermine Plato's penology.

3.   *Punishment as cure*

Any curative theory of punishment must rest on three assumptions:
(1)   That criminality resembles a disease in being bad for the person who has it.
(2)   That the acts designated as crimes are symptoms of some internal disorder.

(3)   That the forms of punishment or treatment proposed can in some way remedy that disorder.

Assumption (1) causes particular problems for those modern penologists who take for granted the utilitarian assumption that an act should be regarded as criminal only if it is harmful to other individuals or to society as a whole. On this view there is no basis — apart from a simple confusion of individual and collective good — for regarding crime as bad for the criminal himself. So the analogy between crime and disease immediately breaks down. Plato is in a much stronger position because he has maintained (a) that the virtues are divine goods and that to be deprived of them is the greatest evil that can befall us, (b) that the just life is pleasanter than the unjust, (c) that the unjust man will be separated from the company of the good and will do badly in later existences, and (d) that no one therefore would voluntarily choose to be unjust. (See chapters 4, 5, 6 above.) If these claims were established, the analogy between injustice and disease would be entirely defensible since injustice clearly would be bad for the unjust man. The difficulty, of course, is that none of them is based on any really firm line of argument.

Assumption (2) is important because the Athenian, like most other legislators, imposes penalties only on those who have committed offences. On a curative theory this requires explanation. Should we not seek to diagnose those with disordered souls so that we may cure them before they commit offences? And why should we assume that the acts designated as criminal arise from disorders in the soul? Might not the same act arise from very different inner conditions?

Plato's theory can go a long way towards meeting these conditions. To begin with he could point to the many devices by which he would seek to educate citizens in the way of virtue. These, he might claim, should be sufficient to cure those whose psychic disorders have yet to result in crime. If a criminal act has been committed, that is *prima facie* evidence that more serious (an unpleasant) methods of cure are required. On the other hand he does not believe that all who commit offences should be punished. As we shall see in the next chapter he distinguishes carefully between damage or injury and injustice. Curative measures are required where the act issues from an unjust state of the soul but simple damage requires only compensation. The Athenian then distinguishes different causes of injustice and goes on to a long account of the laws on homicide and wounding. The general point is that courts are to pay close attention to motive and circumstances of each act and to vary the punishments accordingly. There are indications that he would wish to apply this to the treatment of all crimes though there are only a few cases in which this is made explicit. (See, e.g. the laws on atheism (908a–910e) and on improper advocacy (938b–c).)

These points make it clear that Plato does not simply assume that acts forbidden by law must stem from a diseased state of the soul. Rather he would see the occurrence of these acts as an occasion for investigating whether the perpetrator was suffering from injustice in the soul and for giving appropriate treatment. But it is significant that Plato uses crimes of violence (homicide and wounding) to illustrate his points, for these are the kinds of crime that it is most natural to attribute to psychic disorder and which therefore fit the curative model best. The model is much less natural in the case of most other crimes, e.g. failure to marry, planting trees too close to one's neighbours' property, engaging in retail trade or waging private war. These may be contrary to the particular form of social order the Athenian wishes to impose but they do not, on the face of it, look like symptoms of mental illness. After all, the fact that a legislator has chosen to make an act illegal does nothing to show that those who do it must be suffering from some psychic disorder. The same point can apply to some modern reform theories. Medical treatment may be appropriate for some crimes (e.g. compulsive shoplifting) but one cannot infer that it will be equally appropriate for others (including, e.g., minor motoring offences).

Assumption (3) applies to any curative theory — one must give some grounds for supposing that the treatment given to criminals can cure their evil tendencies — but it poses special problems for a theory like Plato's which proposes to cure criminals by punishing them rather than by psychiatric or similar kinds of treatment. Not only is there no obvious reason why the suffering implicit in punishment should improve our character, it can even be argued that traditional punishments make criminals worse by intensifying their hostility to society. Plato must therefore demonstrate that the kinds of punishment he envisages would have the required effects.

There are hints of an answer to this problem in the *Gorgias*, 504b–505b, and the *Republic*, 591a–b, both of which suggest that the experience of punishment curbs or restrains the desires. These passages could be taken in conjunction with the *Timaeus* doctrine that disorderly motions of the lower soul may affect the reason (42e–44d, 69d–70d; see above chapter 5, section 2). Could one not suppose that punishment somehow brings these motions to order? This idea may be attractive so long as one thinks in terms of corporal punishments which may literally create motions within us, but the Athenian does not normally prescribe corporal punishment for citizens. The physiological passages in which Timaeus argues that the balance of fluids in the body may affect the soul (86b–87b) likewise afford no help because there is no reason to suppose that punishment affects the bodily fluids.

Within the *Laws* there is no explicit account of how punishment cures, though we might construct an account out of some remarks made during the discussion of drinking parties. The Athenian there argues that the fear of disgrace or punishment may stop us fleeing from danger. This 'good' fear may thus help to train us in the habit of fearlessness (646e–648c). This idea could be generalized. Perhaps we initially refrain from crime for fear of punishment and thereby become habituated to just behaviour. The trouble with this suggestion is that it makes the reformative effect of punishment dependent on deterrence. Punishment would not benefit the individual who is punished so much as those other people who are deterred by the example of his punishment and thereby acquire good habits.

This is clearly the major weakness in Plato's account of punishment. Unless he can provide substantial grounds for supposing that punishment remedies the disorders of the soul, there is no reason to accept a curative theory.

4 *The theory in practice*

Even if it was granted, for the sake of argument, that punishments might cure psychic disorders, there would still be serious difficulties in the notion of a penal code based on curative considerations. Conventional codes prescribe punishments *for offences*, but the legislator who aims to cure the criminal should be concerned primarily with the underlying mental condition. We might therefore expect his code to prescribe specific treatments for each kind of *mental disorder*. Alternatively, if he had sufficient confidence in the expertise of the courts, he might leave all treatments to their discretion.

Plato is aware of these points. In Book IX the laws on homicide and wounding involve quite elaborate distinctions between the different states of mind which may have prompted the crime. In each case the main division is between acts done in anger and acts that are fully voluntary. The section is prefaced by a discussion of the causes of injustice (863a–864d) and it looks as if these two laws may be intended as examples of the kind of thing that legislators and courts should aim at in other cases (876a–e, 934a). But Plato seems reluctant to press these points to their logical conclusions. For most of the offences mentioned in the *Laws*, the Athenian assigns a specific penalty without any indication of how it might be varied to suit different mental conditions. Even the laws on homicide and wounding include elements which would fit badly with a strictly curative policy. For example, the penalties are varied, not only according to the mental condition of the offender, but also according to the civic status (slave or free) of the offender and his victim and the degree of family relationship, if any, subsisting between them. If someone kills a free man in anger without premeditation he will be exiled for two years; if he kills a slave he will have to pay double damages to the owner; but if he kills his own parent he will be put to death, unless, curiously enough, the parent manages to forgive the killer before he dies (868e–869a). Considerations of this kind might have some relevance for a curative theory — perhaps the anger of those who kill parents is usually more incurable than that of those who kill strangers or slaves. But it is possible on some occasions that the killing of a stranger could show more serious depravity than the killing of a parent. So there seems no justification for rigid distinctions here. The provision that a parricide may be acquitted by his victim is particularly anomalous since it has no relevance whatever to the curability of the offender.

In 875d–876e there is a digression about the need for courts to exercise discretion. The Athenian's position is that an ideal ruler would rule without laws. In practice this is impossible, but where there are well educated judges, as much as possible should be left to their decision. Since the judges in the new Cretan City will be well educated, one might expect them to be given wide discretion in sentencing. Some of the Athenian's measures do allow for this (847a, 867d–e, 880c, 928c, 941a). These cases however are relatively unusual. The Athenian's general practice is to lay down a particular penalty for each offence without any explicit indication that judges might vary it to suit the mental state of individual offenders.

There are other indications that the Athenian does not adhere single-mindedly to his curative theory. This is evident, for example, in his use of the death penalty which is supposed to be restricted to incurables. The Athenian takes this restriction seriously in his treatment of thefts from temples and public property (854d–e, 941e–942a). Citizens who commit these offences after the education they have received should be executed as beyond cure, but slaves and foreigners may be allowed to live. The rationale of this distinction is clear enough (though one might object to its crudity — can *all* citizens but *no* slaves or foreigners who commit these offences be deemed incurable?) A similar point is made in the case of improper advocacy through avarice (938b–c). It is reasonable, too, to suppose that those who remained unreformed after three convictions for perjury are beyond cure (937c). But in most cases there is no obvious justification, within the Athenian's official theory, for the use of capital punishment. The Athenian decrees the death penalty for offences like harbouring an exile, waging private war, taking bribes (955b–d) and obstructing the judgment of a court (958c), without any attempt to show that those who do these things must be incurable. It is notable, too, that, in spite of the cases just mentioned, in which he acknowledges that slaves are less likely than citizens to be beyond cure, he is normally much more severe on the former.

Other features of the penal code also look troublesomely irrational. In dealing with homicide cases (865a–874c), the Athenian assumes that those who kill others, even accidentally, are polluted by the bloodshed and must therefore be excluded for a time from the haunts of their victims, as well as undergoing ceremonial purification. Thus most killers are required to spend a period in exile. There are even provisions for the trial of animals and inanimate killers (873d–874a). The Athenian repeats stories about the vengeance of the gods and of the souls of the dead even though he officially regards vengeance as irrational (729e, 865d–e, 870d–e, 872e–873a).

Most of the divergencies between the penal code and the official theory could be explained only on the supposition that the Athenian attaches weight to other considerations besides the need to cure the criminal. Even the explicitly penological passages mention deterrence and the need to rid the city of evil men. The latter purpose could be served by sentences of exile (735d–e). The fact that the Athenian so often prefers the death penalty may suggest that deterrent considerations weigh heavily with him. There are even passages which imply that a deterrent function is built into his conception of law. In distinguishing between laws proper and preambles he argued that laws imposing a penalty embody a kind of threat. They may therefore be classified as using force rather than persuasion (721e, 722b; cf. 784c, 853b–c). He illustrates the point by reference to those who fail to marry at the appropriate time. He hopes that the penalty will prevent them seeing the single life as easy and profitable (721d). Clearly at this point deterrent considerations are uppermost in his mind.

The Athenian also expects punishment to have an educational effect. In 631b–632d he argued that the primary task of the legislator is to instruct the citizens in virtue as a whole and he implied that one way of doing this is by the correct distribution of praise and blame, rewards and penalties. The thought must be that penalizing a form of action teaches us that it is wrong, just as rewarding it teaches us that it is right.

Potential offenders are unlikely to be deterred by the threat of punishment unless they know in advance what penalties are likely to follow the crimes they contemplate. So, in its deterrent aspect, punishment presupposes some kind of tariff of penalties for offences. Similarly, if penalties are to have an educational force, instructing us in what is right and wrong, they will need to reflect the seriousness of the offences for which they are prescribed. If the penalties for a type of crime varied from case to case for reasons not obvious to the outsider the effect would be to confuse rather than to strengthen ethical judgements. So, on educational as on deterrent grounds, there are good reasons for discouraging too many individual variations in penalties.

In practice the Athenian seeks, not only to make the citizens virtuous, but also to make the state unified and orderly. From this perspective even some of the more irrational-looking penalties can have a point. For example, slave offenders must be punished severely because only through fear can the slave population be kept in subordination. The belief in pollution could also serve a social purpose by encouraging people to look with horror on unnatural deaths. The fact that the Athenian would exempt from pollution those who kill unintentionally in war, public games or military training and doctors who fail to save their patients' lives (865a–b) suggests this kind of explanation — in these cases a belief in pollution would be socially counterproductive. The same may be true of the passages suggesting that the gods or the souls of the dead avenge themselves on those who have killed. Such a belief may be irrational in itself but it could certainly be useful. Even the provision that animals and inanimate objects which have caused death should be tried like criminals could have a utilitarian basis. Such trials might fulfil functions like those of a modern coroner's court (Macdowell, 1963, pp. 85–9, 143–4).

Once the wider social purposes that punishment might achieve are taken into account, it ceases to be surprising that the Athenian does not carry to its logical conclusion his belief in the curative value of punishment. In practice he expects the legislator to act on considerations that give the penal code a quite different shape from any which a purely curative system would bear. This may be inevitable, since the most plausible accounts of how punishment could cure psychic disorder seem to presuppose that the institution is already accepted on other grounds.

Some modern scholars have held the Athenian's account of the aims of punishment to be particularly enlightened, because it rejects ideas of vengeance and insists on the need to cure the criminal and discourage future crimes. They have then regretted that, by comparison, the actual penal code is reactionary and even barbaric. The assumption here is that it is more enlightened to punish for some future good than as a response to what has happened in the past. But there are powerful moral objections to most forward-looking views of punishment. To punish someone as a deterrent is to treat him, not as an end in himself, but as a means to some supposed social good. 'Curing' or 'reforming' the criminal may in practice mean 'brainwashing him' or remoulding his character to a pattern approved by the authorities. The penal code of the *Laws* highlights these dangers. Although the Athenian's use of quasi-medical terms such as 'curing' suggests that he is concerned with the welfare of the individual criminal, in practice most of the crimes for which he will be punished are not harmful to him as an individual; they are generally offences against the social order or deviations from the approved norms of thought and behaviour. This is especially obvious in the case of offences such as innovation in music (799b) and atheism (908e-909a). The Athenian sees punishment as a mechanism for enforcing social conformity. In some ways it might have been preferable if he had stuck to ideas of vengeance, for although such ideas may be primitive and barbaric they involve no threat to the integrity of the individual.

14

Responsibility

Laws, 731b–d, 734b, 859c–873b, 874b–877c, 878b–879b; *Protagoras*, 352a–358e; *Gorgias*, 466d–468e

Although Plato in the *Laws* no longer seems to accept the Socratic denial of *akrasia*, he still maintains that all injustice is involuntary (731c, 734b, 860d; see above, chapter 5, section 2). This gives rise to a very obvious problem in the construction of the legal code. All legislators have found it necessary to distinguish voluntary from involuntary wrongs. But it looks as though this distinction could not be maintained if all injustice was involuntary. So it seems that Plato must either abandon his belief in the involuntariness of injustice or do without one of the fundamental assumptions of criminal law. He makes the Athenian face this problem fairly and squarely in 859c–864c.

In this context the words 'voluntary' and 'involuntary' are translations of the Greek words *hekon* and *akon*. The Greeks used these words quite freely. Almost any act done with less than whole-hearted enthusiasm could be said to be done *akon*. So besides 'voluntary' and 'involuntary' there are several other pairs of English terms which could translate *hekon* and *akon*, for example 'intentional' and 'unintentional', 'willing' and 'unwilling', 'with his consent' and 'against his will'. Translators use these terms more or less indiscriminately. For most purposes this does not matter, since the average English speaker is equally indiscriminate. But philosophers and jurists sometimes try to give these words precise meanings and to distinguish their meanings very carefully. So those who read the *Laws* in an English version must remember that, since Plato is working in terms of a single pair of opposites, *hekon* and *akon*, any variations are the work of the translator.

1   *The problem*

At 859c the Athenian introduces what we may call 'the paradox of just punishment'. His argument seems to be as follows:

(1)   Anything which is just must also be *kalon* (a difficult word to translate: it can mean 'good', 'noble', 'beautiful' or 'honourable').

(2)   Being justly punished must therefore be *kalon*.

(3)   But the things done to us when we are punished are the very reverse of those normally considered *kalon* (i.e. they are normally considered bad, ignoble or disgraceful).

(4)   Thus there appears to be a contradiction in ordinary ways of speaking.

The Athenian makes it clear that he and his companions will have to take issue with ordinary thought on this question (859c–d), but he does not explain exactly how he would solve the paradox. In the *Gorgias*, 476a–477a, Socrates is made to raise a similar problem. It is solved there by the argument that, since just punishment is *kalon*, it must, in spite of appearances, be good (i.e. beneficial) for the person who undergoes it. No doubt the Athenian has a similar point in mind here, but his language at 860c and 861a suggests that he also means to make some kind of logical point. Perhaps, as Saunders (1968, p. 422) suggests, he means that punishment is good in one aspect though not in another.

At 860c the Athenian claims that a similar inconsistency may appear in his own view that bad men are in all respects involuntarily bad. This belief commits him to saying that injustice is involuntary, which in turn, seems to imply that no one voluntarily does an unjust act. But this conclusion raises serious problems for the Athenian in his role of legislator. It is normal in legislation to distinguish voluntary and involuntary acts of injustice, penalizing the former more heavily than the latter. It looks as though the Athenian's philosophical belief that all injustice is involuntary would invalidate this distinction. Thus there appears to be a contradiction between that belief and the practical requirements incumbent on the Athenian as a legislator.

At this point (861a) the Athenian recalls his treatment of the paradox of just punishment. He seems to be suggesting that the problem of voluntary and involuntary acts of injustice can be solved in the same kind of way. He cannot abandon his belief that injustice is involuntary but he can show that there is some other kind of distinction to be made between acts. The suggestion he offers (861d–862c) is that we should distinguish between (a) acts of injustice and

(b) harms or injuries. People sometimes assume that all injuries are injustices and therefore treat cases in which one man involuntarily injures another as cases of 'involuntary injustice'. The Athenian, on the other hand, would not call such involuntary injuries 'injustice'. Equally, he would claim that there are acts of injustice which, so far from doing harm, actually confer benefits. His point is that what makes an act unjust is not its harmful nature, but the character or disposition from which it stems. Accordingly, he maintains that when harm has been done there will be need for restitution but that cases of injustice call for additional measures to cure the wrongdoer (862d–863a).

It is not difficult to see in outline what the Athenian has in mind and how this connects with his theory of punishment. In his view the legislator, in addition to compensating those who have suffered injury, must also attempt to cure the unjust souls of those who do wrong. This means that he cannot confine his attention to the external aspects of actions but must also consider whether they result from a disordered psychological condition. The kinds of act that we normally call 'involuntary' in everyday life are not the outcome of the agent's choices and do not therefore have any bearing on the state of his soul. Thus they do not call for any special treatment. The Athenian would regard these as mere 'harms'. The acts which are normally called 'voluntary', on the other hand, do stem from the agent's choices and do therefore reveal his mental condition. If these acts are contrary to the requirements of justice they show that the agent has an unjust soul and needs treatment. It is these that the Athenian would call 'acts of injustice'. Thus, even though the Athenian believes that no one voluntarily acquires an unjust soul, he still needs to make a distinction between those acts which are indicative of a bad mental state and those which are not. This is the function of his distinction between acts of injustice and harms. In its practical effect this distinction would be very close to the conventional one between voluntary and involuntary crimes.

Unfortunately, all is not as plain sailing as this would suggest. The Athenian does not simply abandon the conventional distinction between voluntary and involuntary crimes in order to replace it with a distinction between acts of injustice and harms. Rather, he talks as though acts of injustice must be voluntary while mere harms may be involuntary. He attacks the very idea that an involuntary act should be called unjust (862a). In his penal code, too, he insists on the distinction between those illegal acts which are voluntary and those which are not. Thus he seems to be saying both that all injustice is involuntary and that acts of injustice must be voluntary. In other words, he still seems to be left with the contradiction he detected between his belief in the involuntariness of injustice and the assumptions he makes about the requirements of legislation.

2   *The solution*

Before considering how the Athenian might solve his problem, it may be helpful to set out schematically the arguments which generate the apparent contradiction.

First there is the argument to the conclusion that all unjust acts must be involuntary. This seems to be as follows:

(A1)   The unjust man is bad.
(A2)   No one is voluntarily bad.
(A3)   Therefore no one is voluntarily unjust.
(A4)   Therefore no one voluntarily does an unjust act.

Opposed to this is the argument that at least some acts of injustice must be voluntary. This seems to run as follows:

(B1)   The legislator must punish injustice.
(B2)   In doing so he must treat those who act voluntarily more harshly than those who do not.
(B3)   Therefore the legislator's activity presupposes that people voluntarily do unjust acts.

Given the Athenian's commitment to legislation, the conclusions (A4) and (B3) seem to involve him in a contradiction. This contradiction could be avoided either (a) by rejecting at least one premise of one or other of the arguments, or (b) by denying the inference from one or other of the sets of premises to their supposed conclusion, or (c) by showing that the two conclusions do not really contradict one another. The premises (A1), (A2), (B1), (B2) are all accepted by the Athenian more or less explicitly. So is the inference from (A1) and (A2) to (A3). Thus there are only three routes by which the contradiction could be resolved:

(1)   We could reject the inference from (A3) to (A4).
(2)   We could reject the inference from (B1) and (B2) to (B3).
(3)   We could try to interpret the conclusions (A4) and (B3) in such a way that they do not contradict one another.

If he took route (1), the Athenian would be denying the inference from 'No one is voluntarily unjust' to 'No one voluntarily does an unjust act'. This inference is not, in fact, logically compelling as it stands. One could insist that there is a difference between *being* unjust and acting *unjustly*, and that there is, therefore, no inconsistency in saying that the criminal's unjust state is involuntary while the acts which arise out of it are voluntary. This, if I understand him rightly, is the interpretation adopted by Saunders. In his view, the Athenian means to distinguish between the psychological state and the criminal act. The act may be voluntary or involuntary in the sense that one has choice and freedom of action. The state of mind that makes one commit the offence is, on the other hand, always involuntary in that it is not the sort of thing one could ever choose (1968, pp. 423–4; cf. 1970a, pp. 367–8).

One difficulty with this interpretation, as Saunders himself acknowledges, is that the Athenian makes no effort to mark the distinction between states of mind and acts, even though there would be no great linguistic difficulty in doing so. There is also a rather obscure sentence at 860d which can be interpreted in such a way as to make the Athenian deny that there is such a distinction (Shorey, 1928). More importantly, the reasons that the Athenian offers for saying that injustice is always involuntary would seem to apply to unjust acts as well as to unjust states of mind. He believes that injustice is involuntary because no one who really understood what he was doing and who had control over himself would choose to be unjust. But, since unjust behaviour can help to make our souls unjust, the Athenian would presumably say also that no one who really understood what he was doing and who had control over himself would do an unjust deed. Anyone, therefore, who accepts the Athenian's arguments about the involuntariness of injustice ought, it seems, to accept that no unjust acts are voluntary. Thus, if the Athenian thought he could solve the paradox via route (1), he would be seriously muddled.

If the Athenian meant to solve the problem via route (2) he would be accepting that the legislator has to concern himself with both voluntary and involuntary *acts*, but denying that there is such a thing as a voluntary *act of injustice*. There is one obvious way in which one could support this claim. Suppose someone voluntarily committed a crime, let us say an assault, but did not realize that this act was an act of injustice. Could we not then say that what he did was voluntary under the description 'harming someone' but involuntary under the description 'committing an act of injustice'? If that were so, then the legislator's concern to distinguish voluntary and involuntary *acts* would carry no suggestion that there are ever any voluntary *acts of injustice*.

The trouble with this idea is that it runs counter to common sense and to Platonic theory. Common sense suggests that many unjust men realize that they are behaving unjustly. Plato would not, I think, deny this. What he would say is that these people do not realize that their unjust behaviour is bad for them in the sense of being against their true interests. Thus so long as the Athenian sticks to his view that the legislator must distinguish voluntary and involuntary acts he seems committed to saying that there are voluntary *acts of injustice*.

The Athenian could solve his problem via route (3) if he was prepared to admit that, when the word 'voluntarily' appears in his claim that no one voluntarily does an unjust act, it bears a different sense from that which it assumes in the edicts of the legislator. It is not difficult to see why one might wish to say this. As we shall see in the next section, the Athenian believes that we become unjust if our souls are beset by ignorance or are overcome by anger or by pleasures. The ignorance that can make us unjust is not, of course, ignorance of particular facts, but ignorance of what is really good. When the Athenian claims that injustice is involuntary, he is assuming that everyone really wants what is truly good for him. From this it would follow that acts done in ignorance of the good or through the domination of pleasures cannot be what we really want. Hence they can be deemed involuntary. But in saying this kind of thing he is assigning new senses to words such as 'voluntary' and the like. These new senses are of no help to judges in courts of law, for they have to decide whether the acts on which they are called to pass judgment are voluntary in the sense of 'arising out of the agent's underlying mental condition'. For this purpose judges have to know whether the accused actually wanted to do the act, not whether he would have wanted to do it if he had known what was good for him or had had control over his passions. Thus the senses of 'voluntary' and 'involuntary' that are required by legislators and by judges are quite distinct from those involved in the Platonic doctrine that no one is voluntarily unjust. One can admit that there are voluntary acts of injustice in the 'legislator's sense without having to admit that there are such things in the special 'Platonic' sense. In this way the contradiction between the two conclusions, (A4) and (B3) can be removed.

There is, I think, little doubt that the Athenian *ought* to have distinguished the two senses of 'voluntary' and 'involuntary' that I have just described. In the *Gorgias*, 466d–468e, Plato shows his awareness of a closely related point: he distinguishes what a man really wants (the good) from what merely 'seems good' or 'pleases' him. In the present passage, however, there is nothing to suggest that we are expected to make distinctions of this kind. Thus it is impossible to be sure what solution, if any, the Athenian is supposed to have in mind. It may be that Plato himself has not clearly distinguished the different possibilities or perhaps he finds such precision foreign to his immediate purposes.

3   The sources of injustice

At 863a–b the Athenian agrees to give more explanation of his distinction between injustice and harm and between the voluntary and the involuntary. The passage which follows, one of the most controversial in the *Laws*, falls into three sections.

863b–e

This gives a preliminary classification of the causes of error. These are anger, pleasure and ignorance. This classification recalls the tripartite division of the soul (*Republic*, 436a–441c) though the Athenian is unsure whether we should speak of 'parts' or of 'states' of the soul. The point seems to be that injustice may arise through a fault of any of the main parts or tendencies within the soul. Anger and pleasure may both be said to 'overcome' us, though pleasure does so by persuasion and deceit while anger acts by brute force. Ignorance, although it is not said to 'overcome' us, is also a source of error. It may be divided into two kinds, 'simple' and 'double'. The distinguishing mark of the doubly ignorant man is that he erroneously thinks he has knowledge. When accompanied by strength and power this double ignorance is the source of the most serious errors; when it is without power, as in the case of children and the old, it may be treated leniently. The distinction between kinds of ignorance recalls the Socratic doctrine that the greatest ignorance is to think one has knowledge when one does not. It would be interesting to know what kinds of people would count as 'doubly' ignorant. Perhaps those with strength are fanatics, so convinced of their own rightness that they cannot be called to reason, while those without strength are people who make themselves ridiculous through lack of self-awareness.

863e–864b

Here the Athenian says that he is going to give a clear account of justice and injustice, but the passage is remarkably obscure. He begins by saying that the domination of the soul by anger, fear, pleasure, pain, envy and desires is injustice whether or not it leads to actual harm. This seems to be simply a more elaborate restatement of the point that injustice may be due to anger or pleasure. The point is that injustice can consist in an improper domination of the soul by its lower elements. As we would expect, the next sentence seems to describe the kinds of injustice due to ignorance, but it is not all clear what exactly is being said. (A corruption in the manuscripts does not help, though fortunately most recent editors agree in their versions.) Literally translated the sentence reads:

> But if the opinion of what is best, by whatever means a city or private citizens think they can attain it — if this is supreme in their souls and governs every man, then, even if it goes wrong somehow, whatever is done in this way and whatever in each man is obedient to this is to be called just and best for the whole of human life, though many people consider a harm of this kind an involuntary injustice.

The key phrases here are 'the opinion of what is best' and 'if it goes wrong somehow', each of which is susceptible of a variety of interpretations. Three readings of the passage as a whole have some plausibility.

(1) 'The opinion of the good' means 'the *individual's* conception of what is good' and 'if it goes wrong somehow' means 'if that conception is in fact mistaken'. The passage as a whole then says that a person who acts according to his own conception of the good will not be called unjust even though his conception is misguided. This is the favoured interpretation of Ritter (1896, p. 283) and other older commentators who saw it as a recognition (at last!) by Plato of the claims of conscience. On this reading a genuinely conscientious action cannot be called unjust. Unfortunately this neat conversion of Plato into a protestant hero does not square with the intolerance of dissent evinced in the *Laws* and in particular with the attitude to atheists adopted in Book X. It is also unlikely that Plato's contemporaries would have described conscientious but misguided actions as 'involuntary injustice'.

(2) The 'opinion of what is best' means the '*correct* conception of the good' and 'if it goes wrong somehow' means 'if it is erroneous in points of detail'. The character described in the passage would then be someone whose passions and desires are correctly ordered in accordance with the judgements of reason but who makes incorrect decisions on some minor matters. It is possible that Plato would be

sympathetic to such people, but again it is implausible to suppose that his contemporaries would have described them as 'involuntarily unjust'.

(3)   The 'opinion of the best' means 'the correct conception of the good', but 'if it goes wrong somehow' means 'if it happens to adopt the wrong means'. The person described would then be someone of good character who goes wrong through a misjudgement of the particular facts. The doctors who fail to save their patients' lives (865a-b) might be an example. This interpretation would give the best sense to the suggestion that the people here described would often be called 'involuntarily unjust'. After all, this is precisely the kind of case the Athenian seems to have in mind when he distinguishes between injustice and harm (861e-862c). It also makes the Athenian genuinely fufil his promise at 863a to explain, not only the nature of justice and injustice, but also the distinction between the voluntary and the involuntary. His position would be that injustice may arise from a disorder of the lower soul or from an erroneous conception of the good. Where, however, a person goes wrong through ignorance of the particular, he will not be called unjust even though he does harm.

864b-c

This purports to be a résumé of what has gone before. Again we are told that there are three main kinds of error though these are described in a slightly different way. The first kind is painful and is called anger or fear. The second kind consists of pleasures and desires. The third is clearly meant to be ignorance, though a corruption of the text makes the exact description unclear. Saunders makes the Athenian describe this kind of error as involving 'hopes and opinions — a mere shot at the truth about the supreme good'. An alternative and perhaps preferable reading (following des Places and Diès) makes it consist in 'the loss of hopes and true opinion about the good'. Whatever the correct version, it does not look as though the passage is intended to add anything to what has gone before. Ignorance is then divided, in accordance with 863c-d, into (a) simple ignorance, (b) double ignorance with power and (c) double ignorance without power. All acts must also be classified into those done openly with violence, those involving secrecy and fraud, and those involving a combination of the two methods. The point is apparently that judges must take all these points into account in deciding how to treat criminals, but there is no explicit reference to these categories in the ensuing sections of the penal code. Presumably these matters are to be left to the court's discretion.

4 *Responsibility in practice*

The account of the law concerning homicide and woundings and assaults, which occupies the second part of Book IX (864c–882c), illustrates the practical application of Plato's theory of responsibility. The first cases dealt with are those where the accused is insane, senile or infantile. These people are not to be punished, though they will be required to give compensation and, if they have killed someone, they will have to spend a year in exile to avoid pollution (864c–e). Plato often talks as though injustice is a kind of extreme folly or stupidity or even a mental disease. This passage shows that he does not regard the unjust as literally insane; he is prepared to distinguish the mad from the bad.

The Athenian divides both homicides and woundings into three main categories: the voluntary, the involuntary and those done in anger. He nowhere gives a precise account of the criteria which would justify us in regarding an act as involuntary, though in the course of the legislation he does give some examples of the kind of thing he has in mind. Certain categories of exile will be deemed to have returned involuntarily if they are shipwrecked on the coast or brought in forcibly by others (866c–d). Citizens will be excused for losing their weapons in war if this happens as a result of being knocked unconscious, being thrown from a height or being overwhelmed by rush of water during a storm at sea (943d–944d). In all these cases the acts are judged involuntary because they result from an overwhelming external force. Elsewhere the Athenian pays more attention to the circumstances than to the causes of the involuntary act. There are special exemptions for those who involuntarily kill someone (other than an enemy) in a contest or in public games, in war or military training, and for doctors whose patients die. As those who killed in these circumstances would be more likely to do so through accident, mistake or ignorance than as a result of an external force, it looks as though the Athenian would recognize a fairly wide range of excuses.

The most surprising feature of this part of the *Laws* is the treatment of killings and woundings done in anger (866d–869e, 878b–879b). These are placed between the voluntary and the involuntary. In the case of killings in anger there is a further subdivision. The first category includes those done without premeditation on the impulse of the moment and where the killer immediately repents. The second category includes cases where one person seeks to kill another in revenge for some provocation and where there is no repentence (866d–e). The crucial difference lies in the presence or absence of premeditation. Acts done with premeditation are more like those done voluntarily. Those done without premeditation are more like the involuntary and may be treated more leniently. The basic penalty for the first category (killings in anger without premeditation) is two years' exile. The basic penalty for the second category (with premeditation) is three years' exile. Both penalties would be very lenient compared with those for voluntary killings which normally carry the death penalty. But the Athenian recognizes that these rough and ready categories may not do justice to the particular circumstances. So the guardians of the laws may, after due investigation, prolong the term of exile indefinitely (867c–868a).

The treatment of woundings is in general like that of killing but imports some problems of its own (874e, 876e–877c, 878b–879b). The Athenian first suggests a fourfold division into those done (a) involuntarily, (b) in anger, (c) through fear and (d) voluntarily and with premeditation (874e). But the detailed legislation does not give any special place to woundings done in fear. Presumably these are to be lumped together with those done in anger. There is no parallel for the distinction made in the case of killings between acts done in anger with and without premeditation. Perhaps this is dropped for the sake of brevity.

The Athenian's account of killing in anger has been examined in detail by A. D. Woozley (1972) whose main concern is to discover the exact meaning of *hekon* and *akon*, the words I have been translating 'voluntary' and 'involuntary'. Although translators have often rendered these as 'intentional' and 'unintentional' Woozley shows that they cannot mean exactly what a modern jurist or philosopher of mind would mean by those terms. The crucial point is that, although the Athenian thinks of those who act in anger as being between the *hekon* and the *akon*, we certainly could not say that these acts would be between the intentional and the unintentional. Most acts done in anger are fully intentional. Equally the Athenian seems to think that premeditated acts are more like those done *hekon* than are unpremeditated ones, but premeditation is not relevant to whether an act is intentional. For rather more complex reasons, Woozley also argues that *hekon* and *akon* cannot mean exactly the same as 'voluntary' and 'involuntary'. He eventually concludes that an act is done *hekon* if the agent could have helped doing it and *akon* if he could not.

Woozley's article is worth reading for its precise analysis of English words such as 'intentional' and 'voluntary'. But as an account of the *Laws* it is flawed by two assumptions. The first is that one can expect a high degree of precision in Plato's use of the words *hekon* and *akon*. It is true that the English terms Woozley considers have been given very precise meanings but only lawyers and philosophers adhere to these at all closely. The man in the street uses 'voluntary', 'intentional' and the like very freely, often treating them as equivalents. The Greek words in question were, if anything, used even more freely, particularly since there was no tradition of jurisprudence or philosophy that could preserve precise meanings for such terms.

The second dubious assumption is that Plato's concerns are much the same as those of modern jurists. Modern legal practice distinguishes fairly sharply between two questions: (a) 'Did the agent do the act alleged?' and (b) 'Should he therefore be punished, and if so how?'. In the Anglo-American system questions of the first type are for the jury to decide. In most circumstances the jury can find the accused guilty only if it has been shown that he acted knowingly and intentionally. The accused may defend himself by arguing, for example, that the act was accidental and was not therefore done intentionally. Once the accused has been found guilty, the judge has to decide what is to be done to him. Judges often have great freedom in choosing a sentence — from an absolute discharge to imprisonment. The accused may attempt to lessen the sentence by making a plea in mitigation, arguing, for example, that he acted under provocation or that he had hitherto led a blameless life.

Modern practice assumes at least an element of retributivism: it is based on the assumption that men deserve punishment if and only if they have intentionally done wrong. So the question of punishment arises only after it has been found that the accused intentionally broke the law. The penal code of the *Laws*, on the other hand, makes no distinction between the question whether the agent intentionally did wrong and the question of how he should be punished. This is what we would expect in view of Plato's theory of punishment. He rejects any element of retributivism and looks on punishment as a device for doing social good, chiefly by curing the criminal. From this perspective the basic question is simply 'What form of treatment will do most good?' In considering this question one would expect him to distinguish three main kinds of case. First there are cases where what has happened is in no sense indicative of any fault in the agent. This might be either because the act did not arise from his character at all or because he acted in ignorance of the facts. Then there are acts which are fully indicative of serious faults of character. In between these will come those acts which are signs of a fault in the agent but not such a serious fault as might normally be supposed. Within this category there will obviously be many graduations.

The Athenian's treatment of homicide makes it clear that he has this kind of point in mind. He begins by discussing involuntary homicide. As we have seen, he does not explore what makes an act involuntary but it looks as though he has in mind those done unintentionally or through excusable ignorance. At the end of the discussion of homicide he also considers cases which we would call justifiable homicide. Those who kill in these circumstances will be treated as innocent. The crucial point about both these categories is presumably that they are no evidence of a bad character on the part of the agent.

Between 869e and 873b there is a discussion of voluntary homicide. The Athenian makes it clear that these are acts of homicide arising out of a depraved character. They involve all kinds of injustice and are premeditated — they result from yielding to pleasures, desires and envy (869e). There follows a digression on the main causes of injustice — inordinate desire for riches, ambition and guilty fears (869e–870d).

Homicides in anger come between the voluntary and the involuntary, because an act in anger is not normally indicative of totally depraved character. The two classes the Athenian distinguishes here are those done on the spur of the moment as the result of sudden emotion and those where the agent has exacted premeditated revenge for some provocation. It is entirely natural to suppose that the second category would generally be symptomatic of a more serious fault of character than the first. But both would be treated by a modern court as cases where there were mitigating circumstances.

This interpretation is confirmed by what might otherwise seem to be some of the Athenian's more peculiar proposals. Killings in self-defence, for example, are treated as a subclass of those done in anger and carry the same diminished penalties, which is reasonable enough if this category is intended to cover all cases where there are mitigating circumstances. But the normal rule that those who kill in anger receive lesser penalties is not applied to those who kill their parents even in self-defence; the same goes for slaves who kill their masters.

This would be nonsense if the Athenian's primary concern was the degree to which the agent could or could not help doing what he did. The anger a son feels towards his father or a slave towards a free man is no less powerful an emotion than any other. The point must be that in these cases penal policy cannot allow provocation as a mitigating circumstance. Killing one's father is such a terrible thing that one should put up with anything rather than commit this crime. So parricide even under provocation is evidence of a particularly vicious nature. In the case of slaves who kill free men, the Athenian may be thinking not so much of the depravity of character revealed in such acts, as of the need at all costs to prevent slaves becoming insubordinate.

Another anomaly, on Woozley's interpretation, would be in the Athenian's treatment of fear as a cause of crime. In the account of woundings, acts done in fear are treated alongside those done in anger, as coming between the voluntary and the involuntary. But in his treatment of killings he expressly treats murders done through a guilty fear, as in the case of a criminal who kills to conceal his crime, as being prime examples of the voluntary (870c–d). Yet guilty fears are no less compelling than innocent ones. There are, of course, perfectly good reasons, which a modern court would easily understand, for treating the two acts differently. The guilty fear in itself results from depravity of character and there are also good deterrent reasons for being especially hard on this kind of killer.

5 Responsibility and the treatment of criminals

Plato's handling of the problems of responsibility resembles in some respects that of Barbara Wootton (1963). Both authors start from the assumption that the aim of the penal process is to treat crime, and that therefore the only question relevant in deciding whether and how to punish someone, is 'What sort of punishment would cure the condition which led to this crime and prevent its repetition?' Wootton accordingly argues that the notion of responsibility must be eliminated. The concern of the courts should be simply to discover whether the acts alleged to have occurred really did occur. The criminal should then be handed over to a body of experts to determine how he should be treated. Plato's proposals seem less radical but rest on similar assumptions. Questions of the voluntariness or involuntariness of the crime are not particularly relevant in themselves. What counts is whether the act was evidence of depravity. The aim should then be to find an appropriate way of treating this depravity. Plato does not propose the establishment of separate panels of psychiatrists or the like to consider this question, but he does think that ideally it would be left to the discretion of a body of wise and experienced people. The rules he suggests seem to be intended primarily as guidelines for the use of these 'experts'.

Wootton's proposals have been heavily criticized, largely because they would lead to consequences which most of us would find morally unacceptable. One particular objection is that the length and unpleasantness of treatment need not correspond to the seriousness of the condition it is supposed to cure. It is quite conceivable that one who had committed a dreadful murder could be treated quickly and easily while one who had committed a much more minor crime would require a long and unpleasant course of treatment. In this respect Plato does not seem to see the implications of his own position. Although he claims that any kind of treatment may be considered, he in practice takes it for granted that the length and unpleasantness of the sentence will be proportional to the degree of depravity involved in the crime. This is why those who kill in anger on the spur of the moment get lesser sentences. The Athenian could perhaps defend himself by claiming that more serious crimes require heavier sentences for deterrent reasons but this is not necessarily so. As Bentham saw, the logic of deterrence is that, where there were especially strong motives for a crime (e.g. some form of provocation), sentences should be increased in order to outweigh the temptation. So the considerations traditionally regarded as mitigating circumstances should really be seen as aggravating the offence. The fact that Plato fails to see these points suggests that he has not seen the full implications of his own position and has not entirely emancipated himself from retributivism.

15

Religion

Laws, 624a–625b, 715e–718c, 738b–e, 759a–760a, 828a–d, 884–910d;
Phaedrus, 245c–246a; Timaeus, especially 27c–47e, 68e–69d, 92c;
Philebus, 28c–30d; Epinomis

It is not by accident that the word *theos*, 'god' is placed emphatically at
the beginning of the first sentence of the *Laws*. The Athenian and his
companions are on a pilgrimage to the cave where Minos was supposed
to have received the laws of Crete from no less a being than Zeus
himself. The message is pretty obvious: law-giving is a religious task
and must be grounded on an adequate theology. This religious
emphasis is maintained throughout the dialogue. It is particularly
evident in the provisions made for the foundation of temples (738b–e,
761c, 778c–d, 848c–d), for the choice priests and other religious
officials (759a–760a) and for the holding of festivals (771d, 828a–d).
The most striking expression of religious sentiment is in 715e–718c, a
passage that reads more like a piece of prophecy than sober
philosophy. Its doctrine, in so far as it is capable of summary, is that
God controls everything and is the measure of all things. His constant
companion is justice. Anyone who wishes to be truly happy must make
himself like God by being virtuous. The wicked cut themselves off
from God. The first object of worship must therefore be the gods of
Olympus, then those of the underworld, spirits, heroes, household
gods and finally one's parents. In other words, although the beginning
of the speech may suggest monotheistic ideas to us, the Athenian is
lending his support to traditional Greek religion — Plato never seems
to worry over the question whether there is one god or many.

In Book X the supposed need for a law against atheism provides the
opportunity for a more philosophical approach to religion. By way of a
preamble to this law the Athenian offers a long and detailed proof of
the existence of a god or gods.

1   *The dangers of atheism*

The first few pages of Book X (884a–891d) serve as an introduction to the main arguments on the existence and nature of the gods. Their chief purpose is to establish that these matters really are of concern to the legislator. They do this by arguing that atheism or incorrect religious belief is a serious cause of vice, and can result from intellectual error as much as from moral corruption; it is therefore the duty of the legislator to convert the unbeliever. At one level the section is profoundly depressing. The old men give vent to their prejudices, assuming that atheism is necessarily connected with vice, that it is a product of youthful pride and folly and that it must be suppressed. But, even so, the Athenian does insist, against the more simple-minded Cretan, that the existence of the gods cannot be taken as obvious (886a). There is a serious intellectual case for atheism and this must be met in its own terms by argument.

Two passages in this introduction are worth special attention. The first is at 885b, where the Athenian maintains that those who utter impious words or do impious deeds can do so only because they believe one or other of three erroneous doctrines: (a) that there are no gods, (b) that the gods are indifferent to the affairs of men, or (c) that the gods can be won over by prayers and sacrifices. The lawgiver must convince these people of their errors by persuading them (a) that there are gods, (b) that these gods are concerned with the affairs of men and (c) that they cannot be bribed. The Athenian himself follows this plan in 891e–907b.

It is not surprising that a respectable Greek should insist that the gods exist and are not indifferent to human affairs. But the attack on the idea that the gods can be bribed, like the criticism of poets who represent the gods as behaving immorally (886b–c; cf. *Republic*, 377b–392c), shows Plato as a reformer aware of some of the less acceptable aspects of conventional Greek religion. The passage recalls *Republic*, 362d–367e, where Adeimantus lists the same three varieties of erroneous belief about the gods. But there are important differences in the use of the two dialogues make of this classification. In the *Republic* Adeimantus calls on Socrates to show that there are other reasons for being just besides the fear of divine retribution. In the present passage, by contrast, the Athenian assumes that people cannot be expected to behave themselves without this fear. So although the *Laws* officially agrees with the *Republic* in maintaining that virtue is the greatest good, it concedes that, in practice, sanctions are still necessary.

The second passage to dwell on is the Athenian's statement of the case for atheism (888e–890b). The atheists, as he represents them, begin by dividing all things into three categories depending on whether they come about by (a) nature (*phusis*), (b) chance (*tuchē*) or (c) art (*technē*). According to the Athenian the atheists attribute most things in the universe to nature or chance. Art in their view is only a secondary cause and its products, which include politics and legislation, are of little importance. From this they conclude that the gods, as products of art, have no real existence, that the good according to the law (a matter of art) is different from the good according to nature, that justice is a human invention liable to constant controversy and change, and that natural rightness consists, not in subduing oneself to others, as the law demands, but in making oneself master over them.

Attempts have been made to identify a particular thinker or thinkers who might be in Plato's mind here. It seems more likely that he is conflating the doctrines of several different authors. His primary target is the immoralism he had earlier put into the mouths of Callicles and Thrasymachus and which he supposed to be a direct consequence of the sophistic distinction between *nomos* and *phusis*. In this he has almost certainly been unfair. The belief that morality is a human invention does not in itself imply that morality is a thing of no importance, and it is likely that many of those who accepted the *nomos–phusis* distinction would nevertheless have supported customary standards of behaviour — Protagoras, for example, may well have taken this view.

As Plato sees it, this supposed immoralism rested on the attempts of the pre-Socratic philosophers to investigate the universe in a purely naturalistic way without reference to any divine agency. The basic assumptions of these philosophers, as Plato sees them, are embodied in the distinction between nature, chance and art. They conceived each thing to have its own nature or *phusis* so that whatever arose out of its nature might be said to be a product of *phusis*. Art, by contrast, includes everything that involves purpose or intention; but it may be said to make use of nature in the sense that we use the natural properties of things to carry out our purposes. The third category, that of chance, includes everything not directly attributable to either nature or art. Thus it would seem that the art of the chariotmaker makes use of the nature of wood and metal, but if two chariots accidentally collide, that happens by chance, because it is a direct result neither of nature nor of art. The distinction between nature, chance and art therefore cuts across the modern distinction between events which are and events which are not causally determined. Some events which we would regard as causally determined could be attributed to chance.

The Athenian indicates at 889a that he is unwilling to accept the division of the world into the products of nature, chance and art. The reason soon becomes clear: he wants to maintain that everything is ultimately the product of art and that the threefold classification is therefore misconceived. In other words he is going to argue that the world cannot be understood without giving a fundamental place to notions of intention, purpose or design. But the way in which he expresses this aim sounds curious to our ears. He is going to demonstrate that the first existents are not the elements of fire, earth, air and water to which the atheists give the name 'nature', but soul and its works which are to be termed 'art'. It is these that are truly natural (892c-893b). He attempts to prove this by means of an argument from change (893c-897b) that in some respects resembles Aristotle's argument to the first mover and Aquinas' 'first way'. (The most important difference is that Aristotle and Aquinas both believe that the first mover must itself be unchanged: God therefore moves the universe as a final cause by being the object of desire. In Plato, on the other hand, 'soul' moves itself as well as other things and thus seems to operate as an efficient cause.) Having established in this way that soul has priority, the Athenian goes on to argue that the order of the universe shows it to be governed by a soul that possesses goodness and rationality (897b-899b).

2 The priority of soul

The argument for the priority of soul (893c-897b) appears to have the following as its main stages:

(1) Some things are at rest, others in motion (893b-c).
(2) There are two main kinds of motion: (a) that which moves other things but not itself, and (b) that which moves itself as well as moving other things (894b-c).
(3) (a) The first motion cannot be the kind that moves other things without moving itself (894e).
  (b) If there was a state of complete rest then the kind of motion that moves itself would have to be the first to arise out of that state (895a-b).
(4) Therefore the first kind of motion is that which moves itself (895b).
(5) A thing that moves itself is said to be alive (895c).
(6) That which has soul is alive (895c).

(7)   Soul is, by definition, the motion that moves itself (895e–896a).

(8)   Therefore soul is the first source of movement and change in everything (896b–c).

(9)   Therefore soul is prior to material things (896b–c).

(10)   Therefore the attributes of soul are also prior to material things (896c–d).

(11)   Soul, since it is the source of everything, must be the source of values — good and bad, fair and foul, just and unjust (896d).

(12)   Since soul dwells in and governs all moving things, it must govern the universe (896d–e).

Premise (1), that some things are in motion and others at rest, may not be the truism it seems. Parmenides had denied the reality of motion while Heraclitus maintained that everything moves. On the orthodox interpretation Plato's own middle dialogues maintain that the Forms, which are the only reality, are unchanging and unmoving.

Premise (2), the distinction between the motions that are and are not self-moving, is reached after a detailed classification of kinds of motion and change. These appear to be (a) motion in one location (i.e. circular motion like that of a top which revolves while staying in one place), (b) motion in many locations (i.e. when something moves from place to place), (c) combination, (d) separation, (e) increase, (f) diminution, (g) generation, (h) destruction, (i) self-moving motion, and (j) motion that is not self-moving. Two points are worth noting in this obscure passage. Firstly the Athenian talks as though all kinds of change happen as the result of the movement of particles. So under the general heading 'motion' he would seem to include anything whatever that may be said to happen. The second point is that the kinds of motion are not mutually exclusive. In particular, any of the first eight motions could be either self-moving or caused by some other motion. So 'self-moving' and 'non-self-moving' are basic categories into which all motion and changes can be divided.

The non-self-moving motion has the power to move other things but not itself, while the self-moving motion can move both other things and itself. We might put the point by saying that the non-self-moving motion results from a cause other than itself while the self-moving motion does not. Understood in this way it is a truth of logic that all motions are either self-moving or non-self-moving, but the terms carry with them the seeds of dangerous confusion. The obvious examples of self-moving motions are the movements of human beings and animals which depend on knowledge, desires, intentions and the like — i.e. they involve agency. But if 'self-moving' is taken to imply agency, it is no longer a logical truth that all motions are either self-moving or moved by something else. Logically speaking, there is no reason why a totally inanimate thing should not start spontaneously into motion.

Stages (3) and (4) offer two co-ordinate arguments to show that the first motion must be the self-moving variety. The first argument (via 3a) makes the unwarranted assumption that there must be a first motion, i.e. that there cannot be an infinite regress of motions. The second argument (via 3b) assumes that rest is the natural state of things and that movement requires explanation. This would be reasonable enough if one accepted the very natural belief that things in motion are always tending to slow down and stop. There would then be need for some spontaneous motion to keep the universe moving. But, of course, modern physics rejects this belief. Rest stands in need of explanation as much as motion.

The argument in (5), (6) and (7) is confused. We might expect the Athenian to argue: 'To be self-moving is to be alive; to be alive is to have a soul; therefore whatever is self-moving has a soul'. What he in fact says is: '(5) Whatever is self-moving is alive; (6) whatever has soul is alive; (7) soul is by definition self-moving motion.' On this formulation (5) and (6) are redundant because (7) is established directly by appeal to the supposed definition of soul. This obscures an important weakness in the argument. It is probably true that whatever is alive is, in some sense, self-moving, but it does not follow that whatever is self-moving is alive — that would be true only if we took 'self-moving' in a more restricted sense than it has borne so far, so that it implied not merely spontaneous movement but *agency*. Similarly, although everything that has a soul may be alive, it does not follow that everything which is alive has soul, unless, that is, one takes soul in such a wide sense that lower animals and even plants have souls. In *Timaeus*, 77a–b, plants are credited with the lowest (appetitive) kind of soul, but for the purposes of the present argument Plato needs a more restricted sense of 'soul' which implies intelligence.

A notable feature of this passage is an attempt to elucidate the notion of truth by definition (895d–e). The Athenian distinguishes (a) a thing's being or essence (*ousia*), (b) its definition or account (*logos*), and (c) its name. The definition and the name both refer to the same thing. Thus, since the definition of 'soul' is 'the movement that moves itself' we can ask for no stronger proof that the soul is the first source of movement.

From (8) onwards the argument is hopelessly embroiled in the ambiguities of 'self-moving' and 'soul'. Stage (8) itself, 'Soul is the first source of movement', is supposed to be derived from (4), 'The first motion is the self-moving kind', together with (7) 'Soul is the motion that moves itself'. But in (4) 'self-moving' has to mean simply 'moving without a prior cause' whereas in (7) it has to mean something like 'being alive'. To make matters worse, more and more is built into the concept of soul. Up to this point soul has been treated as a kind of motion but in (9), 'Soul is prior to material things', it is suddenly treated as an independent substance, as though there could be motion independently of anything's moving. Stage (10) treats the soul not simply as that which makes things alive but as essentially involving rational capacities. In (11) we learn that because soul is the cause of everything it must be the cause of things good and bad, fair and foul, just and unjust, i.e. of all values, but we have been given no reason for supposing that there are values and no explanation of what kind of existence they have. Stage (12) moves illegitimately from the claim that soul moves everything to the claim that it dwells in and governs the universe.

If this analysis is correct the argument for the priority of the soul breaks down for two main reasons. Firstly, it fails to take seriously the possibility of an infinite regress of motions. Secondly, it confuses 'self-moving motion' with soul in the traditional sense of an independent substance capable of exhibiting agency and personality.

3   From soul to god

By 896e the Athenian has reached the conclusion that the universe is controlled by soul. He then tantalizingly asserts that there must be at least two souls — one responsible for good and another for evil. It has sometimes been supposed that Plato is here postulating the existence of a bad world soul, but this reading has no real support in the text. It would be sufficient for the Athenian's purposes if there were many imperfect souls who, between them, could account for the evil we see in the world. But this passage obliquely refers to one of the main problems in Plato's theology. How, on the supposition that the world is governed by a rational god or gods, can we account for evil? In the *Timaeus* (42e–44d) the doctrine seems to be that there are disorderly movements which resist the control of reason, but then we have the problem, 'Where do these movements come from?' If we suppose that they are inherent in the materials out of which the universe is constructed, we have a counter-example to Plato's claim that all motion is ultimately initiated by soul. The alternative is to postulate some kind of irrational soul, but this disrupts the strong association Plato sees between soul and rationality. We cannot tell how, if at all, he would solve the problem.

The Athenian now turns to the question 'What sort of soul governs the universe? Is it wise and virtuous, or neither of these?' (896e–897c). He argues that the soul or souls that govern the universe must possess both wisdom and virtue because their motion is most like that of *nous* (intelligence, reason or thought). They exhibit motion in one place (i.e. circular motion) which here, as in the *Timaeus* (35a–37c, 40b, 42e–44d), is associated with reason. The connection, to say the least, is not obvious. The Athenian draws attention to the fact that circular motion, like the working of reason, is always movement in the same respects, in the same manner, in the same place, around the same things, in relation to the same things and in accordance with one rule and system (898b). So the fundamental point seems to be that both are, as we say, rule-governed. Unfortunately, we can concede that there is a certain parallelism here without concluding that the universe is under the control of a rational soul. We now explain natural regularities, such as the movements of the heavens, by reference to laws of nature without presupposing that any kind of intelligent activity lies behind them. But even if we conceded that natural regularities result from the activity of some kind of intelligence we would be entitled to infer only that the intelligence governing the movements of the heavens is sufficient to understand these movements. There would be no grounds for attributing any higher degree of intelligence or anything approximating to moral virtue.

Although the Athenian is emphatic that soul moves the universe, he leaves open the question how soul does this (898e–899c). It could be that there are souls within each of the heavenly bodies. Alternatively soul might move the heavenly bodies externally by physical contact or by some other means. Thus he commits himself to no particular view about the number of gods (one or many) or about their precise relations to heavenly bodies (whether we should see these bodies as gods or as things under the control of gods). But he is sure that the soul or souls in question must be divine. In this sense he echoes the remark attributed to Thales, 'Everything is full of gods' (899b).

4   *The significance of the proof*

Book X cannot be intended as a complete account of Plato's theology.

In the *Timaeus*, for example, we learn about a 'demiurge' or 'craftsman' who is the creator both of the world soul and of souls for the heavenly bodies. The *Philebus* (28c-30d) appears to offer a similar picture. The *Laws* gives only fragments of this system, though there are hints of what lies in the background. At 904a the Athenian speaks of a 'King' who governs the universe. This eternal 'King' is distinguished from the gods recognized by law, who are not eternal though they are imperishable. Several times, too, there is a suggestion that soul, although prior to matter, has nevertheless come into being at some point (892a; cf. 967d). The natural inference is that the Athenian really sees soul as the product of the same eternal creative power of reason that Timaeus calls 'the demiurge'.

The Athenian is also somewhat reticent about the world soul. It is natural to see him as referring, in 896e-897a, to a single soul actuating the universe as a whole, but, when he goes on to consider *how* soul moves the heavenly bodies, he concentrates on the individual souls that are supposed to move bodies such as the sun. All this would make sense if the Athenian was presupposing the system of the *Timaeus* while being reluctant to say much about ideas as alien to conventional religion as those of the demiurge and world soul.

There is a related problem about the status of the traditional gods. Elsewhere in the *Laws* the Athenian stresses the importance of traditional patterns of worship and the official object of the present section is to support a belief in the gods recognized by law (885b). But the argument of Book X offers no reason for believing in the traditional deities. The cosmology of the *Timaeus* likewise has no real place for the gods of popular religion, though Timaeus (ironically?) suggests that these gods must exist since some people, who ought to know their own ancestry, claim descent from them (40d-e). The *Epinomis* explicitly avoids laying down any particular doctrine about the nature of the traditional gods, though it allows for the existence of beings with bodies of air or aether who are intermediate between ourselves and the gods of the heavens (984d-985b). However this passage is suspect, because nowhere in the undoubtedly authentic dialogues does Plato treat aether as a separate element. There are thus two possible views of the role of the traditional gods in the *Laws*. One possibility is that they are viewed as intermediate beings, but the more likely alternative is that the Athenian accepts the language of traditional beliefs as a concession to the masses. Ordinary men (including, no doubt, Cleinias and Megillus) would have difficulty in understanding the sophistications of the genuine Platonic theology; so, for their sake, religious sentiments must be expressed in mythological terms.

This distinction between Platonic and popular religion has a wider importance. Plato has been seen as a reactionary in his attitude to scientific knowledge. The great achievement of the pre-Socratic philosophers was, we are told, to seek naturalistic explanations of the world instead of appealing to myths of divine intervention. Particularly admired by those who argue in this way is the materialistic system of the atomists, Democritus and Leucippus. But Plato attacks the work of these philosophers precisely because of their preference for naturalistic rather than theological explanations. Is he not therefore urging a retreat into obscurantism?

In considering this charge is is vital to see that Plato's deities, unlike the gods of popular religion, operate in strict conformity to rational laws. Thus what excites Plato most about astronomy is that the movements of the heavens are comprehensible in geometrical terms. In his view, this rational order is the strongest evidence for the existence of gods and, conversely, to suppose that gods could act irregularly is blasphemy. Plato's religion thus has the opposite effect from the conventional piety of the Greeks. While conventional religion encouraged men to explain events in terms of arbitrary divine activity, Plato's religion requires us to seek the laws underlying natural phenomena. Indeed, since the sole characteristics Plato attributes to the gods are the desire and capacity to organize things in a rational way, his religion amounts to little more than the conviction that the universe is ultimately law-governed. This Platonic insistence that the universe be explained by means of mathematically expressable laws is as important for the development of science as the pre-Socratic philosophers quest for naturalistic rather than mythological explanations. The fact that Plato expresses his belief in theological language makes no difference to its effect on scientific practice. We can see this also in the work of Newton and his followers. They were certainly influenced by the atomists but they were also actuated by a desire to provide the most satisfying mathematical account of the movements of the heavens. Like Plato, they supposed that in doing this they were revealing the workings of the divine mind.

5   *The gods' concern for man*

Once he has established the existence of a god or gods, the Athenian turns his attention to those who say that the gods do not concern themselves with human affairs or that the gods can be bribed. The argument is quite simple. The gods know everything, have all power and are supremely good (901d–e). But if they neglected the affairs of men, that could only be through ignorance, inability or vice. So the gods must care for men (901e–903a). Similarly anyone who supposed that the gods could be bribed would be regarding them as inferior to human governors, which is absurd (905d–907b). The difficulty with all this is that no justification has been given for attributing to the gods the characteristics they are now supposed to have. At most, the earlier arguments could establish only that the gods have the kinds of perfection needed to secure the order of the heavens. It does not follow from this that they must therefore have the moral perfections. Similar problems affect most other systems of natural religion. The god of the philosophers is not the god of conventional religious belief.

Those who hold that the gods are indifferent to human affairs will, the Athenian supposes, have been led to this view by seeing that the wicked apparently prosper. They believe that this could not happen if human affairs were under divine supervision and therefore conclude that the gods have no concern for us (899d–900c). The details of the passage (903b–905d) in which Plato attempts to deal with this version of the problem of evil are obscure, though the main outline is clear enough. The ruler of the universe arranges everything with a view to the preservation and good of the whole. So we men are created not primarily for our own good but for that of the universe of which we are parts. We should not, therefore, complain of our situation, since it must be best both for us and for the universe as a whole. We all have many existences, so it is a simple matter for the ruler of the universe to ensure that, as our characters change, we are transferred to an appropriate place in the cosmos. If we become virtuous we will go to a higher place to live among better souls, and if we become vicious we will move to a lower region to join the worse souls. But we ourselves are responsible for the ways in which our characters change.

In the background of this passage is the assumption that in a rationally organized world the wicked must do badly and the virtuous must prosper. This doctrine is shared by those who defend a retributive theory of punishment. But, since Plato rejects the retributivists' idea that penalties should be inflicted on people simply because they have done wrong, he cannot maintain a conventional doctrine of divine retribution. An alternative, tried in the *Gorgias*, 525b–c, and the *Republic*, 619b–e, is to suppose that divine punishment cures us of vice or deters us from doing wrong in later existences. In view of the account of punishment in the *Laws*, one might expect a similar theory to be tried here, but the Athenian attempts instead to show that wicked souls do badly and virtuous ones prosper, not as the result of being deliberately punished, but as the natural and inevitable outcome of their own choices. Obviously it is impossible to offer any evidence for such a belief — it has to be accepted, if at all, as a matter of faith. But even so, there are problems in Plato's account. He quite illegitimately takes it for granted that, 'because of our common origin', what is good for the universe as a whole must be good for each of us as individuals (903c) — a line of argument pervasive in Plato's thought though nonetheless fallacious. There is also a good deal of obscurity about the notion of souls moving to a better or worse place: 904c–d uses the conventional language of rewards in heaven and punishment in Hades, but 904e–905a offers the neat idea that the punishment of the wicked and the reward of the virtuous may consist simply in being sent to live among souls like themselves and so receiving the same kind of treatment which they give to others — a solution that would give us all the advantages of Heaven and Hell without the difficulties normally implicit in these ideas.

6   *The law against impiety*

The discussion of religion so far has officially been merely a prelude to the law against atheism. The law itself is based on a distinction between two kinds of atheist. There are those who are basically honest but misguided. They openly admit their atheism but maintain their sense of justice. But there are also those who combine their atheism with a corrupt character. They keep their disbelief secret and are liable to impose themselves on the public in all sorts of ways, but particularly, it seems, by going in for bogus magic and religious ceremonies (908b–e, 909b). The penalty for the honest atheists is to be confined for at least five years in a special reformatory. Their only visitors will be members of the nocturnal council who will come to admonish them. Those reformed by this experience will be allowed to return to a normal life, but anyone reconvicted with be put to death. The penalty for the corrupt atheists is solitary confinement for life.

The proposed treatment of the honest atheist has been widely and rightly condemned (though one eighteenth-century writer did suggest that it would be an appropriate way of dealing with David Hume). No doubt Plato expects the members of the nocturnal council to convert the atheist through philosophical argument. But since the atheist's only hope of freedom (and indeed of survival) lies in agreeing with his instructors, the conditions are hardly those of a fair and free discussion. 'Brainwashing' might be a more adequate description.

It is commonplace to contrast Plato's intolerance with the freedom of thought exercised by his master Socrates. All that can be said in mitigation is that he does not require adherence to the detailed doctrines of a dogmatic religion.

16

The Closed Society of the *Laws*

1   *Plato and Popper*

Many readers will be familiar with the bitter onslaught launched against Plato by Sir Karl Popper in *The Open Society and its Enemies*. The basis of Popper's attack rests on his distinction between open and closed forms of society. Popper sees Plato as the first and most brilliant exponent of a philosophical tradition that rejects the open and seeks to return to the closed society.

The closed society, in its archetypal form at least, is characterized by 'its submission to magical forces' (1966, p. 1). It lives in a charmed circle of unchanging taboos, of laws and customs which are felt to be as inevitable as the rising of the sun, or the cycle of the seasons, or similar obvious regularities of nature' (p. 57). Its characteristic intellectual attitude is thus a naive monism that fails to distinguish the man-made and changeable laws of society from the natural laws of the universe (p. 59). Closed societies are collectivist in the sense that they emphasize the significance of some group or collective (e.g. the tribe), without which the individual is nothing at all (p. 9). This collectivism finds strong expressions when writers like Plato present an 'organic' view of the state treating the individual citizens as though they stood in the same relation to the state as do the parts of a human or animal body to the whole (pp. 79–81).

The open society, by contrast 'sets free the critical powers of man' (p. 1) by recognizing the distinction between normative and natural laws. Its characteristic intellectual attitude is thus a critical dualism which appreciates that the laws and customs of a community, unlike the natural laws of the universe, are open to criticism and can be deliberately changed. In this kind of society, individuals are genuinely confronted by personal decisions (pp. 60–1). The collectivism of the closed society is replaced by individualism, i.e. people are important as individuals, not only as tribal heroes or saviours (pp. 100–2, 190). The aim of the law is to protect the freedom of individuals, provided that this does not involve harming others (pp. 110, 114–15).

Popper's criticisms of Plato are based largely on the *Republic*, which Popper sees as a blueprint for political action. The *Laws*, in his view, was written only when Plato had 'given up hope of realizing his political ideal in all its glory' (p. 102), but since he believes that it is still actuated by the same principles, Popper quotes from it freely, though selectively, in support of his conclusions. This mistaken view of the relationship between the *Republic* and the *Laws* enables Popper to make some lurid charges against Plato. In the city of the *Republic*, philosophers rule without check and there is a strict class system based on selective breeding. The whole system could only be imposed by force. So Popper accuses Plato of advocating dictatorship based on violence, of supporting a caste society and of being a racialist. Once it is appreciated that the *Republic* is not a political programme and that one must look to the *Laws* for Plato's practical proposals, these charges lose most of their force. But this does nothing to undermine Popper's fundamental contention that Plato is an enemy of the open society, and a reading of the *Laws* may even strengthen Popper's case.

By now no argument should be needed to show that the city of the *Laws* will be a closed society in that it severely limits personal freedom and initiative. As evidence, one could cite the tight restrictions on the mode of life of the citizens, including the prohibition of trade and commerce, the rigid control of music and the other arts, and the law against atheism. The city will be almost literally a closed society in the sense that foreign contracts will be curtailed so far as possible (704d–705b, 950d–953e).

The closed society, as described by Popper, is a traditional tribal society controlled by a system of law and custom thought to be as permanent and unchallengeable as the laws of the universe. Similarly in the city of laws every part of life will be controlled by law, written and unwritten. The intellectual mechanisms will be geared to demonstrate that these laws instantiate the same rational principles as the movements of the heavens. Criticism of the system will be prohibited (except to the old) and change will be nearly impossible. As in most traditional societies, the interpretation of the law will lie with a body of elders (the guardians of the laws, and the nocturnal council). In all these respects the city of the *Laws* will correspond closely to the kind of tribal society envisaged by Popper. Indeed it would be much more like a traditional society than would the city of the *Republic*. (Tribal rulers do not have the unchecked power granted to the *Republic's* philosopher kings, so Popper's charges of tribalism and dictatorship do not go well together.)

It should perhaps be said here that Popper's description of tribal societies does not in all respects correspond to those offered by historians and anthropologists. In particular, customary law is generally more flexible than Popper allows and primitive peoples are generally aware of the difference between their laws and the laws of the universe; like the Cretans and Spartans they generally ascribe their customs to a remote ancestor. But these points strengthen rather than weaken the case against Plato; he is not just reverting to traditional pattern but going beyond it.

Of course, neither Plato himself nor his imaginary Athenian share what Popper would regard as the primitive cast of mind. They are themselves only too well aware that laws can be changed, but they want the citizens of the new state to be educated so as to find change unthinkable. This contrast between the Athenian's (or Plato's) attitude and that required in the new citizens expresses itself in an ambivalence already noted in the treatment of the nocturnal council. The members of the council will study law, but it is not clear whether their qualifications to do so will rest on experience, like genuine tribal elders, or on philosophical training.

For his charge of collectivism, Popper relies heavily on two key passages from the *Laws*. In the first the Athenian has been describing the ideal but unattainable state in which there is complete community of property. He quotes the dictum 'friends have all things in common' and goes on to argue that, so far as possible, nothing should be private, wives, children and property should all be common. Ideally we should even see, hear and act in common, we should be unanimous in our praise and blame, and be happy and sad at the same things. In short the laws should create the greatest possible unity (739c-d). This is an explicit attack on any theory that attaches importance to the individual. So, although Popper is wrong to suppose that Plato ever considered the community of family and property an attainable ideal, he is justified in citing it as evidence of Plato's collectivism.

The second passage is not only used in support of the charge of collectivism but is also placed at the head of the first chapter as a motto to illustrate Plato's antipathy to the open society. As cited there it reads

The greatest principle of all is that nobody whether male or female, should be without a leader. Nor should the mind of anybody be habituated to letting him do anything at all on his own initiative; neither out of zeal nor playfully. But in war and in the midst of peace to his leader he shall direct his eye and follow him faithfully. And even in the smallest matter he should stand under leadership. For example, he should get up, or move, or wash, or take his meals . . . only if he has been told to do so. In a word, he should teach his soul by long habit, never to dream of acting independently and to become utterly incapable of it. (942c–d)

In context, this passage is a little less horrifying than it seems by itself. The Athenian is describing military service and the references to getting up, moving, washing and taking meals clearly apply to these activities as performed in campaigns or exercises. There is also a problem about Popper's use of the word 'leader' in his translation. The Greek word *archon* certainly can mean 'leader' but it is also the standard word for any kind of ruler, including democratically appointed magistrates. Immediately after the passage quoted, the Athenian goes on to say that the whole experience of the citizen must be one of 'ruling and being ruled' (or 'leading and being led'). The trouble with the translation 'leader' is that it could suggest the demand for unflinching loyalty to a powerful personality (a Führer), whereas what the passage really asks is that the citizen should obey those who for the time being are duly appointed as magistrates or commanders. (Anyone who thinks the passage is evidence of militarism should remember that the dialogue began with an attack on the militaristic systems of Crete and Sparta; see Silverthorne, 1973).

These qualifications may soften the impact of the passage quoted but they do not significantly affect Popper's basic point. The Athenian is arguing that the entire experience of citizens from earliest childhood should train them to accept discipline and the unthinking obedience that this involves. It explicitly suggests that any expression of individuality is undesirable. So Popper is justified in using it as evidence of Plato's opposition to the open society.

2 *Plato's principles*

Although Popper is entirely correct to claim that the kind of state advocated by Plato would be far removed from the ideal of the open society, the general style of his argument could still be misleading in two ways. In the first place Popper's talk of *the* open society suggests that all societies are open or closed and that we have a straight choice between the two models. But, of course, there is in fact no such thing as a completely open or completely closed society. It may not even be possible to rank societies in order of openness and closedness — society A could be more open than society B in one respect and more closed in another. In the second place, Popper's method could lead to the obviously questionable assumption that the more open of two societies is always to be preferred. But there are other values which a reasonable man might seek and these may conflict with the demands of openness; for example if we set a high value on order we may prefer the less open but more orderly of two societies. In short, the unwary reader of Popper's book could get the impression that we have a simple choice between the open and the closed society and that one of these alternatives (the open model) is obviously the right one to choose. In this perspective Plato's preference for a relatively closed society may seem perverse, the product perhaps of a pathological personality.

Popper explains Plato's position in terms of a supposed 'historicist' methodology which led him to adopt the maxim 'Arrest all change'. But if we are to take Plato seriously as a philosopher we should consider what he actually says. In particular, we would expect to explain his proposals in terms of his own explicit account of the aims of legislation (see above, chapter 4).

We saw that the first object of the legislator is to secure internal and external peace. From very early in the *Laws*, the Athenian maintains that this is to be achieved through law. He believes that a code of law must therefore be accepted as a permanent fixture and that the citizens must be so indoctrinated as to accept this code unthinkingly. This argument rests on some basically sound assumptions. The Athenian is right to assume that law must be relatively stable and that it must command the respect of the citizens. Even in a relatively open society like those of modern Britain or America, the constitution can survive only so long as those with political power accept that they must obey its fundamental provisions. They adopt the habits of mind of a closed society but only with respect to the central features of the constitution. The trouble is that the Athenian pushes these points too far. He treats the creation of order as though it were an overriding aim to be pursued at all costs. But even if we accept that order is a fundamental requirement of any society we need not suppose that order must always be maximized at the expense of any other values whatever. Indeed there comes a point at which the pursuit of order becomes self-defeating since the constraints it imposes on the citizens will lead to discontent. So the question is not 'How can we achieve the greatest degree of order?' but 'How can we produce sufficient order to permit the pursuit of other values?'

Plato's assumption that the chief aim of legislation is to make the citizens virtuous and that virtue is objectively discoverable would also lead naturally to a preference for a relatively closed society. It becomes the function of the state to ensure that the citizens conform to a certain pattern of character and behaviour: to give them freedom is simply to allow them to do the wrong thing. But it is important to see exactly why this argument is erroneous. Political thinkers in the liberal tradition sometimes talk mistakenly as though it is possible for the legal code to avoid a commitment to any values. But some values, if only that of liberty, must be incorporated within the legal code and some possible values must be excluded. It is absurd to suggest that a legal system could be impartial between, say, liberal democrats and supporters of Ayatollah Khomeini's brand of Islamic revolution. So Plato's mistake, if he has made one, does not consist in his belief that there are values that a legal code must promote, but rather in the way in which he conceives those values. He implies that the good life demands conformity to established patterns of thought and behaviour. It is this assumption that must be contested by supporters of the open society.

Plato's conformist conception of virtue is closely connected with what Popper calls his 'holism' — his wish to see human beings as parts of larger wholes. Although this picture of humanity has dangerous implications for morals and politics and can lead to the collectivism characteristic of the closed society, it has attractions that are not purely aesthetic. Most human beings feel a need to 'belong', to feel that they have a secure place as members of a social group. These sentiments can undoubtedly encourage the kinds of attitude that Popper would ascribe to members of closed societies. Marx appeals to them when he advocates co-operative rather than competitive modes of economic activity. Popper scorns such feelings as relics of tribalism. It might be more accurate to suggest that they are part of our heritage as social animals. As such they are inescapable. They may sometimes lead to militarism and intolerance but they are also the source of some of our deepest satisfactions. Plato shows his awareness of this in his calls for friendship among the citizens and in some of his proposals for the new city, notably the common meals. It seems likely that any satisfactory form of society will need to take account of them while trying not to suppress individual initiative. The choice between collectivism or individualism is not so clear cut as Popper apparently supposes.

3 *The afterlife of the* Laws

Although the *Republic* has been much more widely read, it is appropriately the *Laws* that has had the greater influence on practical politics. Some of its proposals seem to have been adopted by Greek cities after Plato's death, but its doctrine of the sovereignty of law and accompanying political theory of checks and balances has had a lasting effect. Mediated by writers such as Aristotle, Polybius and Montesquieu, it has had a profound influence on the development of modern democracies. One unfortunate consequence of Popper's concentration on the *Republic* is that he misses Plato's advocacy of this theory altogether. This is the more surprising because Popper himself advocates a theory of checks and balances against what he takes to be Plato's theory of (unchecked) sovereignty. The important question, Popper maintains, is not 'Who should rule?' but 'How can we so organize political institutions that bad and incompetent rulers can be prevented from doing too much damage?' (121). In the *Laws* Plato adopts a mere optimistic view of the capacities of human rulers — he believes that political institutions can be arranged so that the better people hold office — but he knows that even these will not be infallible. So he would agree wholeheartedly with Popper that the chief task is to design political institutions that take account of human frailty. Thus Popper's focus on the *Republic* not only prevents him from acknowledging the chief debt that liberal political thinkers owe to Plato, but also blinds him to these elements in Plato's thought which, on his own account, would be most positive and valuable.

It is perhaps understandable that Popper, living under the shadow of Hitler, should have been obsessed by the threat of dictatorship and should have interpreted Plato accordingly. But civilized ways of life can also be threatened by a loss of confidence in the state and political institutions generally. This danger is perhaps more apparent at a time when our attention is often focussed on political groups who denounce law and the state as irredeemably corrupt without offering any clear account of what could replace them. In the *Laws*, Plato emphatically expresses his own belief in the value of political society. So the message is not, as has so often been supposed, one of despair. He is telling us that a good life is possible, but only if we take the trouble to develop and defend sound political institutions.

APPENDIX

The Constitution

The Assembly

Membership: open to all who bear or have borne arms for the state, i.e. to all adult male citizens (753b); it is not clear whether women would be members (805a–c may imply that they would).

Attendance: compulsory for the top two property classes; optional for the other two except on special occasions (764a).

Functions: the main function is to elect members of the council and other officials; a few other functions are mentioned (767e–768a, 772c–d, 850b, 921e, 943c); but the role of the Assembly is in general very unclear.

The Council (756b–758d)

Membership: ninety members from each property class; membership lasts one year.

Mode of election: very complex; the whole process lasts five days:

Days 1 and 2: candidates from the first and second classes nominated; all citizens required to take part.

Day 3: candidates from the third class nominated; participation is optional for members of the lowest class but compulsory for others.

Day 4: candidates from the lowest class nominated; participation is optional for members of the third and fourth classes but compulsory for members of the two highest classes.

Day 5: an election is held to choose 180 of those nominated from each class; this number is then reduced by lot to ninety from each class.

Functions: conducting the day to day business of the state, summoning the assembly and guarding the city; for these purposes the Council is divided into twelve sections each of which functions for one month; its other responsibilities are left vague (758a–d).

Guardians of the laws (752d–755b)

Membership: thirty-seven citizens aged at least fifty; they hold office for twenty years or until they are seventy.

Mode of election: (1) for elections occurring after the new city has been properly established, each citizen is required to write down the name of the person he thinks most suitable; the names of those thus nominated are exhibited for thirty days during which objections may be made; the 300 who have received most nominations are then selected; a further selection (apparently by election) reduces these to 100; a final election produces the required number of guardians.

(2) special arrangements are to be made for the transitional period when the new city is being established; the most important suggestions are (a) that, to begin with, the guardians should include eighteen from Cnossos (the most important city of Crete) and nineteen of the new colonists; (b) that the first elections should be supervised by a board of 100 colonists and 100 Cnossians; most scholars (e.g. Morrow, 1960, pp. 204–6, 238–40) have supposed that these suggestions are alternatives linked together by an editor, but Saunders (1970b) has suggested that we could make sense of the text as it stands if (a) is the procedure used at the first foundation of the new city, (b) is used when it has been established for a short time, with the procedure described in (1) above being used for subsequent 'normal' elections.

Functions: intended to be the most influential organ of the
                              state; at first three functions are mentioned —
                              guarding the laws, keeping the property registers,
                              and hearing the cases of those charged with not
                              registering property; many other specific func-
                              tions are also mentioned.

Military officers (755b–756b)

Mode of election: candidates for the post of general are nominated
                              by the guardians and three of these are then
                              elected by the soldiers; the procedure is the same
                              for cavalry commanders except that the election is
                              then made by the cavalry men; company
                              commanders are nominated by the generals, but if
                              these nominations are disputed there is an
                              election.

Religious officials (758d–760a)

Priests: chosen by lot but those chosen will be subject to
                              examination to ensure that they are of suitable
                              character.
Expounders: candidates are elected and the Delphic Oracle is
                              then asked to choose three of these.
Temple treasurers: elected by the highest property class.

Country wardens (760a–763c)

Mode of election: five members of each of the twelve tribes are
                              elected; each of these (or possibly each group of
                              five) then chooses twelve young assistants; they
                              hold office for two years.
Functions: each group of country wardens supervises a
                              different area of the country each month; they are
                              responsible for fortifications, public works and
                              police duties; they act as judges in less important
                              matters.

City wardens (763c–e)

Mode of election:	six members of the highest property class are elected; this number is then reduced by lot to three; they hold office for one year.
Functions:	supervision of public works and police duties within the city.

Market wardens (763c–764c)

Mode of election:	ten members of the two highest property classes are elected; this number is reduced by lot to five; they hold office for one year.
Functions:	supervision of the markets.

The minister of education (764c–766b)

Eligibility:	the minister must be at least fifty years old, the father of legitimate children and a guardian of the laws.
Mode of election:	elected by all the officials except members of the Council; term of office five years.
Functions:	overall supervision of education; said to be the most important office of state (766e).

Scrutineers (945b–948b)

Mode of election:	each citizen must propose the name of one man over fifty years of age; of those thus nominated, half (i.e. those who have received most nominations) go forward; the process is repeated until the number of candidates left corresponds to the number of places to be filled; twelve candidates are to be chosen in the first year and three in each subsequent year; they hold office until they are seventy-five.
Functions:	to scrutinize the conduct in office of all officials and to impose penalties when appropriate.

The nocturnal council (951c–952d, 961a–968e)

Membership:	there are slight discrepancies between the two accounts of the membership of this council (951e, 961a); it looks as though it would consist of (a) the ten oldest guardians of the laws together with the present minister of education and those of his predecessors who are still alive, (b) all who have won awards of honour, and (c) those citizens who have been sent abroad to discover whether anything can be learned from other states; each member is also required to bring at least one suitable young man aged at least thirty.
Functions:	to study the nature of virtue (the true end of the state) and to investigate what laws are best calculated to achieve it; more specific functions include re-educating atheists and hearing the reports of those sent abroad to study foreign customs.

THE ADMINISTRATION OF JUSTICE (766d–768c, 855c–856a, 875e–876e, 956b–958c)

Plato follows the Athenian practice of dividing cases into two categories, public and private. The private category includes not only what we would call civil cases but also all those cases where an injury has been done to an individual in his private capacity. Prosecution in such cases is normally the responsibility of the injured party. Public cases are those where harm has been done to the city as a whole. Prosecutions in these cases may be undertaken either by members of the public or by the appropriate board of officials. Procedures are as follows:

Private cases

(1)   In the first case disputes are to be brought to arbitrators whom the parties choose from among their neighbours.
(2)   There is an appeal from the decision of arbitrators to a tribal court — a court consisting of jurors chosen by lot, probably from the whole citizen body but organized in tribes.
(3)   There is appeal from the tribal courts to a supreme court

consisting of one member nominated from among their own number by each board of officials whose period of office lasts for more than one year.

Public cases

The opening and closing stages are before a court of the whole people, but there is an intervening stage in which a detailed examination is carried out by three judges chosen from the highest officials by the prosecutor and defendant, or by the council if they cannot agree on a choice.

Capital cases come before a special court, apparently consisting of the members of the court of select judges (see under 'Private cases' 3) sitting together with the guardians of the laws.

Morrow (1960, pp. 264–70) points out (a) that the precise demarcation between the court of the people and the court of capital cases is left unclear, and (b) that in summarizing the judicial arrangements of the new city, the Athenian suggests that it should be left to the guardians of the laws to decide an appropriate procedure for trying public cases (957a–b). It may therefore be that the arrangements just described do not embody Plato's final thoughts on this topic.

Magisterial justice

Almost all the boards of officials have power to act as courts in cases which come within the sphere which they normally supervise. This competence is normally restricted to cases where the subject of the dispute is below a certain value, but this limit is set quite high compared with contemporary Athenian practice. So the officials have extensive judicial powers. The precise relation of these to the courts described above is in many respects unclear.

Further Reading

General

Summaries of the dialogue with comments are to be found in Grote (1888), Shorey (1933), Taylor (1960a and b), Friedländer (1969), Strauss (1975), and Guthrie (1978). I have found Grote and Guthrie most helpful.

Saunders (1970a) has a useful introduction.

Morrow (1960) has very full and detailed discussions of the institutional proposals and relates these to what is known of contemporary Greek practice.

England (1921) is a fine work of classical scholarship but has little to offer readers whose interests are primarily philosophical.

Müller (1951) argues for a view of the *Laws* as a chaotic product of Plato's decline. The reply by Görgemanns (1960) is particularly helpful. For a summary of the key issues see the reviews (in English) of these two works by Cherniss (1953) and Ostwald (1962).

Saunders (1975b) is a very readable account of the problems of translating the *Laws*.

Saunders (1975a) is a full bibliography of the *Laws*.

2   Law

The nature of law

Morrow (1960), chs. XI and XII, discusses the relation between philosophical and legal issues in the *Laws*.

On Plato as a founder of the natural-law tradition see Maguire (1947), Hall (1956) and Ostwald (1977).

For the development of the natural-law tradition see Aristotle, *Nicomachean Ethics*, V. vii; X. ix; *Rhetoric*, I, xiii, 1373b 1–8; cf. *Physics* II. viii; Cicero, *Republic*, III. xxii. 33; *Laws*, II. iv. 8 to v. 13; Aquinas, *Summa Theologiae*, 1a 2ae. qq. 90–7.

Modern discussions of natural-law theory are summarized in Harris (1980), chs. 2 and 3. Hart (1961), ch. X, criticizes natural-law theories. Fuller (1969) defends a view of law as purposive. Finnis (1980) gives a detailed defence of natural law, taking some account of Plato's contribution.

The aims of legislation

Aristotle's view is close to that of Plato in the *Laws*; see *Nicomachean Ethics*, II. i, 1103b 1-7; V. i; X. ix; *Politics*, VII. ii; VII. xiv, 1333a 30–1334a 10.

On the problem of legal moralism see Mill, *On Liberty*, Berlin (1969) Hart (1962) and Devlin (1965). The issues are summarized in Harris (1980), ch. 10. On Plato's doctrine of persuasion and its relevance to the preambles of the laws see Morrow (1953).

Plato as a legislator

Morrow (1941) and Cairns (1949) assess Plato's merits as a legislator.

Vol. xi of des Places and Diès (1951-6) contains a lengthy account by L. Gernet of the relationship between Plato's code and Greek law in Plato's day. Macdowell (1978) is a convenient source for the law of Athens.

3   *Moral philosophy*

Virtue

Most modern accounts of Plato's moral philosophy neglect the *Laws*. Gould (1955) and Crombie (1962-3), vol. 1, ch. 6, are exceptions to this rule. For the idea of *sophrosune* (self-control) see North (1966).

Dover (1974) is a mine of information on the attitudes of Plato's contemporaries to moral matters.

Gigon (1954) argues for the incoherence of the opening pages of the *Laws*. For a reply see Görgemanns (1960), pp. 113–54.

Aristotle's treatment of moral virtue in *Nicomachean Ethics*, II, is in many respects very close to that of Plato in the *Laws*.

Moral psychology

Dodds (1951), Rees (1957) and Vlastos (1957) discuss the basic principles of Plato's moral psychology as it appears in the later dialogues. Saunders (1962) argues that the *Laws*, like the Republic, maintains a parallelism between the parts of the soul and the parts of the state. Görgemanns (1960), pp. 155–61, considers the roles of reason and passion in the *Laws*.

The possibility of *akrasia*

Most modern commentators have concentrated on the treatment of this problem in the *Protagoras*, together with the *Meno* and *Gorgias*. See Santas (1964) and Gulley (1965). Walsh (1963), O'Brien (1967) and Hackforth (1946) pay more attention to later dialogues including the *Laws*.

Mortimore (1971) includes essays on the problem as it appears in both ancient and modern philosophy.

Aristotle's celebrated account is in *Nicomachean Ethics*, VII. i–ix.

Pleasure and happiness

Most modern discussions of these topics in Plato have concentrated on the *Protagoras*, *Republic* and *Philebus*. Gosling and Taylor (1982) have a rather brief chapter on the *Laws*; see also Görgemanns (1960), pp. 165–92.

Aristotle deals with these topics in *Nicomachean Ethics*, VII. xi–xiv, X. i–v.

For Bentham's felicific calculus see his *Principles of Morals and Legislation*, ch. iv.

4 Politics and society

General accounts

Barker (1960) is still the most helpful account of Plato's political philosophy as a whole and deals very fully with the *Laws*. There are briefer treatments in Crombie (1962–3), vol. 1, ch. 4, and in Hall (1981). Morrow (1962) includes an account of Plato's involvement in Syracuse and of the political implications of the *Letters*.

Almost every page of Aristotle's *Politics* has some bearing on the *Laws*. The notes of Barker (1946) and especially, Saunders (1981a) are valuable in this respect. Of particular interest are Book II, chap. vi, where Aristotle offers some lop-sided and ungenerous criticisms of the *Laws*, and Books VII and VIII, which describe an ideal state not unlike that of the *Laws*.

The open society

Popper (1966) is essential reading, though his treatment of the *Laws* is fragmentary and one-sided. Levinson (1953) is a massive reply to Popper, while Bambrough (1967) includes contributions from both sides of the argument.

Ideal states and utopias

Aristotle, *Politics*, IV. i, discusses the relation between ideal constitutions and what is practicable. He discusses various ideal states, including those of the *Republic* and the *Laws*, in II. i–viii. His own ideal is described in Books VII and VIII.

For modern discussions of utopianism see Popper (1966), ch. 9, and Horsburgh (1956–7).

The mixed constitution

The idea of the mixed constitution as it appears in the *Laws* is discussed in Morrow (1960), ch. X. Aristotle gives his version in *Politics*, IV. ix–xi. The idea has influenced modern thought chiefly through the doctrine of the separation of the powers; see Montesquieu, *L'Esprit des Lois*, XI. 6.

The rule of law

Morrow (1960), ch. XI, discusses Plato's view. For Aristotle's version see *Politics*, III, xi, 1282a 41–b11; III. xvi; IV. iv–vi.

For a modern treatment of the idea of the rule of law see Lucas (1966), pp. 106–43. See also the discussions of the 'inner morality' of the law in Fuller (1969) and of the different kinds of rule that comprise a legal system in Hart (1961), chs IV and V. There is a summary of modern discussions in Harris (1980), ch. XI.

The system of government

Barker (1960), ch. XV, and Morrow (1960), chs. V and VI discuss the political and judicial institutions of the *Laws*. Morrow's discussion is very full and detailed.

On democracy and equality see Aristotle's remarks in *Politics*, II. vi; III. ix; IV. iv; V. i; VI. ii. For a modern introduction to these problems see Benn and Peters (1959), chs. 5 and 15. Lively (1975) and Schumpeter (1950) distinguish different forms of democratic theory. Harvey (1965) places Plato's account of equality in its historical context.

Social organization

Morrow (1960), ch. IV, and Barker (1960), ch. XIV, contain general accounts of the forms of social organization proposed in the *Laws*.

On slavery see Morrow (1939) and Vlastos (1941). Aristotle's discussion in *Politics*, I. iii–vii, makes valuable background reading.

On class structure see Saunders (1961 and 1962) and Wood and Wood (1978), pp. 183–202; cf. Aristotle, *Politics*, IV, iii–iv; IV. xi; VII, viii–x.

On social solidarity see Durkheim (1972), chas. 5 and 6, and Aristotle, *Politics*, III. iv.

5   *Education and the Arts*

For general accounts of these matters as they appear in the *Laws*, Morrow (1960), ch. VII, and Barker (1960), ch. vii. See also Görgemanns (1960), ch. 1. Bury (1937) is a wide-ranging discussion of education in the *Laws*. Sargeaunt (1922–3) concentrates on the role of song and dance and on the idea of man as God's playfellow.

For the theory of music and the other arts see Tate (1928 and 1932), Verdenius (1949), Schipper (1963) and Crombie (1962–3), vol. 1, pp. 190–3.

The educational system of Aristotle's ideal city in many respects resembles that of the *Laws*; see *Politics*, VII, xiii–xvi, and VIII.

6 *Punishment and Responsibility*

Plato's theory of punishment is discussed in Adkins (1960), pp. 299–312, Schuchman (1963), Huby (1972), ch. 7, Saunders (1973a, 1976, and 1981b), and Mackenzie (1981). These all have some bearing on Plato's conception of responsibility.

Woozley (1972) and Saunders (1973b) discuss the theory of responsibility as it appears in Plato's treatment of killings in anger.

For modern discussions of the problem of punishment see Honderich (1976) and Acton (1969). Wootton (1963) has a theory of punishment and responsibility which in some ways resembles Plato's. She is criticized by Hart (1968), esp. ch. VIII, and Flew (1973).

Plato's account of the causes of injustice is discussed in O'Brien (1957) and Saunders (1968); see also the items on *akrasia* cited in 3 above.

Aristotle's scattered remarks on punishment sometimes imply agreement with Plato and sometimes suggest other approaches; see *Nicomachean Ethics*, II, iii, 1104b 14–18; III. v, 1113b 21 to 1114a 3; V. iv, 1132b 34; V. xi, 1138a 4–14; X. ix, 1179b 31 to 1180a 13; cf. Sorabji (1980), ch. 18.

Aristotle's discussion of responsibility in *Nicomachean Ethics*, V. viii, has a close bearing on the *Laws*; see also *Nicomachean Ethics*, III, i–v.

For contemporary Greek practices and attitudes see Dover (1974), pp. 144–60 and Macdowell (1963), chs. 1 and 12.

7 *Religion and Cosmology*

For general accounts of religion in the *Laws* see Barker (1960), pp. 422– and Morrow (1960), ch. VIII.

Kaufmann (1958), s. 44, and Craig (1980), ch. 1, offer critiques of the argument for the existence of god(s).

The following treat the theology and cosmology of the *Laws* in connection with Plato's doctrine as it appears in other dialogues: Hackforth (1936), Solmsen (1942), esp. chs. VIII–X, Dodds (1951), ch. VII, Skemp (1967), Demos (1968).

On the explanation of evil see Vlastos (1939), Cherniss (1954) and Mohr (1978). Saunders (1973a) connects the account of the soul's progress after death with the penology of the *Laws*.

Vlastos (1975) gives an account of Plato's cosmology, criticizing the religious assemptions that underlie it.

Aristotle's argument to the first mover is in some respects parallel to the argument of *Laws*, X, though it also exhibits important differences: see *Metaphysics*, XII. vi–ix; *Physics*, VII–VIII.

8 *Metaphysics and epistemology*

On the philosophical method advocated in the later dialogues see Crombie (1962-3), vol. II, ch. 3, iv and v, the articles by Ackrill and Lloyd in Allen (1965), and Sayre (1969).

On the Forms in the later dialogues see Crombie (1962-3), vol. II, pp. 257-61, Owen (1953), Cherniss (1957). Cherniss (1953), Görgemanns (1960), pp. 218-26, and Guthrie (1978), pp. 378-81, discuss the evidence for the Forms in the *Laws*.

Select Bibliography

This includes all the works referred to in the text or mentioned in the suggestions for Further Reading. For a full bibliography of the *Laws* see Saunders (1975a).

Acton, H.B. (ed.) (1969), *The Philosophy of Punishment*, London: Macmillan.

Adkins, A.W.H. (1960), *Merit and Responsibility*, Oxford: Clarendon Press.

Allen, R.E. (ed.) (1965), *Studies in Plato's Metaphysics*, London: Routledge.

Bambrough, R. (ed.) (1967), *Plato, Popper and Politics*, Cambridge: Cambridge University Press.

Barker, E. (1946), *The Politics of Aristotle*, translated with introduction, notes and appendices, London: Oxford University Press.

(1960), *Greek Political Theory*, 5th edn, London: Methuen.

Benn, S.I. and Peters, R.S. (1959), *Social Principles and the Democratic State*, London: Allen & Unwin.

Berlin, I. (1969), 'John Stuart Mill and the ends of life', in *Four essays on Liberty*, London: Oxford University Press.

Bury, R.G. (1926), *Plato with an English Translation*, vols. IX and X, *Laws*, Loeb Classical Library, Cambridge, Mass.: Harvard University Press, London: Heinemann.

(1937), 'The theory of education in Plato's Laws', *Revue des Études Grecques*, 50, pp. 304-20.

Cairns, H. (1949), 'Plato's theory of Law', in *Legal Philosophy from Plato to Hegel*, Baltimore: Johns Hopkins University Press, pp. 29-76; also in Friedländer (1969).

Cherniss, H.F. (1953), Review of Müller (1951), *Gnomon*, 25, pp. 367-89; reprinted in Cherniss (1977).

(1954), 'The sources of evil according to Plato', *Proceedings of the American Philological Society*, 98, pp. 23-30; reprinted in Vlastos (1972) and in Cherniss (1977).

(1957), 'The relation of the Timaeus to Plato's later dialogues', *American Journal of Philology*, 78, pp. 225-66; also in Allen (1965) and Cherniss (1977).

(1977), *Selected Papers*, Leiden: Brill.

Craig, W.L. (1980), *The Cosmological Argument from Plato to Leibniz*, London: Macmillan.

Crombie, I.M. (1962–3), *An Examination of Plato's Doctrines*, 2 vols., London : Routledge.

Demos, R. (1968), 'Plato's doctrine of the psyche as self-moving motion', *Journal of the History of Philosophy*, 6, pp. 133–45.

des Places, É. and Diès, A. (1951–6), *Platon, Oeuvres Complètes*, vols. XI–XII, Budé edn, Paris: Société d'Édition 'Les Belles Lettres'.

Devlin, P. (1965), *The Enforcement of Morality*, Oxford: Clarendon Press.

Dodds, E.R. (1951), *The Greeks and the Irrational*, Berkeley and Los Angeles: University of California Press.

Dover, K.J. (1974), *Greek Popular Morality in the time of Plato and Aristotle*, Oxford: Blackwell.

Durkheim, E. (1972), *Selected Writings*, ed. A. Giddens, Cambridge: Cambridge University Press.

England, E.B. (1921), *The Laws of Plato*, 2 vols., Manchester: Manchester University Press.

Engels, F. (1972), 'Socialism, utopian and scientific', in R.C. Tucker (ed.), *The Marx Engels Reader*, New York: Norton, pp. 605–39.

Finnis, J. (1980), *Natural Law and Natural Rights*, Oxford: Clarendon Press.

Flew, A.G.N. (1973), *Crime or Disease?* London: Macmillan.

Friedländer, P. (1969), *Plato*, vol. III, trans, H. Meyerhoff, Princeton: Princeton University Press.

Fuller, L. (1969), *The Morality of Law*, revised edn, New Haven and London: Yale University Press.

Gigon, O. (1954), 'Das Einleitungsgespräch der Gesetze Platons', *Museum Helveticum*, 11, 201–3.

Görgemanns, H. (1960), *Beiträge zur Interpretation von Platons Nomoi*, *Zetemata* series, no 25, Munich: Beck.

Gosling, J. and Taylor, C.C.W. (1982), *The Greeks on Pleasure*, Oxford: Clarendon Press.

Gould, J. (1955), *The Development of Plato's Ethics*, Cambridge: Cambridge University Press.

Grote, G. (1888), *Plato and the Other Companions of Socrates*, new edn, vol. IV, London: John Murray.

Gulley, N. (1965), 'The interpretation of "No one does wrong willingly" in Plato's dialogues', *Phronesis*, X, pp. 82–6.

Guthrie, W.K.C. (1978), *History of Greek Philosophy*, vol. V, Cambridge: Cambridge University Press.

◊Hackforth, R. (1936), 'Plato's theism', *Classical Quarterly*, 30, pp. 4–9, reprinted in Allen (1965).

(1946), 'Moral evil and ignorance in Plato's ethics', *Classical Quarterly*, 40, pp. 118-20.

Hall, J. (1956), 'Plato's legal philosophy', *Indiana Law Journal*, 31, pp. 171-206.

Hall, R. (1981), *Plato*, London: Allen & Unwin.

Harris, J.W. (1980), *Legal Philosophies*, London: Butterworth.

Hart, H.L.A. (1961), *The Concept of Law*, Oxford: Clarendon Press.

(1968), *Punishment and Responsibility*, Oxford: Clarendon Press.

Harvey, F.D. (1965), 'Two kinds of equality', *Classica et Mediaevalia*, XXVI, pp. 101-46.

Honderich, T. (1976), *Punishment: the supposed justifications*, revised edn, Harmondsworth: Penguin.

Horsburgh, H.J.N. (1956-7), 'The relevance of the utopian', *Ethics*, LXVII, pp. 127-38.

Huby, P. (1972), *Plato and Modern Morality*, London: Macmillan.

Jowett, B. (1953), *The Dialogues of Plato*, 4th edn, vol. IV, Oxford: Clarendon Press.

Kaufman, W. (1958), *Critique of Religion and Philosophy*, London: Faber.

Levinson, R.B. (1953), *In Defense of Plato*, Cambridge, Mass.: Harvard University Press.

Lively, J. (1975), *Democracy*, Oxford: Blackwell.

Lucas, J.R. (1966), *The Principles of Politics*, Oxford: Clarendon Press.

MacDowell, D.M. (1963), *The Athenian Homicide Law in the Age of the Orators*, Manchester: Manchester University Press.

(1978), *The Law in Classical Athens*, London: Thames & Hudson.

Mackenzie, M.A. (1981), *Plato on Punishment*, Berkeley, Los Angeles and London: University of California Press.

Maguire, J.P. (1947), 'Plato's theory of natural law', *Yale Classical Studies*, 10, pp. 151-78.

Mohr, R.D. (1978), 'Plato's final thoughts on evil', *Mind*, LXXXVII, pp. 522-5.

Morrow, G.R. (1939), 'Plato and Greek slavery', *Mind*, 48, pp. 186-201.

(1941), 'Plato and the rule of law', *Philosophical Review*, 50, pp. 105-26; reprinted in Vlastos (1972).

(1953), 'Plato's conception of persuasion', *Philosophical Review*, 62, pp. 234-50.

(1960), *Plato's Cretan City*, Princeton: Princeton University Press.

(1962), *Plato's Epistles*, Indianapolis: Bobbs Merrill.

Mortimore, G.W. (ed.) (1971), *Weakness of Will*, London: Macmillan.

Müller, G. (1951), *Studien zu den platonischen Nomoi*, Zetemata series, no. 3, Munich: Beck, revised edn, 1968.

North, H. (1966), *Sophrosune*, Ithaca: Cornell University Press.

O'Brien, M.J. (1957), 'Plato and the "good conscience"', *Laws* 863e5–864b7', *Transactions of the American Philological Association*, 88, pp. 81–7.

(1967), *The Socratic Paradoxes and the Greek Mind*, Chapel Hill: University of North Carolina Press.

Ostwald, M. (1962), Review of Görgemanns (1960), *Gnomon*, 34, pp. 231–41.

(1969), *Nomos and the Beginnings of Athenian Democracy*, Oxford: Clarendon Press.

(1977), 'Plato on law and nature', in North (ed.), *Interpretations of Plato*, *Memnosyne Supplement*, 50.

Owen, G.E.L. (1953), 'The place of the *Timaeus* in Plato's dialogues', *Classical Quarterly*, 3, pp. 79–95; reprinted in Allen (1965).

Pangle, T. (1980), *The Laws of Plato*, translated with notes and interpretive essay, New York: Basic Books.

Popper, K.R. (1966), *The Open Society and its Enemies*, vol. 1, Plato, 5th edn, London: Routledge.

(1976), *Unended Quest*, London: Fontana.

Quinton, A. (ed.) (1967), *Political Philosophy*, London: Oxford University Press.

Rees, D.A. (1957), 'Bipartition of the soul in the early Academy', *Journal of Hellenic Studies*, 77, pp. 112–18.

Ritter, C. (1896), *Platons Gesetze*, Kommentar zum Griechischen Texte, Munich: Beck.

Santas, G. (1964), 'The Socratic paradoxes', *Philosophical Review*, 73, 147–64.

Sargeaunt, G.M. (1922–3), 'Two studies in Plato's *Laws*', *Hibbert Journal*, 21, pp. 493–502, 669–79.

Saunders, T.J. (1961), 'The property classes and the value of the *klēros* in Plato's *Laws*', *Eranos*, 59, pp. 29–39.

(1962), 'The structure of the soul and the state in Plato's *Laws*', *Eranos*, 60, pp. 37–55.

(1968), 'The Socratic paradoxes in Plato's *Laws*', *Hermes*, 96, pp. 421–34.

(1970a), *Plato, the Laws*, Harmondsworth: Penguin.

(1970b), 'The alleged double version in the sixth book of the *Laws*', *Classical Quarterly*, 20, pp. 230–6.

(1972), 'Notes on the Laws of Plato', *Bulletin of the Institute of Classical Studies*, supplementary papers, 28.

(1973a), 'Penology and Eschatology in Plato's *Timaeus* and *Laws*', *Classical Quarterly*, 23, pp. 232–44.

(1973b), 'Plato on killing in anger: a reply to Professor Woozley', *Philosophical Quarterly*, 23, pp. 350–6.

(1975a), *Bibliography on Plato's Laws, 1920–1970, with additional citations through 1975*, New York: Arno. New edn, 1979.

(1975b), 'The penguinification of Plato', *Greece and Rome*, 22, pp. 19–28.

(1976), 'Plato's clockwork orange', *Durham University Journal*, LXVIII, pp. 113–17.

(1981a), revised edn of Aristotle's *Politics*, trans. Sinclair, Harmondsworth: Penguin.

(1981b), 'Protagoras and Plato on punishment', in G.B. Kerferd (ed.), *The Sophists and their Legacy, Hermes*, einzelschriften, 44, 129–41.

Sayre, K. (1969), *Plato's Analytic Method*, Chicago: Chicago University Press.

Schipper, E.W. (1963), 'Mimesis in the arts in Plato's *Laws*', *Journal of Aesthetics and Art Criticism*, 32, pp. 199–202.

Schuchman, P. (1963), 'Comments on the criminal code of Plato's *Laws*', *Journal of the History of Ideas*, 24, pp. 25–40.

Schumpeter, J. (1950), *Capitalism, Socialism and Democracy*, 3rd edn, London: Allen & Unwin; a portion of this is reprinted as 'Two concepts of democracy' in Quinton (1967).

Shorey, P. (1928), review of Bury (1926), *Classical Philology*, 23, pp. 403–5.

(1933), *What Plato Said*, Chicago: University of Chicago Press.

Silverthorne, M.J. (1973), 'Militarism in the *Laws?*' *Symbolae Osloenses*, 49, pp. 29–38.

Skemp, J.B. (1967), *The Theory of Motion in Plato's Later Dialogues*, enlarged edn, Amsterdam: Hakkert.

Solmsen, F. (1942), *Plato's Theology*, Ithaca: Cornell University Press.

Sorabji, R. (1980), *Necessity, Cause and Blame: perspectives on Aristotle's theory*, London: Duckworth.

Strauss, L. (1975), *The Argument and the Action of Plato's Laws*, Chicago: University of Chicago Press.

Tate, J. (1928), 'Imitation in Plato's Republic', *Classical Quarterly*, 22, pp. 16–23.

(1932), 'Plato and imitation', *Classical Quarterly*, 26, pp. 161–9.

Taylor, A.E. (1960a), *Plato, the Laws*, Everyman edn, London: Dent. (1960b), *Plato the Man and his Work*, 7th edn, London: Methuen.

Verdenius, W.J. (1949), *Mimesis, Plato's doctrine of artistic imitation and its meaning to us*, Leiden: Brill.

Vlastos, G. (1939), 'The disorderly motion in the Timaeus', *Classical Quarterly*, 33, pp. 71–83; also in Allen (1965).

(1941), 'Slavery in Plato's thought', *Philosophical Review*, 50, pp. 289–304; reprinted in Vlastos (1981).

(1957), 'Socratic knowledge and Platonic pessimism', *Philosophical Review*, 66, pp. 226–38; also in Vlastos (1981).

(1972) (ed.), *Plato*, vol. II, Modern Studies in Philosophy, London: Macmillan.

(1975), *Plato's Universe*, Oxford: Clarendon Press.

(1981), *Platonic Studies*, revised edn, Princeton: Princeton University Press.

Walsh, J. (1963), *Aristotle's Conception of Moral Weakness*, New York and London: Columbia University Press.

Wood, E.M. and Wood, N. (1978), *Class Ideology and Ancient Political Theory*, Oxford: Blackwell.

Wootton, B. (1963), *Crime and the Criminal Law*, London: Stevens.

Woozley, A.D. (1972), 'Plato on killing in anger', *Philosophical Quarterly*, 22, pp. 303–17.

Index